FIFTH AMENDMENT

PRIVILEGE AGAINST SELF-INCRIMINATION

"A person shall not be compelled in any criminal case to be a witness against himself."

CONFESSIONS

An accused's Fifth Amendment's rights are violated when prosecution uses at trial evidence of the accused's own incriminating words that were "deliberately elicited" after commencement of adversarial proceedings in the absence of the defendant's counsel.

CUSTODIAL INTERROGATION

"Custodial interrogation" refers to questioning initiated by law enforcement officers after the person has been taken into custody or otherwise deprived of his freedom in a significant way.

1. Custody: The standard is whether, based upon the totality of the circumstances, and assessed objectively, there was a formal arrest or restraint of freedom of movement of the degree associated with a formal arrest. Objective indicia of custody include, but are not limited to:
   a. Formal arrest.
   b. Prolonged detention.
   c. Demeanor of police officers (e.g., confrontational questioning) and the ratio of officers to suspects. *Thompson v. Keohane*, 516 U.S. 99 (1995).
2. Interrogation: Interrogation is any direct or express questioning about the crime being investigated. *Illinois v. Perkins*, 496 U.S. 292 (1990).

INTERROGATIONS

Miranda v. Arizona, 384 U.S. 436 (1966).

Rule: Any statement, whether inculpatory or exculpatory, made by a suspect as the result of custodial interrogation may not be used against the suspect in a criminal trial, unless it is shown that the police provided procedural safeguards to secure the suspectís Fifth Amendment privilege against self-incrimination.

EXCLUSIONARY RULE

1. Impeachment of defendant: Statements obtained in violation of *Miranda* may be used nonetheless to impeach defendant at trial if he testifies inconsistently with the custodial statement.
2. The "fruit of the poisonous tree" doctrine does not apply to *Miranda* violations.

COERCED CONFESSIONS

1. Rule: A statement obtained by police from a suspect as the result of coercion is inadmissible at trial in violation of the Due Process Clause and the Fifth Amendment privilege against self-incrimination.

---

2. State action is required (i.e., a government agent, such as police, must be coercing the confession).
3. Factors in determining voluntariness:
   a. Use or threatened use of force;
   b. Use of psychological pressure;
   c. Promise of leniency in exchange for a confession; and
   d. Use of deception to secure a confession. *Spano v. N.Y.*, 360 U.S. 315 (1959).

MIRANDA WARNINGS

1. *Miranda v. Arizona*, 384 U.S. 436 (1966): For a confession to be admissible under the Fifth Amendment privilege against self-incrimination, a person in custody must, prior to interrogation, be informed in substance, that:
   a. He has the right to remain silent;
   b. Anything he says can and will be used against him in court;
   c. He has the right to the presence of an attorney; and
   d. If he cannot afford an attorney, one will be appointed for him if he so desires.
2. The above warning must be given:
   a. When anyone is in custody by a government agent and accused of a crime; and
   b. Prior to an interrogation by the police.

USE OF CONFESSION

Use of confession for impeachment: Statements obtained in violation of the *Miranda* warnings may be used to impeach the defendant's trial testimony but may not be used as evidence of guilt. Subsequent confessions are valid.

WAIVER

1. Waiver: Accused may waive the privilege against self-incrimination and/or right to counsel. Waiver must be:
   a. Voluntary;
   b. Knowing; and
   c. Intelligent. *Moran v. Burbine*, 475 U.S. (1986).
2. Waiver may occur only after the full *Miranda* warnings have been given.
3. Prosecution must prove the validity of a waiver by a preponderance of the evidence.
4. Waiver must be expressly stated or implied by the accused's words or conduct. Exceptions: *Oregon v. Elstad*, 470 U.S. 298 (1985).
   a. Public safety: Need not be given in a situation where there is a threat to public safety.
   b. Covert interrogation: Not required when the suspect is unaware that he is speaking with a law enforcement officer.
   c. Booking questions: Need not be given prior to routine booking questions.

CONFESSIONS

1. Fourth Amendment: "Harmless error test"– voluntariness.
2. Fifth Amendment: Privilege against Compelled Self-Incrimination.
3. Sixth Amendment: Right to Counsel.

RIGHT TO SILENCE

Suspect may enforce this right in any manner and at any time prior to or during questioning by indicating that he wishes to remain silent. Interrogation must then cease. The invocation of this right after receiving Miranda warnings may not be used against the defendant at trial (e.g., prosecution cannot argue that defendant must be guilty because he remained silent during questioning). *Doyle v. Ohio*, 426 U.S. 610 (1976); but see *Fletcher v. Weir*, 455 U.S. 603 (1982).

RIGHT TO ASSISTANCE OF COUNSEL

1. If the accused indicates that he wishes to consult an attorney at any time prior to or during questioning, interrogation must cease.
2. Police may not reinstate communication unless the accused's counsel is present.
3. The cease-interrogation rule does not apply:
   a. Unless the accused's request for an attorney is unambiguous; or
   b. If the accused's request for counsel cannot be reasonably construed as an expression of a desire for assistance in dealing with the custodial interrogation.

GOVERNMENT AGENT

1. A waiver is not applicable in the case of secret interrogations, i.e., the use of an undercover agent to elicit incriminating information.
2. The government must demonstrate the intentional relinquishment or abandonment of a known right or privilege.
3. Once right to counsel attaches, if defendant requests assistance of counsel, deliberate elicitation must cease until the defendant talks .... communication.

.... the police: .... 01 (1964).
1. Intentionally seek to ...... .minating information from the accused either via formal interrogation or use of an undercover agent;
2. Intentionally create a situation likely to induce the accused to make incriminating statements; or
3. Knowingly exploit an opportunity to confront the accused without counsel present.

DOUBLE JEOPARDY

IN GENERAL

- Under the Fifth Amendment, a person may not be retried for the same criminal offense once jeopardy has attached.
- Jeopardy attaches in a jury trial at the empaneling and swearing in of the jury.
- In bench trials, jeopardy attaches when the first witness is sworn in.

Double Jeopardy continues on page 4

TWO TYPICAL SEARCHES

1. Searches conducted pursuant to a warrant.
2. Valid warrantless searches. *Illinois v. Rodriguez*, 497 U.S. 177 (1990).

▼

1. SEARCHES CONDUCTED PURSUANT TO A WARRANT

1. Warrant must show probable cause [see Probable Cause box on page 1].
   a. Use of informers: "Totality of the circumstances" test.
   b. Going "behind the face" of the affidavit.
2. A search warrant will be held invalid if it meets all prongs of the following three-pronged test:
   a. A false statement was included in the affidavit by the affiant (officer applying for warrant);
   b. Affiant intentionally or recklessly included the false statement; and
   c. The false statement was material to the finding of probable cause.

▼

2. WARRANTLESS SEARCHES: Valid Exceptions to the Warrant Requirement

1. Search Incident to an Arrest.
2. "Automobile" Exception.
3. Plain View.
4. Consent.
5. Stop and Frisk.
6. Hot Pursuit.
7. Administrative Searches.

▼

"SHOCKS THE CONSCIENCE" TEST

1. "Shocks the conscience" test: Due process requires evidence to be obtained in a manner that does not offend one's "sense of justice." *Rochin v. California*, 342 U.S. 165 (1952).
2. Body searches invoke privacy rights and their "reasonableness" requires a balancing between the public's need for the evidence against the gravity of the invasions.

HABEAS CORPUS

COLLATERAL ATTACK

1. No right to counsel for indigents.
2. Preponderance of evidence standard to show an unlawful detention.
3. State may appeal if the writ is granted.

SENTENCING AND PUNISHMENT

SENTENCING

1. Right to counsel.
2. Right to confrontation and cross-examination.
3. Re-sentencing and reconviction after appeal.
   a. If a harsher sentence is imposed, the reasons must be stated on the record.
   b. Exceptions:
      i. Trial de novo.
      ii. Jury sentencing.

SEARCH INCIDENT TO AN ARREST

1. Incident to a lawful arrest, the police may search the person (or an area within the arm span of the person) to obtain weapons. *Chimel v. California*, 395 U.S. 752 (1969).
2. If person being searched is in an automobile, the search incident to an arrest may include the entire passenger compartment of car (including glove compartment, but not the trunk or any containers).
3. Search must be contemporaneous in time and place with an arrest.
4. Note that if the underlying arrest was not lawful, the subsequent evidence found may be suppressed based on Fourth Amendment issues.

Note: A police officer does not need probable cause to conduct a search incident to a lawful arrest. However, the police officer needs probable cause to seize any object he finds during the search.

"AUTOMOBILE" EXCEPTION

If the police have probable cause to believe that a vehicle contains evidence of a crime, they may search the entire vehicle or any container that might reasonably contain the item for which they had probable cause to search. (Contrast this to a search incident to an arrest.) *Chambers v. Maroney*, 399 U.S. 42 (1970).

However, the police are limited in their search by evidence for which they are looking. If the police have probable cause to believe that an ice chest in the trunk contains contraband, they may search only that ice chest, not the rest of the car. On the other hand, if the probable cause is fairly broad and calls for contraband that may be anywhere in the car, they may search the entire car.

PLAIN VIEW

The police may make a warrantless seizure of evidence in plain view (*Horton v. California*, 496 U.S. 128 (1990)) when they:
1. Are legitimately on the premises.
2. Discover contraband, evidence, fruits, or instrumentalities of crime.
3. See such evidence in plain view.
4. Have probable cause to believe that such item is an instrumentality of a crime or evidence of such.

CONSENT

1. The police may search a person or the premises under the authority of that person if given consent. This is the most popular method of a warrantless search by the police.
2. The consent given must be voluntary and intelligent. However, a voluntary and intelligent consent is not predicated on the person giving the consent knowing that he may withhold consent.
3. The scope of the search is limited by the scope of the consent.
4. Any person with an apparent equal right to use or occupy the property may consent to a search. Any evidence found in such a search may be used against others who reside at the premises or other owners. *Bumper v. North Carolina*, 391 U.S. 543 (1968).

STOP AND FRISK

A police officer may stop a person for arrest if he has a reasonable suspicion based on articulable facts. Stop equals detainment, but does not equal arrest. *Terry v. Ohio*, 392 U.S. 1 (1968).

HOT PURSUIT

Police in "hot pursuit" of a fleeing felon may make a warrantless search and seizure, and may also seize (without a warrant) evidence likely to disappear before a warrant can be obtained. While in pursuit, police may even pursue the suspect into a private dwelling, but must reasonably consider whether or not those inside the dwelling will be harmed.

ADMINISTRATIVE SEARCHES

Agencies may obtain warrants for searches of private residences and commercial buildings. The standard is much lower—a showing of a general and neutral enforcement plan will justify issuance of a warrant.

PUNISHMENT

The Eighth Amendment prohibits "cruel and unusual" punishment.

1. Punishment grossly disproportionate to the offense.
2. Death penalty: Not in itself cruel and unusual; however, the judge or jury must have reasonable discretion, full information regarding defendants, and guidance.
   a. May not be imposed for rape of an adult woman.
   b. May not be imposed for felony murder, unless defendant acted with reckless indifference to human life.

SIXTH AMENDMENT

RIGHT TO COUNSEL

Attaches when adversarial judicial proceedings begin. *Powell v. Alabama*, 287 U.S. 45 (1932).

Examples: Formal charge, preliminary hearing, indictment, or arraignment.

▼

"CRITICAL STAGE"

The state does not have to provide an attorney throughout the criminal process, only at a "critical stage" of the proceedings. *Coleman v. Alabama*, 399 U.S. 1 (1970).

CRIMINAL PROCEDURE

Bill of Rights: First eight Amendments to the Constitution of the United States. The states are bound to follow these rules based on the Due Process Clause of the Fourteenth Amendment.

Two exceptions:

1. Right to indictment by a grand jury.
2. Right to reasonable bail.

EXCLUSIONARY RULE

IN GENERAL

The exclusionary rule prohibits introduction of evidence obtained in violation of a defendant's Fourth, Fifth, and/or Sixth Amendment rights. Illegally obtained evidence is inadmissible at trial. Evidence so obtained, however, may be used for impeachment purposes.

"FRUIT OF THE POISONOUS TREE"

All evidence ("fruit of the poisonous tree") obtained from the exploitation of illegally obtained evidence must also be inadmissible at trial. *Wong Sun v. United States*, 371 U.S. 471 (1963).

Exceptions to the "fruit of the poisonous tree" doctrine:

1. Evidence obtained from an independent source.
2. An intervening act of free will by the defendant.
3. Inevitable discovery.

LIMITATIONS ON THE EXCLUSIONARY RULE

1. Inapplicable to grand juries (unless in violation of the federal wiretapping statute), civil proceedings, internal agency rules, and parole revocation proceedings.
2. Good faith reliance on law, defective search warrant, or clerical error.
3. Impeachment purposes.
4. *Miranda* violations. *United States v. Leon*, 468 U.S. 897 (1984).

HARMLESS ERROR TEST

If illegal evidence is admitted, a resulting conviction should be overturned on appeal unless the government can show beyond a reasonable doubt that the error was harmless.

OTHER CONCERNS

The admissibility of evidence or a confession is determined by a judge outside the hearing of a jury. The government bears the burden of establishing the admissibility of the evidence by preponderance of the evidence.

FOURTH AMENDMENT

FOURTH AMENDMENT

"The right of the people to be secure in their persons, houses, papers, and effects, against unreasonable searches and seizures, shall not be violated, and no Warrants shall issue, but upon probable cause, supported by Oath or affirmation, and particularly describing the place to be searched, and the persons or things to be seized."

REASONABLENESS

1. The Fourth Amendment provides that people should be free from unreasonable searches and seizures. Governmental seizures of persons, including arrests, are seizures within the scope of the Fourth Amendment and so must be reasonable.
2. The Fourth Amendment protects the privacy interests of people, not places. *Katz v. United States*, 389 U.S. 347 (1967).

AUTOMOBILE STOPS

Police may not randomly stop a single automobile for license and registration checks. *Delaware v. Prouse*, 440 U.S. 648 (1979).

SEARCH

An important factor in determining the legality of a search under the Fourth Amendment is ascertaining the reasonable expectation of privacy by the person being subjected to that search. *Bond v. United States*, 529 U.S. 334 (2000).

INCORPORATION OF THE "BILL OF RIGHTS"

The Fourteenth Amendment incorporates many of the rights in the Bill of Rights to apply not only to the federal government but also to the states rights.

1. These rights include the following:
   a. Fourth Amendment – prohibition against unreasonable searches and seizures and the exclusionary rule;
   b. Fifth Amendment – prohibition against compulsory self-incrimination;
   c. Sixth Amendment – right to a speedy trial, a public trial, and a trial by jury, to confront witnesses, to a compulsory process, to the assistance of counsel;
   d. Eighth Amendment – prohibition against cruel and unusual punishment.
2. The rights do not include:
   a. Right to grand jury indictment; or
   b. Eighth Amendment prohibition against excessive bail.

PROBABLE CAUSE

Probable cause is the existence of trustworthy facts or knowledge sufficient for a reasonable person to believe that the suspect has committed or is committing a crime.

1. "Stop and Frisk": If police have a reasonable suspicion of criminal activity or involvement in a completed crime, supported by articulable facts, they may detain a person for investigative purposes. *Terry v. Ohio*, 392 U.S. 1 (1968).
2. If the police have reasonable suspicion that the detainee is armed and dangerous, they may frisk the detainee for weapons.
   a. Duration: The detention must be no longer than necessary to conduct a limited investigation to verify the suspicion. If during the detention, probable cause arises, the detention becomes an arrest.

SEIZURE

1. Arrests: An arrest occurs when the police take a person into custody against his will for purposes of criminal prosecution.
   a. An arrest must be based on probable cause. *California v. Hodari D.*, 499 U.S. 621 (1991).
   b. An arrest warrant is generally NOT required for arresting a suspect in a public place.
   c. An arrest warrant is required for a non-emergency arrest of a person in his home.

EVIDENTIARY SEARCH AND SEIZURE

IN GENERAL

1. A proper search requires a valid warrant under the Fourth Amendment, unless the search is one of the valid warrantless searches.
2. Reasonable Expectation of Privacy: In order to contest a search, the person being searched must establish standing. Standing is established through the person showing that he had a legitimate expectation of privacy and that there was governmental conduct involved.
   a. Legitimate Expectation of Privacy.
      i. A right to possession of the place searched.
      ii. The place searched was his home whether or not he owned or had a right to possession of it.
      iii. He was an overnight guest of the owner of the place searched.
   b. Governmental Conduct: Constitutional guidelines for a reasonable search and seizure are limited to actions taken by a government agent. If a non-government agent enacted the search without state authority, a Fourth Amendment challenge cannot be made.
      i. If the crime is induced by governmental conduct that "shocks the conscience," it violates due process.

Evidentiary Search and Seizure continues on page 2 ▶

SEPARATE SOVEREIGNS

The constitutional prohibition against double jeopardy does not apply to trials by separate sovereigns. Thus, one may be tried for the same conduct by both state and federal government or even by two states. However, municipalities are not considered a separate sovereign for the purposes of double jeopardy analysis. *Heath v. Alabama*, 474 U.S. 82 (1985).

Example: A woman is falsely charged with the murder of her husband in the state of Washington. The woman is subsequently convicted of that charge by a vindictive jury. In time, however, she finds out that her husband is alive and well in Louisiana. Based on erroneous legal advice given by a disbarred fellow prisoner, the convicted murderer escapes to Louisiana and kills her husband. The woman is brought to trial in Louisiana. She raises the defense of double jeopardy. Her defense will fail because two sovereigns, in this case, Washington and Louisiana, may try and convict her of the same crime—murder of her husband.

REPROSECUTION

1. After mistrial: *United States v. Perez*, 22 U.S. 579 (1824); *United States v. Dinitz*, 424 U.S. 600 (1976).
    a. Definition: A mistrial is a judicial determination of a trial before a verdict is reached; it is granted on the motion of either party or on the court's own motion that a new trial be held.
    b. Mistrial over the defendant's objection bars prosecution unless there is a "manifest necessity."
    c. Verdict of conviction could be reached but would have to be reversed on appeal due to an obvious procedural error.
    d. Mistrial with defendant's consent: Defendant may not object to re-prosecution.
    e. Exception: the Double Jeopardy Clause bars re-prosecution after a mistrial is declared if the prosecutor or judge intended to provoke the mistrial motion.
2. After acquittal: *Ball v. United States*, 163 U.S. 662 (1896); *Green v. United States*, 355 U.S. 184 (1957).
    a. Definition: Verdict of not guilty by judge or jury or any ruling by a judge that represents a resolution in the defendant's favor of some or all of the factual elements charged.
    b. Rule: Defendant may not be re-prosecuted.
3. After dismissal: *United States v. Scott*, 437 U.S. 82 (1978).
    a. Definition: Judicial termination of a trial before a verdict is reached, but does not involve a resolution of any factual element of the offense charged.
    b. Rule: Re-prosecution after dismissal made on defendant's motion or without objection therefrom is not barred.
4. After conviction: *United States v. Tateo*, 377 U.S. 463 (1964).
    a. Rule: Re-prosecution of a defendant who successfully appeals his conviction on the basis of prejudicial error is not barred.
        i. Exception: Reversal of a conviction obtained on the sole ground that the evidence was insufficient to sustain the guilty verdict.

---

b. Multiple punishment: The government is not barred from convicting and imposing punishment on a person in a single proceeding for violation of separate statutory provisions that constitute the same offense if the legislature so permits.
c. Collateral estoppel: Prosecutor may not re-litigate an issue of ultimate fact in a second prosecution if it has once been determined by a valid and final judgment in the defendant's favor. Test is whether a rational jury could have based its verdict upon an issue other than that which the prosecutor seeks to foreclose from consideration.

ENTRAPMENT

IN GENERAL

1. Entrapment applies when a government agents acts improperly with respect to the defendant. It can be raised either as a defense at trial or as a pretrial motion thereby barring prosecution of the entrapped party. *United States v. Russell*, 411 U.S. 423 (1973).
2. Conduct may be so outrageous in some circumstances to constitute a violation of due process. Jurisdictions employ either a subjective or an objective test.
    a. Subjective test: entrapment is proved if a government agent implants in the mind of an innocent person the disposition to commit the offense and induces its commission so that the government may prosecute. *Sherman v. United States*, 356 U.S. 369 (1958).
    b. Objective test: Entrapment is proved if police conduct falls below commonly accepted standards for the proper use of government power.

TRIAL

RIGHT TO FAIR TRIAL

1. Right to trial by jury. *Duncan v. Louisiana*, 391 U.S. 145 (1968).
    a. Only for "serious" offenses, i.e., those with the possibility of imprisonment for more than 6 months.
    b. No jury trial required for civil contempt. Where no penalty is authorized, if the actual sentence is more than 6 months, the right to a jury trial arises.
    c. No constitutional right to 12 jurors, but there must be at least 6.
    d. No right that the jury verdict be unanimous if there are 12 jurors; for 6-person juries, decision must be unanimous.
    e. Right to have the jury selected from a cross-section of the community
        i. Defendant may contest the fact that a significant segment of the community has been omitted, even if he is not a member of such segment.
        ii. Applies only to venire: there is no right to proportional cross-section of community on the defendant's particular jury.
    f. Prosecution may not use peremptory challenges to exclude potential jurors solely because of race or gender. *Batson v. Kentucky*, 476 U.S. 79 (1986).

RIGHT TO CONFRONT WITNESS

1. Defendant has the right to confront witnesses in a criminal prosecution. This right is not absolute:
    a. Defendant may be removed if he is disruptive.
    b. Defendant is not deprived of his right if he voluntarily leaves the courtroom during the proceedings.
2. Confessions of co-defendants are inadmissible, unless:
    a. References to the defendant can be removed;
    b. The co-conspirator is a witness; or
    c. It is used in rebuttal of defendant's allegation that his own confession was the result of coercion.
3. Statements made at prior judicial proceedings may be admitted if:
    a. Witness is unavailable following a good-faith effort on the part of the prosecution; and
    b. Defendant had an opportunity to cross-examine.

▼

RIGHT TO COUNSEL

1. Right to Appointed Counsel at Trial: "In all criminal prosecutions, the accused shall enjoy the right to…have the assistance of counsel for his defense."
    a. Indigents: Right to counsel does NOT apply in all criminal prosecutions.
    b. Felonies: Defendant has right to counsel in felony criminal trials; the accused is entitled to court-appointed attorney if he cannot afford one.
    c. Misdemeanors: An indigent is entitled to the assistance of counsel in any trial in which a sentence of imprisonment may be imposed.
2. Right of Self-Representation: Must be asserted in a timely fashion or it is LOST; Court may appoint "standby counsel" to take over during trial if necessary.
3. Right to Appointed Counsel on Appeal: The Sixth Amendment is limited to prosecutions. The defendant is entitled to the assistance of counsel under the Fourteenth Amendment Due Process and Equal Protection Clauses for a first appeal but not for subsequent appeals. *Douglas v. California*, 372 U.S. 353 (1963).
4. Right to Effective Representation of Counsel: The Sixth Amendment also requires that counsel provide effective representation of the client. *Strickland v. Washington*, 466 U.S. 668 (1984).
    a. Representation is ineffective if counsel's conduct "so undermines the proper functioning of the adversarial process that the trial cannot be relied on as having produced a just result."
    b. Test:
        i. Deficient representation: Defendant must identify acts or omissions depriving him of effective assistance, based on objective, prevailing norms.
        ii. Prejudice: Defendant must show a reasonable probability that but for such acts or omissions the result would have been different.

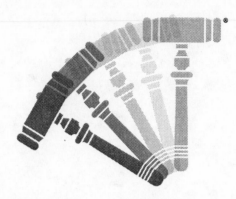

Casenote® Legal Briefs

CRIMINAL PROCEDURE

Keyed to Courses Using

Kamisar, LaFave, Israel, King, Kerr, and Primus's
Modern Criminal Procedure:
Cases, Comments, and Questions
Fourteenth Edition

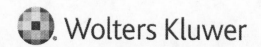

Copyright © 2016 CCH Incorporated. All Rights Reserved.

Published by Wolters Kluwer in New York.

Wolters Kluwer Legal & Regulatory US serves customers worldwide with CCH, Aspen Publishers, and Kluwer Law International products. (www.WKLegaledu.com)

No part of this publication may be reproduced or transmitted in any form or by any means, electronic or mechanical, including photocopy, recording, or utilized by any information storage and retrieval system, without written permission from the publisher. For information about permissions or to request permissions online, visit us at www.WKLegaledu.com, or a written request may be faxed to our permissions department at 212-771-0803.

To contact Customer Service, e-mail customer.service@wolterskluwer.com, call 1-800-234-1660, fax 1-800-901-9075, or mail correspondence to:

Wolters Kluwer
Attn: Order Department
P.O. Box 990
Frederick, MD 21705

Printed in the United States of America.

1 2 3 4 5 6 7 8 9 0

ISBN 978-1-4548-7332-7

About Wolters Kluwer Legal & Regulatory US

Wolters Kluwer Legal & Regulatory US delivers expert content and solutions in the areas of law, corporate compliance, health compliance, reimbursement, and legal education. Its practical solutions help customers successfully navigate the demands of a changing environment to drive their daily activities, enhance decision quality and inspire confident outcomes.

Serving customers worldwide, its legal and regulatory portfolio includes products under the Aspen Publishers, CCH Incorporated, Kluwer Law International, ftwilliam.com and MediRegs names. They are regarded as exceptional and trusted resources for general legal and practice-specific knowledge, compliance and risk management, dynamic workflow solutions, and expert commentary.

Format for the Casenote® Legal Brief

Nature of Case: This section identifies the form of action (e.g., breach of contract, negligence, battery), the type of proceeding (e.g., demurrer, appeal from trial court's jury instructions), or the relief sought (e.g., damages, injunction, criminal sanctions).

Fact Summary: This is included to refresh your memory and can be used as a quick reminder of the facts.

Rule of Law: Summarizes the general principle of law that the case illustrates. It may be used for instant recall of the court's holding and for classroom discussion or home review.

Facts: This section contains all relevant facts of the case, including the contentions of the parties and the lower court holdings. It is written in a logical order to give the student a clear understanding of the case. The plaintiff and defendant are identified by their proper names throughout and are always labeled with a (P) or (D).

Palsgraf v. Long Island R.R. Co.

Injured bystander (P) v. Railroad company (D)

N.Y. Ct. App., 248 N.Y. 339, 162 N.E. 99 (1928).

NATURE OF CASE: Appeal from judgment affirming verdict for plaintiff seeking damages for personal injury.

FACT SUMMARY: Helen Palsgraf (P) was injured on R.R.'s (D) train platform when R.R.'s (D) guard helped a passenger aboard a moving train, causing his package to fall on the tracks. The package contained fireworks which exploded, creating a shock that tipped a scale onto Palsgraf (P).

🏛 RULE OF LAW
The risk reasonably to be perceived defines the duty to be obeyed.

FACTS: Helen Palsgraf (P) purchased a ticket to Rockaway Beach from R.R. (D) and was waiting on the train platform. As she waited, two men ran to catch a train that was pulling out from the platform. The first man jumped aboard, but the second man, who appeared as if he might fall, was helped aboard by the guard on the train who had kept the door open so they could jump aboard. A guard on the platform also helped by pushing him onto the train. The man was carrying a package wrapped in newspaper. In the process, the man dropped his package, which fell on the tracks. The package contained fireworks and exploded. The shock of the explosion was apparently of great enough strength to tip over some scales at the other end of the platform, which fell on Palsgraf (P) and injured her. A jury awarded her damages, and R.R. (D) appealed.

ISSUE: Does the risk reasonably to be perceived define the duty to be obeyed?

HOLDING AND DECISION: (Cardozo, C.J.) Yes. The risk reasonably to be perceived defines the duty to be obeyed. If there is no foreseeable hazard to the injured party as the result of a seemingly innocent act, the act does not become a tort because it happened to be a wrong as to another. If the wrong was not willful, the plaintiff must show that the act as to her had such great and apparent possibilities of danger as to entitle her to protection. Negligence in the abstract is not enough upon which to base liability. Negligence is a relative concept, evolving out of the common law doctrine of trespass on the case. To establish liability, the defendant must owe a legal duty of reasonable care to the injured party. A cause of action in tort will lie where harm,

though unintended, could have been averted or avoided by observance of such a duty. The scope of the duty is limited by the range of danger that a reasonable person could foresee. In this case, there was nothing to suggest from the appearance of the parcel or otherwise that the parcel contained fireworks. The guard could not reasonably have had any warning of a threat to Palsgraf (P), and R.R. (D) therefore cannot be held liable. Judgment is reversed in favor of R.R. (D).

DISSENT: (Andrews, J.) The concept that there is no negligence unless R.R. (D) owes a legal duty to take care as to Palsgraf (P) herself is too narrow. Everyone owes to the world at large the duty of refraining from those acts that may unreasonably threaten the safety of others. If the guard's action was negligent as to those nearby, it was also negligent as to those outside what might be termed the "danger zone." For Palsgraf (P) to recover, R.R.'s (D) negligence must have been the proximate cause of her injury, a question of fact for the jury.

▶ ANALYSIS
The majority defined the limit of the defendant's liability in terms of the danger that a reasonable person in defendant's situation would have perceived. The dissent argued that the limitation should not be placed on liability, but rather on damages. Judge Andrews suggested that only injuries that would not have happened but for R.R.'s (D) negligence should be compensable. Both the majority and dissent recognized the policy-driven need to limit liability for negligent acts, seeking, in the words of Judge Andrews, to define a framework "that will be practical and in keeping with the general understanding of mankind." The Restatement (Second) of Torts has accepted Judge Cardozo's view.

Quicknotes
FORESEEABILITY A reasonable expectation that change is the probable result of certain acts or omissions.

NEGLIGENCE Conduct falling below the standard of care that a reasonable person would demonstrate under similar conditions.

PROXIMATE CAUSE The natural sequence of events without which an injury would not have been sustained.

Party ID: Quick identification of the relationship between the parties.

Concurrence/Dissent: All concurrences and dissents are briefed whenever they are included by the casebook editor.

Analysis: This last paragraph gives you a broad understanding of where the case "fits in" with other cases in the section of the book and with the entire course. It is a hornbook-style discussion indicating whether the case is a majority or minority opinion and comparing the principal case with other cases in the casebook. It may also provide analysis from restatements, uniform codes, and law review articles. The analysis will prove to be invaluable to classroom discussion.

Issue: The issue is a concise question that brings out the essence of the opinion as it relates to the section of the casebook in which the case appears. Both substantive and procedural issues are included if relevant to the decision.

Holding and Decision: This section offers a clear and in-depth discussion of the rule of the case and the court's rationale. It is written in easy-to-understand language and answers the issue presented by applying the law to the facts of the case. When relevant, it includes a thorough discussion of the exceptions to the case as listed by the court, any major cites to the other cases on point, and the names of the judges who wrote the decisions.

Quicknotes: Conveniently defines legal terms found in the case and summarizes the nature of any statutes, codes, or rules referred to in the text.

Wolters Kluwer Legal & Regulatory US is proud to offer *Casenote® Legal Briefs*—continuing thirty years of publishing America's best-selling legal briefs.

Casenote® Legal Briefs are designed to help you save time when briefing assigned cases. Organized under convenient headings, they show you how to abstract the basic facts and holdings from the text of the actual opinions handed down by the courts. Used as part of a rigorous study regimen, they can help you spend more time analyzing and critiquing points of law than on copying bits and pieces of judicial opinions into your notebook or outline.

Casenote® Legal Briefs should never be used as a substitute for assigned casebook readings. They work best when read as a follow-up to reviewing the underlying opinions themselves. Students who try to avoid reading and digesting the judicial opinions in their casebooks or online sources will end up shortchanging themselves in the long run. The ability to absorb, critique, and restate the dynamic and complex elements of case law decisions is crucial to your success in law school and beyond. It cannot be developed vicariously.

Casenote® Legal Briefs represents but one of the many offerings in Legal Education's Study Aid Timeline, which includes:

- *Casenote® Legal Briefs*
- *Emanuel® Law Outlines*
- Emanuel® *Law in a Flash* Flash Cards
- Emanuel® *CrunchTime®* Series

Each of these series is designed to provide you with easy-to-understand explanations of complex points of law. Each volume offers guidance on the principles of legal analysis and, consulted regularly, will hone your ability to spot relevant issues. We have titles that will help you prepare for class, prepare for your exams, and enhance your general comprehension of the law along the way.

To find out more about our law school tools for success, visit us at *www.WKLegaledu.com* or email us at *legaledu@wolterskluwer.com*. We'll be happy to assist you.

How to Brief a Case

A. Decide on a Format and Stick to It

Structure is essential to a good brief. It enables you to arrange systematically the related parts that are scattered throughout most cases, thus making manageable and understandable what might otherwise seem to be an endless and unfathomable sea of information. There are, of course, an unlimited number of formats that can be utilized. However, it is best to find one that suits your needs and stick to it. Consistency breeds both efficiency and the security that when called upon you will know where to look in your brief for the information you are asked to give.

Any format, as long as it presents the essential elements of a case in an organized fashion, can be used. Experience, however, has led *Casenote® Legal Briefs* to develop and utilize the following format because of its logical flow and universal applicability.

NATURE OF CASE: This is a brief statement of the legal character and procedural status of the case (e.g., "Appeal of a burglary conviction").

There are many different alternatives open to a litigant dissatisfied with a court ruling. The key to determining which one has been used is to discover *who is asking this court for what.*

This first entry in the brief should be kept as *short as possible.* Use the court's terminology if you understand it. But since jurisdictions vary as to the titles of pleadings, the best entry is the one that addresses who wants what in this proceeding, not the one that sounds most like the court's language.

RULE OF LAW: A statement of the general principle of law that the case illustrates (e.g., "An acceptance that varies any term of the offer is considered a rejection and counteroffer").

Determining the rule of law of a case is a procedure similar to determining the issue of the case. Avoid being fooled by red herrings; there may be a few rules of law mentioned in the case excerpt, but usually only one is *the* rule with which the casebook editor is concerned. The techniques used to locate the issue, described below, may also be utilized to find the rule of law. Generally, your best guide is simply the chapter heading. It is a clue to the point the casebook editor seeks to make and should be kept in mind when reading every case in the respective section.

FACTS: A synopsis of only the essential facts of the case, i.e., those bearing upon or leading up to the issue.

The facts entry should be a short statement of the events and transactions that led one party to initiate legal proceedings against another in the first place. While some cases conveniently state the salient facts at the beginning of the decision, in other instances they will have to be culled from hiding places throughout the text, even from concurring and dissenting opinions. Some of the "facts" will often be in dispute and should be so noted. Conflicting evidence may be briefly pointed up. "Hard" facts must be included. Both must be *relevant* in order to be listed in the facts entry. It is impossible to tell what is relevant until the entire case is read, as the ultimate determination of the rights and liabilities of the parties may turn on something buried deep in the opinion.

Generally, the facts entry should not be longer than three to five *short* sentences.

It is often helpful to identify the role played by a party in a given context. For example, in a construction contract case the identification of a party as the "contractor" or "builder" alleviates the need to tell that that party was the one who was supposed to have built the house.

It is always helpful, and a good general practice, to identify the "plaintiff" and the "defendant." This may seem elementary and uncomplicated, but, especially in view of the creative editing practiced by some casebook editors, it is sometimes a difficult or even impossible task. Bear in mind that the *party presently* seeking something from this court may not be the plaintiff, and that sometimes only the cross-claim of a defendant is treated in the excerpt. Confusing or misaligning the parties can ruin your analysis and understanding of the case.

ISSUE: A statement of the general legal question answered by or illustrated in the case. For clarity, the issue is best put in the form of a question capable of a "yes" or "no" answer. In reality, the issue is simply the Rule of Law put in the form of a question (e.g., "May an offer be accepted by performance?").

The major problem presented in discerning what is *the* issue in the case is that an opinion usually purports to raise and answer several questions. However, except for rare cases, only one such question is really the issue in the case. Collateral issues not necessary to the resolution of the matter in controversy are handled by the court by language known as *"obiter dictum"* or merely *"dictum."* While dicta may be included later in the brief, they have no place under the issue heading.

To find the issue, ask *who wants what* and then go on to ask *why did that party succeed or fail in getting it.* Once this is determined, the "why" should be turned into a question.

The complexity of the issues in the cases will vary, but in all cases a single-sentence question should sum up the issue. *In a few cases,* there will be two, or even more rarely, three issues of equal importance to the resolution of the case. Each should be expressed in a single-sentence question.

Since many issues are resolved by a court in coming to a final disposition of a case, the casebook editor will reproduce the portion of the opinion containing the issue or issues most relevant to the area of law under scrutiny. A noted law professor gave this advice: "Close the book; look at the title on the cover." Chances are, if it is Property, you need not concern yourself with whether, for example, the federal government's treatment of the plaintiff's land really raises a federal question sufficient to support jurisdiction on this ground in federal court.

The same rule applies to chapter headings designating sub-areas within the subjects. They tip you off as to what the text is designed to teach. The cases are arranged in a casebook to show a progression or development of the law, so that the preceding cases may also help.

It is also most important to remember to *read the notes and questions* at the end of a case to determine what the editors wanted you to have gleaned from it.

HOLDING AND DECISION: This section should succinctly explain the rationale of the court in arriving at its decision. In capsulizing the "reasoning" of the court, it should always include an application of the general rule or rules of law to the specific facts of the case. Hidden justifications come to light in this entry: the reasons for the state of the law, the public policies, the biases and prejudices, those considerations that influence the justices' thinking and, ultimately, the outcome of the case. At the end, there should be a short indication of the disposition or procedural resolution of the case (e.g., "Decision of the trial court for Mr. Smith (P) reversed").

The foregoing format is designed to help you "digest" the reams of case material with which you will be faced in your law school career. Once mastered by practice, it will place at your fingertips the information the authors of your casebooks have sought to impart to you in case-by-case illustration and analysis.

B. Be as Economical as Possible in Briefing Cases

Once armed with a format that encourages succinctness, it is as important to be economical with regard to the time spent on the actual reading of the case as it is to be economical in the writing of the brief itself. This does not mean "skimming" a case. Rather, it means reading the case with an "eye" trained to recognize into which "section" of your brief a particular passage or line fits and having a system for quickly and precisely marking the case so that the passages fitting any one particular part of

the brief can be easily identified and brought together in a concise and accurate manner when the brief is actually written.

It is of no use to simply repeat everything in the opinion of the court; record only enough information to trigger your recollection of what the court said. Nevertheless, an accurate statement of the "law of the case," i.e., the legal principle applied to the facts, is absolutely essential to class preparation and to learning the law under the case method.

To that end, it is important to develop a "shorthand" that you can use to make marginal notations. These notations will tell you at a glance in which section of the brief you will be placing that particular passage or portion of the opinion.

Some students prefer to underline all the salient portions of the opinion (with a pencil or colored underliner marker), making marginal notations as they go along. Others prefer the color-coded method of underlining, utilizing different colors of markers to underline the salient portions of the case, each separate color being used to represent a different section of the brief. For example, blue underlining could be used for passages relating to the rule of law, yellow for those relating to the issue, and green for those relating to the holding and decision, etc. While it has its advocates, the color-coded method can be confusing and time-consuming (all that time spent on changing colored markers). Furthermore, it can interfere with the continuity and concentration many students deem essential to the reading of a case for maximum comprehension. In the end, however, it is a matter of personal preference and style. Just remember, whatever method you use, underlining must be used sparingly or its value is lost.

If you take the marginal notation route, an efficient and easy method is to go along underlining the key portions of the case and placing in the margin alongside them the following "markers" to indicate where a particular passage or line "belongs" in the brief you will write:

N   (NATURE OF CASE)
RL   (RULE OF LAW)
I   (ISSUE)
HL   (HOLDING AND DECISION, relates to the RULE OF LAW behind the decision)
HR   (HOLDING AND DECISION, gives the RATIONALE or reasoning behind the decision)
HA   (HOLDING AND DECISION, applies the general principle(s) of law to the facts of the case to arrive at the decision)

Remember that a particular passage may well contain information necessary to more than one part of your brief, in which case you simply note that in the margin. If you are using the color-coded underlining method instead of marginal notation, simply make asterisks or checks in the margin next to the passage in question in the colors that indicate the additional sections of the brief where it might be utilized.

The economy of utilizing "shorthand" in marking cases for briefing can be maintained in the actual brief writing process itself by utilizing "law student shorthand" within the brief. There are many commonly used words and phrases for which abbreviations can be substituted in your briefs (and in your class notes also). You can develop abbreviations that are personal to you and which will save you a lot of time. A reference list of briefing abbreviations can be found on page x of this book.

C. Use Both the Briefing Process and the Brief as a Learning Tool

Now that you have a format and the tools for briefing cases efficiently, the most important thing is to make the time spent in briefing profitable to you and to make the most advantageous use of the briefs you create. Of course, the briefs are invaluable for classroom reference when you are called upon to explain or analyze a particular case. However, they are also useful in reviewing for exams. A quick glance at the fact summary should bring the case to mind, and a rereading of the rule of law should enable you to go over the underlying legal concept in your mind, how it was applied in that particular case, and how it might apply in other factual settings.

As to the value to be derived from engaging in the briefing process itself, there is an immediate benefit that arises from being forced to sift through the essential facts and reasoning from the court's opinion and to succinctly express them in your own words in your brief. The process ensures that you understand the case and the point that it illustrates, and that means you will be ready to absorb further analysis and information brought forth in class. It also ensures you will have something to say when called upon in class. The briefing process helps develop a mental agility for getting to the *gist* of a case and for identifying, expounding on, and applying the legal concepts and issues found there. The briefing process is the mental process on which you must rely in taking law school examinations; it is also the mental process upon which a lawyer relies in serving his clients and in making his living.

Abbreviations for Briefs

acceptance	acp	offer	O
affirmed	aff	offeree	OE
answer	ans	offeror	OR
assumption of risk	a/r	ordinance	ord
attorney	atty	pain and suffering	p/s
beyond a reasonable doubt	b/r/d	parol evidence	p/e
bona fide purchaser	BFP	plaintiff	P
breach of contract	br/k	prima facie	p/f
cause of action	c/a	probable cause	p/c
common law	c/l	proximate cause	px/c
Constitution	Con	real property	r/p
constitutional	con	reasonable doubt	r/d
contract	K	reasonable man	r/m
contributory negligence	c/n	rebuttable presumption	rb/p
cross	x	remanded	rem
cross-complaint	x/c	res ipsa loquitur	RIL
cross-examination	x/ex	respondeat superior	r/s
cruel and unusual punishment	c/u/p	Restatement	RS
defendant	D	reversed	rev
dismissed	dis	Rule Against Perpetuities	RAP
double jeopardy	d/j	search and seizure	s/s
due process	d/p	search warrant	s/w
equal protection	e/p	self-defense	s/d
equity	eq	specific performance	s/p
evidence	ev	statute	S
exclude	exc	statute of frauds	S/F
exclusionary rule	exc/r	statute of limitations	S/L
felony	f/n	summary judgment	s/j
freedom of speech	f/s	tenancy at will	t/w
good faith	g/f	tenancy in common	t/c
habeas corpus	h/c	tenant	t
hearsay	hr	third party	TP
husband	H	third party beneficiary	TPB
injunction	inj	transferred intent	TI
in loco parentis	ILP	unconscionable	uncon
inter vivos	I/v	unconstitutional	unconst
joint tenancy	j/t	undue influence	u/e
judgment	judgt	Uniform Commercial Code	UCC
jurisdiction	jur	unilateral	uni
last clear chance	LCC	vendee	VE
long-arm statute	LAS	vendor	VR
majority view	maj	versus	v
meeting of minds	MOM	void for vagueness	VFV
minority view	min	weight of authority	w/a
Miranda rule	Mir/r	weight of the evidence	w/e
Miranda warnings	Mir/w	wife	W
negligence	neg	with	w/
notice	ntc	within	w/i
nuisance	nus	without	w/o
obligation	ob	without prejudice	w/o/p
obscene	obs	wrongful death	wr/d

Table of Cases

CHAPTER 4

The Right to Counsel

Quick Reference Rules of Law

Betts v. Brady

Farmhand (D) v. Court (P)

316 U.S. 455 (1942).

NATURE OF CASE: Criminal prosecution for robbery.

FACT SUMMARY: Betts (D) was indicted for robbery and his request to have counsel appointed for his trial was denied under a local law which allowed appointed counsel only for rape and murder cases.

🏛 RULE OF LAW
The right to counsel is not fully applicable to the states because the Sixth Amendment's guarantee of counsel is not completely incorporated by the Fourteenth Amendment, but the failure to appoint counsel is a violation of due process, if, under the circumstances of the case, it results in a conviction that is lacking in fundamental fairness.

FACTS: Betts (D), an indigent, was indicted for robbery. He was an unemployed farmhand of ordinary intelligence but uneducated. He requested to have counsel appointed for him because he was too poor to afford an attorney, but his request was denied under a local rule that allowed the appointment of counsel only in rape and murder cases. Betts's (D) defense to the charge was the presentation of an alibi, so the only issue involved in the trial was the veracity of the prosecution and defense witnesses. Betts (D) elected to have a trial without a jury and didn't take the stand in his own defense; the trial resulted in a conviction and an eight-year sentence.

ISSUE: Is the state's failure to appoint counsel for an indigent defendant a violation of the Fourteenth Amendment guarantee of due process?

HOLDING AND DECISION: (Roberts, J.) No. The Fourteenth Amendment's guarantee of due process does not require the appointment of counsel for indigent defendants in all criminal cases. Under the Sixth Amendment, which applies only to federal courts, appointment of counsel is required for all criminal cases if the defendant is unable to afford counsel and he does not intentionally and competently waive his right to counsel. But the Fourteenth Amendment does not incorporate all aspects of the Sixth Amendment, so the federal rule of appointment of counsel for all criminal cases is not applicable to the states. The Sixth Amendment is not fully incorporated because the appointment of counsel is not a fundamental right essential to preserve the fairness of all trials. This proposition is shown by the fact that in most states the appointment of counsel is not considered required for all cases but is essentially a question of legislative policy. However, in most states the court does have the power to appoint

counsel where it is necessary in the interest of fairness. Affirmed.

DISSENT: (Black, J.) First, the Fourteenth Amendment makes the Sixth Amendment guarantee of counsel fully applicable to the states, but this view is not accepted by the majority. Nonetheless, even if the majority's view of incomplete incorporation is adopted, the nature of the offense and the circumstances of the trial show that the denial of counsel was a violation of due process.

▶ ANALYSIS

This case is important only for historical reasons because its holding that the Sixth Amendment is not fully applicable to the states through the Fourteenth Amendment was reversed in the following case of *Gideon v. Wainwright,* 72 U.S. 335 (1963). But the rule had vitality until 1963. Under the *Betts* rule, the Court was willing to find special circumstances which made the denial of appointed counsel violation of due process.

■▬■

Quicknotes

PROCEDURAL DUE PROCESS The constitutional mandate that if the state or federal government acts so as to deny a citizen of a life, liberty or property interest the individual is first entitled to notice and the right to be heard.

RIGHT TO COUNSEL Right conferred by the Sixth Amendment that the accused shall be provided effective legal assistance in a criminal proceeding.

■▬■

Gideon v. Wainwright

Non-capital felon (D) v. Court (P)

372 U.S. 335 (1963).

NATURE OF CASE: Appeal of denial of petition for habeas corpus relief.

FACT SUMMARY: Gideon (D) appealed his criminal conviction for a noncapital felony on the grounds that the trial court's refusal to appoint counsel for him was unconstitutional.

> ## 🏛 RULE OF LAW
> The right to counsel is one of those rights that is "fundamental and essential to a fair trial" and is thus made obligatory upon the states by the Fourteenth Amendment.

FACTS: Gideon (D) was convicted of a noncapital felony after the Florida trial court refused to appoint counsel for him because the law allowed such appointment only in capital cases. His petition for habeas corpus relief was denied, but the United States Supreme Court granted certiorari to consider his contention that the denial of appointed counsel had been unconstitutional.

ISSUE: Is the right to counsel a fundamental right that is made obligatory upon the states by the Fourteenth Amendment?

HOLDING AND DECISION: (Black, J.) Yes. A provision of the Bill of Rights that is "fundamental and essential to a fair trial" is made obligatory upon the states by the Fourteenth Amendment. *Betts v. Brady*, 316 U.S. 455 (1942), was correct in so assuming. However, the *Betts* Court was wrong in concluding that the Sixth Amendment's guarantee of counsel is not one of those fundamental rights. It is. In deciding it was not, the *Betts* Court made an abrupt break with its own well-considered precedents. Today, this Court returns to these old precedents by recognizing that the right to counsel of one charged with a crime, is deemed fundamental and essential to a fair trial in our country. Reversed.

CONCURRENCE: (Clark, J.) The Constitution makes no distinction between capital and noncapital cases. It requires due process for a deprivation of "liberty" just as for a deprivation of "life."

CONCURRENCE: (Harlan, J.) While *Betts* should be overruled, to say that it represented "an abrupt break with well-considered precedents" is wrong. *Betts* recognized that special circumstances similar to those which made denial of counsel unconstitutional in capital cases could exist in noncapital cases, but it required they be shown in order to establish a denial of due process. The special circumstances rule has been abandoned in capital cases and it is time it now be abandoned in noncapital cases which carry the possibility of a substantial prison sentence.

▌ ANALYSIS

The flip side of the right to have counsel is the right not to have counsel, i.e., self-representation. The American Bar Association has taken the position that the right to counsel is so fundamental that except in the simplest trials the court should appoint "standby counsel" when a defendant chooses to represent himself. Most courts that have addressed the issue have decided that a defendant need not specifically be informed of his right to represent himself.

━━

Quicknotes

PROCEDURAL DUE PROCESS The constitutional mandate that if the state or federal government acts so as to deny a citizen of a life, liberty or property interest the individual is first entitled to notice and the right to be heard.

RIGHT TO COUNSEL Right conferred by the Sixth Amendment that the accused shall be provided effective legal assistance in a criminal proceeding.

━━

Rothgery v. Gillespie County

Individual (P) v. State (D)

554 U.S. 191 (2008).

NATURE OF CASE: Appeal from lower court decision in favor of the state.

FACT SUMMARY: Using erroneous information, the State (D) charged Rothgery (P) with unlawful possession of a firearm by a felon. The State (D) arraigned Rothgery (P) without the assistance of counsel and subsequently jailed Rothgery (P) for a short time before he posted a security bond.

RULE OF LAW
A criminal defendant's initial appearance before a judicial officer, where he learns of the charges against him, constitutes the start of adversarial proceedings that triggers the attachment of the Sixth Amendment's right to counsel.

FACTS: Using erroneous information, Texas police arrested Rothgery (P) for unlawful possession of a firearm. The police brought him before a magistrate judge for an Article 15.17 hearing. At the hearing, the magistrate judge found probable cause existed and set bail at $5,000. The State (D) then jailed Rothgery (P) before he posted a security bond. Six months later, a grand jury formally indicted Rothgery (P) for the same charge. After his rearrest, the State (D) jailed Rothgery (P) for three weeks until he was able to post bail. The State (D) then assigned him a lawyer. The lawyer proved to the State (P) that the charges were erroneous. The State (D) agreed and dismissed all charges. Rothgery (P) then brought this action against the State (D) under 42 U.S.C. 1983, alleging that the State's (D) unwritten policy of denying indigent defendants with counsel until a formal indictment issued, well after initial arraignment, violated his Sixth Amendment right to counsel. The district court granted the State (D) summary judgment and the Fifth Circuit Court of Appeals affirmed. Rothgery (P) appealed to the United States Supreme Court.

ISSUE: Does a criminal defendant's initial appearance before a judicial officer, where he learns of the charges against him, constitute the start of adversarial proceedings that triggers the attachment of the Sixth Amendment's right to counsel?

HOLDING AND DECISION: (Souter, J.) Yes. A criminal defendant's initial appearance before a judicial officer, where he learns of the charges against him, constitutes the start of adversarial proceedings that triggers the attachment of the Sixth Amendment's right to counsel. The court has previously held that the Sixth Amendment right to counsel attaches at the initiation of criminal proceedings, whether that initiation is in the form of an indictment,

arraignment, preliminary hearing, or some other hearing wherein the defendant is formally charged. Typically, an arraignment is the initial appearance. The issue here is whether Texas's Article 15.17 hearing is an initial appearance. It clearly qualifies. At the hearing, the State (D) informed Rothgery (P) of the charges against him and set bail. Once attachment occurs, the state must appoint counsel during any critical stage of the post-attachment proceedings. The Court shall not consider at this time whether the six-month delay in appointment of counsel for Rothgery (P) specifically constituted a violation of his right to counsel. Reversed.

CONCURRENCE: (Roberts, C.J.) The Court is bound by multiple precedents which have found that the Sixth Amendment right attaches at the point of the initial hearing. Justice Alito, however, correctly points out in his concurrence the distinction between the time the right attaches and the circumstances when counsel must be provided to the defendant.

CONCURRENCE: (Alito, J.) The Court's opinion is correct that Rothgery's (P) right to counsel attached at the Article 15.17 hearing. However, there is a distinction between when the right to counsel attaches and the state's duty to supply counsel post-attachment. The moment of attachment is not the same as a criminal defendant's substantive entitlement to assistance of counsel. The state need only supply counsel at those pretrial and trial events that may prejudice the outcome of the defendant's prosecution. These are referred to as critical stages of the prosecution, such as a police lineup or pretrial interrogations and of course the trial itself.

DISSENT: (Thomas, J.) The commencement of a criminal prosecution referred to in the Sixth Amendment occurs when the state files formal criminal charges in court to try and punish the defendant. Rothgery's (P) appearance before the magistrate here did not commence a criminal prosecution. No formal charges were filed. The only document submitted at the time was an affidavit from a police officer. Our prior decisions have used the term "arraignment" as the usual time when the right to counsel attaches. However, there is a difference between an informal hearing before a magistrate after an arrest and a formal arraignment post-indictment where the defendant enters a plea. The latter proceeding should be when the right to counsel arises.

Continued on next page.

▶ *ANALYSIS*

Justice Alito's concurrence is critical to an understanding of the Sixth Amendment's right to counsel. Eight of the nine judges agreed that the right attaches at the initial appearance, regardless of the form of that appearance. That was the sole question at issue here. It is a different analysis as to when the state must provide counsel to an indigent defendant throughout the prosecution.

■━━■

Quicknotes

RIGHT TO COUNSEL Right conferred by the Sixth Amendment that the accused shall be provided effective legal assistance in a criminal proceeding.

SIXTH AMENDMENT Provides the right to a speedy and public trial by impartial jury, the right to be informed of the accusation, the right to confront witnesses, and the right to have the assistance of counsel in all criminal prosecutions.

■━━■

Ross v. Moffitt

Forgery convict (D) v. Court (P)

417 U.S. 600 (1974).

NATURE OF CASE: Appeal from a conviction for forgery.

FACT SUMMARY: Ross (D) contended that he was entitled to appointed counsel to represent him in a petition for discretionary review by the state supreme court.

🏛 RULE OF LAW
There is no constitutional right to appointed counsel for discretionary appellate proceedings.

FACTS: Ross (D) was convicted of forgery in a North Carolina state court. He was represented at trial and in his appeal of right to the intermediate appellate court by a public defender. He was denied such representation in his discretionary appeal to the state supreme court. The United States Supreme Court granted review.

ISSUE: Is there a constitutional right to appointed counsel for discretionary appellate proceedings?

HOLDING AND DECISION: (Rehnquist, J.) No. There is no constitutional right to appointed counsel for discretionary appellate proceedings. At the trial stage, the state's responsibility is to ensure the defendant's rights are protected. The state has channeled resources toward convicting a defendant, thus in an adversarial arena it is only just that counsel be appointed. However, on appeal, the defendant initiates the process in order to overturn a lower court. The defendant is thus not in need of protection from state action. He is the aggressor. No constitutional right exists in this circumstance. Affirmed.

DISSENT: (Douglas, J.) The indigent defendant, whose liberty is at stake, is at a great disadvantage on appeal whether such is of right or discretionary. He is entitled to appointed counsel.

▶ ANALYSIS

This case rejects the equal protection argument that wealthy defendants have a better chance in discretionary appeal than indigent defendants. Wealth is not a suspect classification and thus indigence does not necessarily entitle the defendant to increased access to appellate review.

■ ▬ ■

Quicknotes

EQUAL PROTECTION A constitutional guarantee that no person shall be denied the same protection of the laws enjoyed by other persons in life circumstances.

SUSPECT CLASSIFICATION A class of persons that have historically been subject to discriminatory treatment; statutes drawing a distinction between persons based on a suspect classification, i.e., race, nationality or alienage, are subject to a strict scrutiny standard of review.

■ ▬ ■

Faretta v. California

Grand theft defendant (D) v. State (P)

422 U.S. 806 (1975).

NATURE OF CASE: Appeal from conviction for grand theft.

FACT SUMMARY: Faretta (D) was convicted following a trial court's refusal to allow him to represent himself.

🏛 RULE OF LAW
A criminal defendant has a Sixth Amendment right to conduct a pro se defense.

FACTS: Faretta (D) was charged with grand theft. Before trial, he indicated that he wished to conduct his own defense. Faretta (D) was a high school graduate and had once before represented himself. The trial court compelled him to allow an attorney to represent him, and he was convicted. Faretta's (D) appeals were rejected in the state courts. Faretta (D) appealed to the United States Supreme Court.

ISSUE: Does a criminal defendant have a Sixth Amendment right to conduct a pro se defense?

HOLDING AND DECISION: (Stewart, J.) Yes. A criminal defendant has a Sixth Amendment right to conduct a pro se defense. The protections afforded a defendant in the Sixth Amendment are personal to him. The right to counsel is just that—a right. Rights may be waived. To thrust counsel upon an unwilling defendant would violate the language of the Amendment. As long as waiver of counsel is intelligently made, the state cannot force one upon a defendant. Reversed.

DISSENT: (Burger, C.J.) The Sixth Amendment guarantees a defendant a full defense, and allowing a defendant to waive the right to counsel violates this spirit.

DISSENT: (Blackmun, J.) The overriding interest in any criminal prosecution is that justice be done. Without counsel justice often will not be done to a defendant.

▌ ANALYSIS

The rule here was later lessened somewhat. In *McKaskle v. Wiggins,* 465 U.S. 168 (1984), the Court held that a court could force a defendant to have counsel in a consultant role while conducting his defense. Obviously, where consultation ends and outright representation starts is not a question easily answered.

Quicknotes

GRAND THEFT The illegal taking of another's property with the intent to deprive the owner thereof, the value of which is greater than the statutory amount.

PRO SE DEFENSE Representing oneself at trial rather than retaining a lawyer.

■■■

United States v. Gonzalez-Lopez

Federal government (P) v. Alleged drug distributor (D)

548 U.S. 140 (2006).

NATURE OF CASE: Appeal from vacated conviction for distribution of illegal drugs.

FACT SUMMARY: Gonzalez-Lopez (D) contended that the district court's erroneous denial of application for admission *pro hac vice* by Low, his counsel of choice, entitled him to a reversal of his conviction on drug charges.

🏛 RULE OF LAW
A trial court's erroneous deprivation of a criminal defendant's choice of counsel entitles him to reversal of his conviction.

FACTS: Gonzalez-Lopez (D) hired attorney Low, a California attorney, to represent him on a federal drug charge in federal court in Missouri. The district court denied Low's application for admission *pro hac vice* on the ground that he had violated a professional conduct rule in that jurisdiction and then, with one exception, prevented Gonzalez-Lopez (D) from meeting or consulting with Low throughout the trial. Instead, a local attorney represented Gonzalez-Lopez (D). The jury found Gonzalez-Lopez (D) guilty. The court of appeals reversed, holding that the district court erred in interpreting the disciplinary rule, that the court's refusal to admit Low therefore violated Gonzalez-Lopez's (D) Sixth Amendment right to paid counsel of his choosing, and that this violation was not subject to harmless error review. The Government (P) conceded that the district court had erroneously deprived Gonzalez-Lopez (D) of his counsel of choice. The United States Supreme Court granted certiorari.

ISSUE: Does a trial court's erroneous deprivation of a criminal defendant's choice of counsel entitle him to reversal of his conviction?

HOLDING AND DECISION: (Scalia, J.) Yes. A trial court's erroneous deprivation of a criminal defendant's choice of counsel entitles him to reversal of his conviction. Although the Government (P) conceded that the district court's error violated Gonzalez-Lopez's (D) Sixth Amendment right to counsel of choice, it nonetheless contends that the violation is not "complete" unless the defendant can show that substitute counsel was ineffective to the extent that his performance was deficient and the defendant was prejudiced by it—or the defendant can demonstrate that substitute counsel's performance, while not deficient, was not as good as what his counsel of choice would have provided, creating a "reasonable probability that . . . the result . . . would have been different." To support these propositions, the Government (P) emphasizes that the right to counsel is accorded to ensure that the

accused receive a fair trial, and asserts that a trial is not unfair unless a defendant has been prejudiced. The right to counsel of choice, however, does not require that a trial be fair, but that a particular guarantee of fairness be provided, namely, that the accused be defended by the counsel he believes to be best. The Due Process Clause requires that a trial be fair, but the elements of fairness can also be found in the Counsel Clause. The right provided in that Clause was violated here; no additional showing of prejudice is required to make the violation "complete." While prejudice is required for a showing of ineffective counsel, which is derived from the Sixth Amendment's purpose of ensuring a fair trial, choice of counsel does not derive from this purpose. Instead, it is a root constitutional principle, so that its violation does not require more than a showing that the defendant was deprived of his counsel of choice. This Sixth Amendment violation is also not subject to harmless-error analysis, as the court of appeals correctly held. The erroneous deprivation of the right to counsel of choice qualifies as structural error, "with consequences that are necessarily unquantifiable and indeterminate." Different attorneys will pursue different strategies with regard to myriad trial matters, and the choice of attorney will affect whether and on what terms the defendant cooperates with the prosecution, plea bargains, or decides to go to trial. It is impossible to know what different choices the rejected counsel would have made, and then to quantify the impact of those different choices on the outcome of the proceedings. To do so would require speculation. This inquiry is not comparable to that required to show that a counsel's deficient performance prejudiced a defendant. Notwithstanding these rulings, nothing in this opinion should be construed as casting any doubt, or qualifying in any way, the Court's previous holdings limiting the right to counsel of choice and recognizing trial courts' authority to establish criteria for admitting lawyers to argue before them. However broad a trial court's discretion may be, it is conceded here that the district court erred, and the ensuing choice of counsel violation is not subject to harmless-error review. Affirmed.

DISSENT: (Alito, J.) Instead of the per se rule that the majority adopts, defendants denied their first choice of counsel should be required to show that the error affected the quality of their representation. The majority errs in concluding that the Sixth Amendment protects a defendant's choice of counsel; instead, it protects the right to have the assistance of that counsel. It follows, therefore, that if the quality of that assistance is not adversely affected,

Continued on next page.

there is no constitutional violation. Such an interpretation is supported by the Sixth Amendment itself, which focuses on assistance of counsel, rather than on counsel's identity. Further, a defendant's right to counsel of choice has always been limited by various factors, as where the chosen counsel may not practice before the court hearing the case, or by conflict-of-interest rules. Under this understanding, a defendant would not have to show that the second-choice attorney was constitutionally ineffective, but would be entitled to a new trial if the he could show an identifiable difference in the quality of representation between the disqualified counsel and the attorney who represents the defendant at trial. Even if, however, the majority's rule is correct, it does not follow that it will always require reversal. Instead, reversal should occur only where fundamental unfairness has been shown—and such unfairness does not flow inexorably from the denial of first-choice counsel. The majority's focus on the trial error/structural defect dichotomy is misleading since the touchstone of structural error is fundamental unfairness. Thus, reversal should not be automatic where constitutional error does not necessarily result in such unfairness. Otherwise, the majority's per se rule gives the defendant a second bite at the apple even if second-choice counsel was "brilliant." Requiring some showing of prejudice, or permitting harmless-error review would avoid such an anomalous result.

▌ *ANALYSIS*

It should be kept in mind that the right to counsel of choice is not implicated where the defendant must have appointed counsel. In such situations, the court does not violate the defendant's choice of counsel right if it denies the appointment of a specific requested attorney.

■━━■

Quicknotes

DUE PROCESS CLAUSE Clauses, found in the Fifth and Fourteenth Amendments to the United States Constitution, providing that no person shall be deprived of "life, liberty, or property, without due process of law."

HARMLESS ERROR An error taking place during trial that does not require the reviewing court to overturn or modify the trial court's judgment, in that, it did not affect the appellant's substantial rights or the disposition of the action.

PRO HAC VICE Applicable to a specific occasion; the use or application of a condition for the limited duration of a single situation.

■━━■

CHAPTER 5

The Performance of Counsel

Quick Reference Rules of Law

Strickland v. Washington

Confessing convict (D) v. State (P)

466 U.S. 668 (1984).

NATURE OF CASE: Appeal from denial of writ of habeas corpus.

FACT SUMMARY: Strickland (D) contended he was denied effective assistance of counsel when his attorney failed to present character evidence that might have reduced his sentence.

RULE OF LAW
A defendant must, in order to show he was denied the effective assistance of counsel, establish that: (1) counsel's performance was deficient and (2) the deficient performance prejudiced the defense.

FACTS: Strickland (D) confessed to several crimes including murder, torture, and kidnapping. After he was convicted, he stated at the sentencing hearing that he was sorry for and regretted his crimes. His appointed counsel chose not to introduce any character evidence and to allow the court to pass sentence based solely on Strickland's (D) statements. The attorney knew the judge favored such repentance and that introducing character evidence would subject Strickland (D) to cross-examination. Strickland (D) was sentenced to death. He petitioned the district court for a writ of habeas corpus, contending he was denied effective assistance of counsel. The district court found that any errors made by counsel were not prejudicial and denied the writ. The court of appeals reversed, and the United States Supreme Court granted certiorari.

ISSUE: Must a defendant show that his defense was prejudiced by his counsel's deficient performance in order to sustain a claim he was denied effective assistance of counsel?

HOLDING AND DECISION: (O'Connor, J.) Yes. In order to establish that he was denied effective assistance of counsel, a defendant must show: (1) counsel's performance was deficient and (2) the deficient performance prejudiced his defense. This requires that the defendant show that counsel's errors were so serious as to deprive him of a fair trial. In this case, Strickland's (D) counsel gave him reasonably effective assistance by pursuing a reasonable defense strategy. Further, any further character evidence submitted at the hearing would have been cumulative and ineffective. Therefore, any errors committed were not prejudicial. As a result, Strickland (D) failed to establish he was denied effective counsel. Reversed.

DISSENT: (Marshall, J.) The prejudice standard here established by the majority is so malleable that, in practice, it will either have no grip at all or will yield excessive variation in the manner in which the Sixth Amendment is interpreted and applied by different courts. To tell lawyers and lower courts that counsel for a criminal defendant must behave "reasonably" and must act like "a reasonably competent attorney" is to tell them almost nothing.

ANALYSIS

In this case, the Court stated that the "benchmark for judging any claim of ineffectiveness must be whether counsel's conduct so undermined the proper functioning of the adversarial process that the trial cannot be relied on as having produced a just result." From this point of departure, it broke the test down to two parts: performance and prejudice.

Quicknotes

CERTIORARI A discretionary writ issued by a superior court to an inferior court in order to review the lower court's decisions; the Supreme Court's writ ordering such review.

CHARACTER EVIDENCE Evidence of someone's moral standing in a community based on reputation.

WRIT OF HABEAS CORPUS A proceeding in which a defendant brings a writ to compel a judicial determination of whether he is lawfully being held in custody.

Harrington v. Richter

State (P) v. Convicted felon (D)

562 U.S. 86 (2011).

NATURE OF CASE: Review of petition for habeas corpus relief.

FACT SUMMARY: Richter (D) was convicted of several counts, including murder, but argued on appeal his criminal defense attorney provided ineffective assistance for failure to consult certain experts. Richter's (D) conviction was affirmed at each step. Richter (D) sought habeas corpus relief in the federal system after being denied relief in the state courts.

🏛 RULE OF LAW
Federal habeas relief may be granted when the earlier state court decision involved an unreasonable application of clearly established federal law.

FACTS: Joshua Johnson told police he was in bed and Patrick Klein was in the living room when two men broke into his house, shot him and Klein, and stole a gun safe, weapons, and cash. Evidence at the scene corroborated Johnson's account. Blood spatter and pools of blood were in the kitchen, the living room, and in the doorway to Johnson's bedroom. Investigators did not take samples from the bedroom doorway blood pool. When investigators searched Richter's (D) residence, they found a gun safe and ammunition that matched the caliber weapons used to shoot Johnson and Klein. Klein died of his injuries. Richter (P) initially denied involvement but then produced one of the weapons and told a version of events that differed from Johnson's. Richter (D) and Christian Branscombe were tried on several charges, including murder. In his opening statement, Richter's (D) defense attorney indicated Branscombe shot Johnson in self-defense and Klein was killed in the crossfire in the bedroom doorway. The prosecution had not intended to introduce forensic evidence related to the blood samples, but changed course after the defense opening statement. Defense counsel elicited damaging testimony during cross-examination of the prosecution experts. Defense also called seven witnesses to testify to Richter's (D) version of events. The jury nonetheless convicted Richter (D) on all counts and the California Court of Appeals affirmed. The California Supreme Court denied review and Richter (D) did not file for review by the United States Supreme Court. As permitted under California law, Richter (D) later filed a direct petition with the California Supreme Court for habeas corpus relief. He argued ineffective assistance of counsel because defense counsel failed to consult experts in serology, pathology, or blood spatter patterns to confirm his account rather than Johnson's. The California Supreme Court denied Richter's (D) petition in a one-sentence summary order and Richter (D) filed in the United States District Court. The District Court denied his petition and a three-judge panel of the Court of Appeals for the Ninth Circuit affirmed. The Court of Appeals then granted rehearing en banc and reversed. The Court of Appeals considered preliminarily whether the federal habeas statute applied to Richter's (D) petition but determined the California decision was an unreasonable application of *Strickland v. Washington*, 466 U.S. 668 (1984), because Richter's (D) defense counsel was deficient for failing to consult blood experts. The United States Supreme Court granted review.

ISSUE: May federal habeas relief be granted when the earlier state court decision involved an incorrect application of clearly established federal law?

HOLDING AND DECISION: (Kennedy, J.) Yes. Federal habeas relief may be granted when the earlier state court decision involved an unreasonable application of clearly established federal law. When evaluating the application of the *Strickland* standard, the question is not whether the earlier state court incorrectly evaluated the merits of the claim but whether the state court unreasonably applied federal law. A state court determination on the merits precludes federal habeas relief so long as "fair-minded jurists could disagree" on the correctness of the state court decision. Here, the Court of Appeals disagreed with the state court's decision but determined that their disagreement equaled state court's unreasonable application of *Strickland*. That is not correct. Federal habeas relief for persons in state custody is available pursuant to 28 U.S.C. § 2254, as amended by the Antiterrorism and Effective Death Penalty Act of 1996 (AEDPA). Richter (P) argued the summary order did not address the merits, but his arguments fail. Section 2254(d) applies to his petition; habeas relief is not available to him unless he demonstrates the earlier state court's decision was contrary to clearly established federal law, involved an unreasonable application of clearly established federal law, or was based on an *unreasonable* determination of facts in light of the record. The Court of Appeals relied on the second exception involving unreasonable application. The Court of Appeals determined the California Supreme Court's decision on Richter's (D) ineffective assistance of counsel claim unreasonably applied the holding in *Strickland*. The Court of Appeals reviewed the case de novo, found a *Strickland* violation, and declared the state court's decision unreasonable. AEDPA requires more; the court must evaluate the basis for the state court's decision and then ask whether

Continued on next page.

fair-minded jurists might disagree the decision was inconsistent with clearly established federal law. The Court of Appeals ignored the second step. *Strickland* and § 2254(d) are "highly deferential" and the question is not whether counsel's actions were reasonable but whether there is any reasonable argument counsel satisfied *Strickland* standards. There are reasons Richter's (D) counsel may have chosen not to consult blood experts. Perhaps counsel did not want to confirm his client's guilt or transform the case into a battle of the experts. Richter's (D) counsel made a mistake in thinking the prosecution would not present forensic evidence but the prosecution did not make that decision until trial began and that may not be so fundamental a mistake to call the trial's fairness into doubt. It was not unreasonable for the California Supreme Court to determine Richter's (D) evidence of prejudice fell short of showing a substantial likelihood of a different result but for counsel's actions. Further, there was sufficient evidence in support of guilt rather than Richter's (D) version. The California Supreme Court decision required more deference than it received. Reversed and remanded.

CONCURRENCE: (Ginsburg, J.) Richter's (D) counsel did not meet the *Strickland* standard because he was deficient in failing to consult blood experts. Counsel's lapse was not so serious as to deprive Richter (D) of a fair trial.

▶ ANALYSIS

Federal habeas relief is not meant to be another opportunity to appeal the lower conviction but to correct serious deficiencies in a state court action. The AEDPA tightened review even further to ensure the thousands of habeas petitions filed each year do not result in an automatic federal relitigation of state court convictions. Even if the federal courts would have arrived at a different conclusion, the state court's decision is entitled to deference if it arises out of a legitimate basis.

∎▬∎

Quicknotes

DE NOVO The review of a lower court decision by an appellate court, which is hearing the case as if it had not been previously heard and as if no judgment had been rendered.

HABEAS CORPUS A proceeding in which a defendant brings a writ to compel a judicial determination of whether he is lawfully being held in custody.

INEFFECTIVE ASSISTANCE OF COUNSEL A claim brought by an accused in which it must be determined whether the attorney's rendering of representation was such that the ultimate disposition of the case may not be relied upon as fair.

∎▬∎

Hurrell-Harring v. State of New York

Class of criminal defendants (P) v. State (D)

N.Y. Ct. App., 15 N.Y.3d 8, 904 N.Y.S.2d 296, 930 N.E.2d 217 (2010).

NATURE OF CASE: Appeal from lower court decisions in favor of the state.

FACT SUMMARY: A class of 20 indigent individuals charged with crimes brought a class-action lawsuit against the State of New York on the grounds the general performance of their court-appointed attorneys was so deficient that it violated the state's obligation to provide indigent individuals with counsel.

> ## 🏛 RULE OF LAW
> Where the general performance of court-appointed attorneys is deficient, criminal defendants may bring a class-action suit alleging that the state has violated its constitutional obligation to provide them with counsel.

FACTS: A group of 20 indigent individuals (the class) (P) charged with various crimes brought suit against the State of New York (D) arising from the general poor, and in some cases, nonexistent performance of their court-appointed attorneys. The class-action complaint alleged 10 of the 20 criminal defendants had no attorneys at their arraignments. Other allegations include the general unavailability of the attorneys to their clients, the waiver of legal rights without prior consent, and the existence of prejudicial conflicts of interest on the part of some of the attorneys. The class (P) sought a declaratory judgment that their right to counsel has been violated. The class does not seek any relief specific to their individual criminal cases. The lower court granted the State's (D) motion to dismiss and the class (P) appealed.

ISSUE: Where the general performance of court-appointed attorneys is deficient, may criminal defendants bring a class-action suit alleging that the state has violated its constitutional obligation to provide them with counsel?

HOLDING AND DECISION: (Lippman, C.J.) Yes. Where the general performance of court-appointed attorneys is deficient, criminal defendants may bring a class-action suit alleging that the state has violated its constitutional obligation to provide them with counsel. The State (D) argues these are actually claims for ineffective assistance of counsel. Accordingly, their argument is that due to the distinct factual nature of such cases, they may not be treated as a class but only on a case-by-case basis. Moreover, the State (P) argues such claims cannot be brought until after the criminal matter has concluded, at which time a more complete review of counsel's performance may occur. The State (D) is incorrect. The class (P) is alleging outright nonrepresentation by the court-appointed attorneys. All of the allegations of the complaint, which must be taken as true at the motion to dismiss stage, relate to a basic denial of their right to an attorney, not to the alleged defective performances of those attorneys. While later development of the facts through discovery may lead to a different outcome, the class (P) at this stage must be entitled to litigate their claim. Reversed.

DISSENT: (Pigott, J.) The complaint raises basic issues of ineffective assistance of counsel, from improper waiver of rights, nonresponsiveness, and failure to appear at hearings. These claims do not rise to the level of systemic denial of the class's (P) right to counsel. This action should be dismissed and the individuals should refile their claims separately.

▶ ANALYSIS

There is no consensus throughout the states on how to handle these cases brought on behalf of criminal defendants alleging systemic constitutional violations. Some states, like New York, have allowed them to proceed under a violation of the general right to counsel theory. Other courts have reviewed them under the preliminary injunction standard, including whether any irreparable harm will result if action is not taken to remedy the alleged claims.

━■━

Quicknotes

MOTION TO DISMISS Motion to terminate an action based on the adequacy of the pleadings, improper service or venue, etc.

RIGHT TO COUNSEL Right conferred by the Sixth Amendment that the accused shall be provided effective legal assistance in a criminal proceeding.

━■━

Wheat v. United States

Drug conspirator (D) v. Federal government (P)

486 U.S. 153 (1988).

NATURE OF CASE: Appeal from conviction for conspiracy.

FACT SUMMARY: Wheat (D) contended he was deprived of his right to counsel when the district court disqualified his attorney of choice for conflict of interest.

🏛 RULE OF LAW
A criminal defendant is not entitled to have counsel of his choice where his representation would create an inherent conflict of interest.

FACTS: Wheat (D) was arrested along with Gomez-Barajas and Bravo on drug conspiracy charges. Iredale, an attorney, represented both Gomez-Barajas and Bravo. Bravo pled guilty, and Gomez-Barajas was acquitted. Gomez-Barajas was scheduled to be tried separately on the other charge; however, he offered to plead guilty pursuant to a plea bargain. After this agreement was made, but before it was accepted by the court, Wheat (D) sought to have Iredale represent him. The Government (P) moved to disqualify Iredale on the basis that such representation would require the cross-examination of Gomez-Barajas and Bravo and thus presented a conflict of interest. The court denied the request for Iredale to represent Wheat (D), rejecting Wheat's (D) contention that the denial violated his constitutional right to counsel. Wheat (D) was convicted and appealed. The court of appeals affirmed and the United States Supreme Court granted a hearing.

ISSUE: Is a criminal defendant entitled to have counsel of his own choice where his representation would create an inherent conflict of interest?

HOLDING AND DECISION: (Rehnquist, C.J.) No. A criminal defendant is not entitled to have counsel of his choice where his representation creates an inherent conflict of interest. The right to counsel does not always include the right to counsel of choice. In this case, representation of all three co-conspirators would incurably compromise counsel's ability to represent all his clients. As a result, the representation was properly denied. Affirmed.

DISSENT: (Marshall, J.) A constitutional right to counsel of choice exists and is fully applicable in this case. The right to control the defense rests solely with the defendant. Thus, such right overcomes any potential conflict of interest.

DISSENT: (Stevens, J.) The majority here gives inadequate weight to the informed and voluntary character of the clients' waiver of their right to conflict-free representa-

tion. Specifically, the majority virtually ignores the fact that the additional counsel representing petitioner had provided him with sound advice concerning the wisdom of a waiver and would have remained available during the trial to assist in the defense.

▶ ANALYSIS

In general, counsel may represent conflicting interests after full disclosure and a written waiver. Some cases, such as this one, present such a pronounced conflict that such cannot be waived. It is felt that while the right to counsel of choice is upheld, the right to effective counsel is sacrificed.

■━■

Quicknotes

CONFLICT OF INTEREST Refers to ethical problems that arise, or may be anticipated to arise, between an attorney and his client if the interests of the attorney, another client or a third party conflict with those of the present client.

CROSS EXAMINATION The interrogation of a witness by an adverse party either to further inquire as to the subject matter of the direct examination or to call into question the witness's credibility.

■━■

Arrest, Search, and Seizure

Quick Reference Rules of Law

Wolf v. Colorado

Abortion physician (D) v. State (P)

338 U.S. 25 (1949).

NATURE OF CASE: Appeal from conviction of conspiracy to commit abortion.

FACT SUMMARY: Dr. Wolf (D) was convicted of conspiracy to commit abortion, such conviction resting in part upon evidence seized from his office.

🏛 RULE OF LAW
In a prosecution in a state court for a state crime, the Fourteenth Amendment does not forbid the admission of evidence obtained by an unreasonable search and seizure.

FACTS: Appointment books were seized from Dr. Wolf's (D) office. Partly on the basis of this evidence, Dr. Wolf (D) was convicted in a state court of conspiracy to commit abortion. Under Colorado law, evidence seized in an unreasonable search and seizure is admissible against the accused. Had the case been brought in federal court, the evidence would have been inadmissible under the exclusionary rule as being in violation of Dr. Wolf's (D) Fourth Amendment rights.

ISSUE: Does a conviction by a state court for a state offense deny a defendant his due process rights under the Fourteenth Amendment solely because evidence was obtained by a search and seizure which was illegal under the Fourth Amendment, and thus would have been excluded if the case had been brought in a federal court?

HOLDING AND DECISION: (Frankfurter, J.) No. While the Fourth Amendment's prohibition against unreasonable searches and seizures is incorporated under the due process clause of the Fourteenth Amendment and thus is binding upon the states, the federal exclusionary rule is not binding on the states. The exclusion of illegally obtained evidence is not fundamental to the concept of ordered liberty. It is merely one means of securing compliance with the Fourth Amendment and thus deterring unreasonable searches and seizures. The states are free to fashion other remedies to deter violations of defendants' due process rights, as long as they do indeed provide some means of redress. It is not a departure from the basic standards of individual rights to remand such individuals to the remedies of private action and to such protection as the internal discipline of the police. While it is true that exclusion of such evidence is an effective means of deterring unreasonable searches, the Supreme Court will not condemn a state's reliance upon methods which, if consistently enforced, would be equally effective. The public opinion within the state can be more effectively exerted against the local police than can local opinion against federal officers. Affirmed.

CONCURRENCE: (Black, J.) The exclusionary rule is not a command of the Fourth Amendment, but is merely a judicially created rule of evidence and thus should not be incorporated within the Fourteenth Amendment.

DISSENT: (Murphy, J.) There are no real alternative remedies to the exclusionary rule, and thus the exclusionary rule must be binding on the states. District attorneys would not prosecute themselves or those working for them for illegally obtaining evidence. An action for trespass is subject to far too many defenses, and also provides little inducement in the way of damages to discourage illegal searches and seizures.

DISSENT: (Douglas, J.) Without the exclusionary rule, the Fourth Amendment loses its meaning and validity.

▶ ANALYSIS

In *Weeks v. United States*, 232 U.S. 383 (1914), the Supreme Court first held that, under the Fourth Amendment, evidence obtained by federal officials by means of an unreasonable search and seizure is inadmissible as evidence in a federal court. Evidence procured by state officials in violation of the Fourth Amendment is also inadmissible in federal court (*Elkins v. United States*, 364 U.S. 206 (1960)). In *Wolf*, the Court established two basic propositions: first, the Fourth Amendment's prohibition against unreasonable search and seizure is binding on the states through the Due Process Clause of the Fourteenth Amendment; and second, the rule of *Weeks*, excluding all evidence seized in an unreasonable search, is not commanded by the Fourth Amendment but is a judicially created rule of evidence for federal courts and is, therefore, not binding on the states. Under *Wolf*, then, although unreasonable search and seizure by state officials is unconstitutional, it is permissible for the state courts to use such illegally obtained evidence in state trials, if the state has some procedure other than the exclusionary rule to discourage unreasonable searches. Although this case held that the exclusionary rule is not implicit in the Fourteenth Amendment's concept of ordered liberty and fundamental justice, the following case of *Mapp v. Ohio*, 67 U.S. 643 (1961), using the same standard, overturned *Wolf* and found that the exclusionary rule was a part of the Fourteenth Amendment, binding on the states.

◼️◼️

Continued on next page.

Quicknotes

EXCLUSIONARY RULE A rule precluding the introduction at trial of evidence unlawfully obtained in violation of the federal constitutional safeguards against unreasonable searches and seizures.

PROCEDURAL DUE PROCESS The constitutional mandate that if the state or federal government acts so as to deny a citizen of a life, liberty or property interest, the individual is first entitled to notice and the right to be heard.

Mapp v. Ohio

Homeowner (D) v. State (P)

367 U.S. 643 (1961).

NATURE OF CASE: Certiorari from conviction of possession of lewd and lascivious materials.

FACT SUMMARY: Evidence obtained when officers broke into and conducted an unlawful search of Miss Mapp's (D) home, was used for her conviction by an Ohio state court of possession of lewd and lascivious materials.

> 🏛 **RULE OF LAW**
> The Fourth Amendment is incorporated in the Fourteenth Amendment Due Process Clause, and requires that the state courts exclude evidence obtained by unlawful searches and seizures.

FACTS: On May 23, 1957, three Cleveland police officers arrived at Miss Mapp's (D) home pursuant to information that a person wanted for questioning in connection with a bombing and a large amount of "policy paraphernalia" could be found there. When Miss Mapp (D), after telephoning her attorney, refused to allow the officers in without a search warrant, they waited for more officers and then forcibly broke into the house. The officers then proceeded to conduct a warrantless search of Miss Mapp's (D) entire house. At her subsequent trial, evidence seized from this search was used to convict her of the possession of lewd and lascivious books, pictures, and photographs. The Supreme Court of Ohio found that her conviction was valid, even though it was based upon unlawfully seized evidence. Thereupon, Miss Mapp (D) was granted certiorari by the United States Supreme Court.

ISSUE: Can evidence obtained in an unlawful search and seizure be used as evidence in a state trial of the accused?

HOLDING AND DECISION: (Clark, J.) No. The Fourth Amendment is incorporated by the Fourteenth Amendment Due Process Clause, and requires that state courts exclude evidence obtained by unlawful searches and seizures. The Fourth Amendment right to be free from unreasonable searches and seizures was first extended to the states under the Fourteenth Amendment in *Wolf v. Colorado*, 338 U.S. 25 (1949). Although this Court refused in *Wolf* to apply the exclusionary rule to the states as essential to the protection of that right, it was well established even then, by this Court, in *Weeks*, 232 U.S. 383 (1914), that in federal prosecutions, the Fourth Amendment bars the use of any evidence secured through any illegal search and seizure. Today, for compelling reasons, the same sanction of exclusion must be applied to the states. First, as a minor consideration, it must be recognized that *Wolf* was based upon factual considerations no longer true today. At the time of *Wolf*, two-thirds of the states were opposed to the use of the exclusionary rule, but today more than half have wholly or partially adopted it. Second, and more important, the exclusionary rule is essential to the protection of the right to be free from unreasonable searches and seizures, and to the integrity of the judiciary. The purpose of the exclusionary rule is "to compel respect for the constitutional guaranty in the only effectively available way—by removing the incentive to disregard it." Without this rule, the Fourth and Fourteenth Amendments' protection against unreasonable searches and seizures would be a valueless "form of words." Furthermore, the "judicial integrity" of our system requires that government, for its own preservation, observe its own laws, especially the charter of its own existence. Miss Mapp's (D) conviction must be reversed. Reversed.

DISSENT: (Harlan, J.) There are several problems with the Court's decision today. First, the pivotal issue is not a reexamination of *Wolf*, but whether the "mere knowing possession of obscene materials" can be considered criminal, consistent with the rights of the free thought and expression. Second, even if the issue is the reexamination of *Wolf*, this Court's reasoning that the basic federal remedy for a violation of the Fourth Amendment rights must apply to the states is unjustifiable. *Wolf* did not hold that the Fourth Amendment, as such, is applicable to the states through the Fourteenth Amendment, but only that problem does not involve the substantive commands of the Fourth Amendment, but the flexible Due Process Clause of the Fourteenth Amendment. The Court should refrain from hindering the states in their own criminal law enforcement with the adamant exclusionary rule.

▶ **ANALYSIS**

This case illustrates the trend of the Supreme Court in incorporating the Bill of Rights into the Due Process Clause of the Fourteenth Amendment. However, the Court has not applied a "total incorporation theory," as it did here, to all of those rights so far incorporated. For example, in the case of the right to a trial by jury, the federal requirement of a unanimous verdict of the twelve-man jury for conviction is not applicable to the states, although the right to a jury trial is, because such a requirement is not "essential" to the right. Note, finally that the Fourth Amendment applies only to the government (state

Continued on next page.

or federal), and as such the prosecution may use evidence obtained by private parties even if the methods such parties used were illegal.

■■■■

Quicknotes

BILL OF RIGHTS Refers to the first ten Amendments to the federal Constitution, setting forth individual rights and liberties.

EXCLUSIONARY RULE A rule precluding the introduction at trial of evidence unlawfully obtained in violation of the federal constitutional safeguards against unreasonable searches and seizures.

FOURTEENTH AMENDMENT DUE PROCESS CLAUSE Provides that protections mandated by the U.S. Constitution and observed by the federal government are equally applicable, and therefore must be observed by the States.

FOURTH AMENDMENT Provides that persons be secure as to their person and private belongings against unreasonable searches and seizures.

PRIVILEGE AGAINST SELF-INCRIMINATION A privilege guaranteed by the Fifth Amendment to the federal Constitution in a criminal proceeding for communications made by an accused and protecting an accused or witness from having to give testimony that may incriminate himself.

■■■■

United States v. Leon

Federal government (P) v. Owner of illegally seized evidence (D)

468 U.S. 897 (1984).

NATURE OF CASE: Appeal from the suppression of evidence.

FACT SUMMARY: The court of appeals held that evidence seized pursuant to a facially valid warrant had to be suppressed due to a lack of probable cause to issue the warrant even though the police had acted in good faith.

RULE OF LAW

The Fourth Amendment does not require exclusion of evidence seized pursuant to a facially valid warrant where the police have acted in good faith.

FACTS: The district court granted Leon's (D) motion to suppress evidence seized on good faith pursuant to a facially valid warrant issued by the neutral magistrate which was subsequently found to be based on an affidavit that did not sufficiently establish probable cause. The court of appeals affirmed, refusing to recognize a good-faith exception to the exclusionary rule. The United States Supreme Court granted certiorari.

ISSUE: Does the Fourth Amendment require exclusion of evidence seized pursuant to a facially valid warrant where the police have acted in good faith?

HOLDING AND DECISION: (White, J.) No. The Fourth Amendment does not require exclusion of evidence seized pursuant to a facially valid warrant where the police have acted in good faith. The exclusionary rule is applied only in cases where it would be consistent with its rationale. The rule is imposed to deter police conduct that denies the defendant his constitutional rights. Where the police act in good faith, under the authorization of a neutral and detached magistrate, the deterrent purpose does not apply. As a result, the rule should not be applied in this case. Reversed.

CONCURRENCE: (Blackmun, J.) Because the Court correctly recognized that the exclusionary rule is not constitutionally mandated, it correctly limited its scope to cases where the deterrent purpose will be served.

DISSENT: (Brennan, J.) The exclusionary rule is indirectly compelled by the Fourth Amendment. Also, the good-faith exception will simply allow police to infringe on constitutional rights by limiting the information included in affidavits supporting search warrants.

▶ ANALYSIS

The Court stated in this case that suppression remains a viable tool if the magistrate or judge, in issuing a warrant, was misled by information in an affidavit that the affiant knew was false. Suppression will also be allowed where the police could not have acted in good faith because the warrant was obviously invalid.

■■■■

Quicknotes

AFFIDAVIT A declaration of facts written and affirmed before a witness.

EXCLUSIONARY RULE A rule precluding the introduction at trial of evidence unlawfully obtained in violation of the federal constitutional safeguards against unreasonable searches and seizures.

GOOD-FAITH EXCEPTION TO WARRANT REQUIREMENT The exception to the rule that evidence obtained as the result of an unlawful search and seizure is nevertheless admissible at trial if the officers had a reasonable, good-faith belief that they acted pursuant to legal authority.

PROBABLE CAUSE A reasonable basis for believing that a crime has been committed.

■■■■

Hudson v. Michigan

Convicted felon (D) v. State (P)

547 U.S. 586 (2006).

NATURE OF CASE: Appeal of lower court refusal to exclude evidence obtained following a knock-and-announce violation.

FACT SUMMARY: Police (P) entered and searched a home after failing to knock and announce. They found drugs and a firearm in their search, and Hudson (D) moved at trial to exclude the evidence based on the knock-and-announce violation.

RULE OF LAW
Violation of the knock-and-announce rule does not require the suppression of all evidence found in a warranted search.

FACTS: Police (P) entered and searched Hudson's (D) home with a warrant but failed to knock first, and only waited three to five seconds after announcing themselves before entering. Hudson (D) was convicted in state court for possessing cocaine and a firearm. Hudson (D) argued that the evidence against him was seized in violation of the "knock and announce" rule of the Fourth Amendment, which requires the police to knock, announce their presence, and wait 20 to 30 seconds before executing a search warrant, except in exigent circumstances. The trial judge granted Hudson's (D) motion to suppress the evidence on the basis of the knock-and-announce rule. The Michigan Court of Appeals reversed, holding that it was bound by two cases decided by the Michigan Supreme Court that created an "exception" to the suppression of evidence obtained in violation of the knock-and-announce rule when the evidence would inevitably have been discovered.

ISSUE: Does violation of the knock-and-announce rule require the suppression of all evidence found in a warranted search?

HOLDING AND DECISION: (Scalia, J.) No. Violation of the knock-and-announce rule does not require the suppression of all evidence found in a warranted search. Evidence seized in violation of the knock-and-announce rule can be used against a defendant in a later criminal trial without violating the Fourth Amendment, and judges cannot suppress such evidence for a knock-and-announce violation alone. The purpose of the knock-and-announce rule is to protect police officers from surprising residents who might retaliate in presumed self-defense, to protect private property from damage, and to protect the privacy and dignity of residents. The knock-and-announce rule has never purported to protect one's interest in preventing the government from seeing or taking evidence described in a warrant. In addition, the cost of excluding evidence based on knock-and-announce

violations would be serious, amounting to providing dangerous criminals with a get-out-of-jail-free card. Affirmed.

CONCURRENCE: (Kennedy, J.) The knock-and-announce requirement protects rights and expectations linked to ancient principles in our constitutional order. The majority opinion does not suggest that violations of the knock-and-announce requirement are trivial or beyond the law's concern. In addition, the decision determines only that in the specific context of the knock-and-announce requirement, a violation is not sufficiently related to the later discovery of evidence to justify suppression.

DISSENT: (Breyer, J.) Settled case law by this Court established that the Fourth Amendment normally requires police officers to knock and announce their presence before entering a dwelling. The majority opinion holds that evidence seized from a home following a violation of this requirement need not be suppressed. As a result, the Court destroys the strongest legal incentive to comply with the Constitution's knock-and-announce requirement. At the very least, eliminating the exclusionary rule from consideration for knock-and-announce violations will cause some government agents to find it less risky to violate the rule.

ANALYSIS

This case is premised on the insufficient connection between the failure by the police to knock and announce and the evidence found in the house, thus rendering exclusion of that evidence based on the violation unjustifiable. The case might stand for a broader application of the rule, which might curb altogether the exclusionary rule based on knock-and-announce violations.

■■■

Quicknotes

EXIGENT CIRCUMSTANCES Circumstances requiring an extraordinary or immediate response; an exception to the prohibition on a warrantless arrest or search when police officers believe probable cause to exist and there is no time for obtaining a warrant.

FOURTH AMENDMENT Provides that persons be secure as to their person and private belongings against unreasonable searches and seizures.

KNOCK AND ANNOUNCE Requirement that a police officer must first knock and announce his intention before he enters an individual's home in the execution of a valid warrant.

■■■

Herring v. United States

Individual (D) v. Federal government (P)

555 U.S. 135 (2009).

NATURE OF CASE: Appeal from Eleventh Circuit Court of Appeals in favor of government.

FACT SUMMARY: After receiving information from a neighboring county that Herring (D) had an outstanding warrant against him, police officers in Coffee County arrested Herring (D). A search of his vehicle revealed a gun and illegal drugs. The police then learned the warrant had previously been recalled.

🏛 RULE OF LAW
When police mistakes leading to an unlawful search are the result of isolated negligence attenuated from the search, rather than systemic error or reckless disregard of constitutional requirements, the exclusionary rule does not apply.

FACTS: Police in Coffee County investigated whether Herring (D) had any outstanding warrants against him. A search of a neighboring county's database initially revealed that Herring (D) had a warrant against him for failure to appear for a felony charge. Acting on the information, the police officers arrested Herring (D). A search of his vehicle incident to his arrest turned up a gun and illegal drugs. Shortly after the search, police dispatch informed the arresting officers that the warrant had actually been recalled five months earlier and was no longer valid. Federal charges were subsequently brought against Herring (D) and he moved to suppress the evidence from the search on the grounds the arrest and search were in violation of his Fourth Amendment rights. The trial court and Eleventh Circuit Court of Appeals found that because the mistake was caused by the mere negligence of the police record keeping system, the exclusionary rule did not apply. Herring (D) appealed.

ISSUE: When police mistakes leading to an unlawful search are the result of isolated negligence attenuated from the search, rather than systemic error or reckless disregard of constitutional requirements, does the exclusionary rule apply?

HOLDING AND DECISION: (Roberts, C.J.) No. When police mistakes leading to an unlawful search are the result of isolated negligence attenuated from the search, rather than systemic error or reckless disregard of constitutional requirements, the exclusionary rule does not apply. The mere fact that a search is unreasonable does not mean the exclusionary rule automatically applies. The Court has previously held the rule does not apply when police reasonably relied upon an invalid warrant issued by a court. The only issue here is whether negligence by the police, as opposed to others, will lead to the suppression of evidence. The Court holds that it should not. The exclusionary rule was created to deter police misconduct. The conduct must have a deliberate or indifferent nature to invoke the exclusionary rule. Those circumstances are not present here. An error arising from nonrecurring negligence, as opposed to systemic negligence, does not implicate the concerns the exclusionary rule was designed to protect. Affirmed.

DISSENT: (Ginsburg, J.) The Court's decision may lead to the arrest of innocent persons based upon information that is negligently maintained. Police departments across the country will have little incentive to ensure the accuracy of their warrant databases. The exclusionary rule is the only remedy Herring (D) and others in his situation have. A subsequent lawsuit against the police for wrongful arrest will be barred by qualified immunity. Just as in tort law, the risk of exclusion of evidence would encourage police departments at the state and federal level to monitor the warrant databases and ensure their accuracy.

DISSENT: (Breyer, J.) Distinguishing between police errors and judicial errors is easier for reviewing courts to adjudicate, rather than the Chief Justice's case-by-case review of each alleged error to determine the level of culpability. The exclusionary rule should be applied whenever the police personnel are responsible for the error.

▌ ANALYSIS

A debate has ensued over the scope of this five to four decision. Some commentators believe the scope is limited to police errors in regard to record keeping only. However, others believe police departments may rely on the decision to argue that any of their good-faith mistakes will prohibit the application of the exclusionary rule. It does appear though that the holding concerns only those isolated and negligent mistakes that are "attenuated from the search." The precise contours of this "attenuation" factor have yet to be defined.

■▬■

Quicknotes

EXCLUSIONARY RULE A rule precluding the introduction at trial of evidence unlawfully obtained in violation of the federal constitutional safeguards against unreasonable searches and seizures.

WARRANT An order issued by a court directing an officer to undertake a certain act (e.g., arrest or search).

■▬■

Katz v. United States

Telephone better (D) v. Federal government (P)

389 U.S. 347 (1967).

NATURE OF CASE: Appeal from criminal conviction for transmitting betting information over the phone.

FACT SUMMARY: Katz (D) was arrested for transmitting wagering information by telephone to another state. At his trial, the government introduced recordings of his conversation made by attaching a listening and recording device to the outside of a phone booth.

🏛 RULE OF LAW
The Fourth Amendment protects a person from search and seizure if, under the circumstances, he has a justifiable expectation of privacy, regardless of whether an actual physical trespass occurred.

FACTS: Katz (D) was arrested and convicted for transmitting betting information by telephone to another state in violation of a federal statute. At his trial, the prosecution introduced recordings of phone conversations Katz (D) had made. These recordings were made by attaching a listening and recording device to the outside of a phone booth that Katz (D) used to make his calls. There was no search warrant. The Government (P) used this device only after it had made an investigation that indicated the phone booth was being used to transmit such information, and the Government (P) only recorded conversations that Katz (D) personally had.

ISSUE: Is the attachment of a listening device to the outside of a public telephone booth a search and seizure within the meaning of the Fourth Amendment?

HOLDING AND DECISION: (Stewart, J.) Yes. The Fourth Amendment protects persons' justifiable expectations of privacy, and protects people and not places. Whatever a person knowingly exposes to the public, even in his own home, is therefore not protected by the Fourth Amendment, but what a person keeps private, even in a public place, may be protected. Earlier cases stated that surveillance, without a trespass or seizure of a material object, is outside of the Fourth Amendment and now these cases must be overturned. Even though the phone booth was a public place, and there was no physical trespass (the device was on the outside of the booth), there was a search because the Government (P) violated the privacy upon which Katz (D) justifiably relied. There also is a seizure even though no tangible property was taken because the recording of a statement overheard, even if there is no trespass, is a seizure. The remaining question, then, is whether the government complied with the constitutional standards of the Fourth Amendment. Although the Government (P) reasonably believed that the phone booth was being illegally used, and their

search and seizure was carefully limited both in scope and duration, the action cannot be upheld because there was no search warrant issued. A search warrant is a safeguard in several ways: a neutral magistrate, on the basis of information presented to him, determines whether a warrant should issue; the search warrant carefully limits the scope of the search; and the government must report back on the evidence it finds. Without such safeguards, even if the search was in fact reasonable, it cannot be upheld. Reversed.

CONCURRENCE: (Harlan, J.) In order to be protected by the Fourth Amendment, a person must have an actual subjective expectation of privacy and, also, that expectation of privacy must be reasonable.

DISSENT: (Black, J.) When the Fourth Amendment was adopted, eavesdropping was a common practice, and if the framers of the Constitution wished to limit that procedure, they would have used appropriate language. This case, then, goes against the plain meaning of the Fourth Amendment, which was solely aimed at limiting the practice of breaking into buildings and seizing tangible property. Therefore, wiretapping, which is a form of eavesdropping, is not subject to the Fourth Amendment.

▶ ANALYSIS

Katz rejects the old rule that held that there was no search unless there was a physical trespass and substitutes a new rule based on the defendant's expectation of privacy. One facet of this privacy concept is the place involved—for example, if, unlike Katz (D), the defendant was engaged in conversation in a public place that was audible to others, there would be no search within the meaning of the Fourth Amendment. Also, the privacy concept turns on the action of the defendant. If the defendant had engaged in a loud conversation, even in his own home, which was audible to a person standing outside his door, there would be no search since the conversation was exposed by the defendant to the public.

▆▆▆

Quicknotes

EXPECTATION OF PRIVACY Requirement that in order to invoke the Fourth Amendment's protection against unreasonable searches and seizures, the individual must have a reasonable expectation of privacy in respect to the location searched or thing seized.

▆▆▆

United States v. Jones

Federal government (P) v. Individual (D)

565 U.S. ___, 132 S. Ct. 945 (2012).

NATURE OF CASE: Appeal from intermediate appellate court decision in favor of the defendant.

FACT SUMMARY: Government agents installed a GPS tracking device on the undercarriage of a vehicle owned by Jones (D), who was suspected of trafficking in narcotics, and then monitored the vehicle's movements for a period of 28 days.

🏛 RULE OF LAW

The government's installation of a GPS device on an individual's vehicle and the government's use of the device to track the location of that vehicle constitute a search under the Fourth Amendment.

FACTS: Government agents installed a GPS tracking device on the undercarriage of Jones's (D) vehicle for a period of 28 days. The device was able to track the location of the vehicle to within 50 feet. The district court judge denied Jones's (D) motion to suppress the GPS evidence and a jury convicted him. The Court of Appeals for the D.C. Circuit then reversed, finding that the evidence obtained by the use of the GPS device without a warrant violated the Fourth Amendment. The Government (P) appealed to the United States Supreme Court.

ISSUE: Does the government's installation of a GPS device on an individual's vehicle and the government's use of the device to track the location of that vehicle constitute a search under the Fourth Amendment?

HOLDING AND DECISION: (Scalia, J.) Yes. The government's installation of a GPS device on an individual's vehicle and the government's use of the device to track the location of that vehicle constitute a search under the Fourth Amendment. The Government (P) argues that no search occurred because Jones (D) had no reasonable expectation of privacy in the area of the vehicle accessed by government agents or in the location of the vehicle on public roads. However, this case need not be analyzed on the reasonable expectation of privacy theory. Instead, the government's physical trespass in the form of attaching a device to one's vehicle constitutes the search. One's private vehicle is protected by the Fourth Amendment's prohibition of unreasonable searches of one's "person, houses, papers and effects." The more general unreasonable expectation of privacy theory did not replace the original trespass to property theory of unreasonable searches. Rather, it is supplemental to the original understanding of the Fourth Amendment. It is enough for this case to focus narrowly upon the government's trespass upon Jones's (D) "effects", i.e., his vehicle, to find that a search occurred. Affirmed.

CONCURRENCE: (Sotomayor, J.) The Government's (P) physical invasion of Jones's (D) personal property constituted a search. However, this Court may need to utilize the more general reasonable expectation of privacy theory in other cases because many forms of electronic surveillance do not include a physical intrusion.

CONCURRENCE: (Alito, J.) The Court should have analyzed this under the broader reasonable expectation of privacy theory rather than the simple trespass to property theory. Reliance on the narrow trespass theory will not provide any guidance to law enforcement for those surveillance cases where there is no physical intrusion.

▶ ANALYSIS

While the judgment in this case was unanimous, the Court was split five to four on how to analyze the use of the GPS tracking device. The federal agents' intrusion upon the personal property of Jones (D) was the significant factor in this case. As the concurring justices note, however, the issue remains undecided on how far law enforcement can go with electronic or even Internet searches that do not include a physical intrusion.

■=■

Quicknotes

FOURTH AMENDMENT Provides that persons be secure as to their person and private belongings against unreasonable searches and seizures.

SEARCH AND SEIZURE An inspection conducted in order to obtain evidence to be utilized for the prosecution of a crime and the subsequent taking of such evidence.

■=■

Florida v. Jardines

State (P) v. Marijuana grower (D)

133 S. Ct. 1409 (2013).

NATURE OF CASE: Review of Fourth Amendment search criminal case.

FACT SUMMARY: Police brought a drug-detection dog to Jardines's (D) home. The dog "alerted" to the scent of marijuana at the front door. Police then obtained a search warrant for Jardines's (D) home and seized marijuana plants.

🏛 RULE OF LAW
The curtilage is part of a private home for Fourth Amendment purposes and it is impermissible to enter the curtilage with a trained police dog for search purposes without express or implied permission from the homeowner.

FACTS: Police observed Jardines's (D) home on an unverified tip. They brought a trained drug-sniffing dog and approached the home. The dog "alerted" at the front door. Police then obtained a warrant to search the residence. The search revealed marijuana plants, but the evidence was excluded in the lower court as fruit of an unreasonable search.

ISSUE: Is the curtilage part of a private home for Fourth Amendment purposes and is it impermissible to enter the curtilage with a trained police dog for search purposes without express or implied permission from the homeowner?

HOLDING AND DECISION: (Scalia, J.) Yes. The curtilage is part of a private home for Fourth Amendment purposes and it is impermissible to enter the curtilage with a trained police dog for search purposes without express or implied permission from the homeowner. The home is first among equals for Fourth Amendment purposes. Man's right to retreat to his home would have very little practical value if the state's agents could search side yards and porches for evidence with impunity. There is no doubt here the detectives entered the curtilage, which is the area immediately surrounding and associated with the home. The issue then becomes whether the intrusion into a constitutionally protected area occurred with leave from Jardines (D). It did not. The habits of the country may provide an implicit license to a visitor to approach a home. A front door knocker allows for "solicitors, hawkers and peddlers of all kinds." Officers can knock on a front door and speak with the homeowner. There is no customary invitation for a trained police dog to explore the area looking for incriminating evidence. The State (P) relies on this Court's cases finding the subjective intent of the officer is irrelevant. Those cases, however, deal with objectively reasonable searches so the officer's real reason for the

search does not vitiate the objective reasonableness. Here, the objective basis for the officers' behavior was to conduct a search and no one believes they had a license to do so. The Court need not consider whether the officers violated Jardines's (D) expectation of privacy under *Katz v. United States*, 389 U.S. 347 (1967), because the officers conducted a search by physically intruding on Jardines's (D) property. *Katz's* reasonable-expectations test adds to, not substitutes for, the property-based understanding of the Fourth Amendment. [Decision not stated in the excerpt.]

CONCURRENCE: (Kagan, J.) The Court could have arrived at the same decision by considering Jardines's (D) privacy interests. Privacy expectations are heightened in the home and surrounding area and it was an invasion of Jardines's (D) privacy for the officers to invade those expectations when searching with a trained canine assistant.

DISSENT: (Alito, J.) The Court's decision relies on trespass law that is nowhere to be found in Anglo-American jurisprudence. The majority finds Detective Bartelt committed a trespass when he engaged in an otherwise lawful visit to Jardines's (D) home but brought his dog. Trespass law provides no support for such a holding. The police are permitted to "knock and talk". They are permitted to see, hear, and smell what can be detected from their lawful vantage point. The Court states Bartelt had the objective purpose of conducting a search. There is no meaningful way to distinguish between the objective purpose of a "knock and talk" and what occurred here. The dog is the difference here. There is not a single case that holds a visitor commits a trespass when accompanied by a dog on a leash. The Court's trespass rule today is a newly struck counterfeit.

▶ ANALYSIS

The Court's decision was a narrow one involving drug-sniffing dogs, but technological advancements continue to change state agencies' ability to collect evidence. The Court acknowledges officers may approach a private residence for the purpose of speaking with a resident and may even gather evidence from that "knock and talk." In the future, officers may have technological advances providing a greater ability to see, hear, and smell. The Court may have to reconsider what constitutes an impermissible intrusion resulting in an impermissible search.

■▬■

Continued on next page.

Quicknotes

CURTILAGE   Those buildings or structures that are directly connected to, or in proximity with, a family dwelling.

SEARCH   An inspection conducted in order to obtain evidence to be utilized for the prosecution of a crime.

━━━

Illinois v. Gates

State (P) v. Drug trafficker (D)

462 U.S. 213 (1983).

NATURE OF CASE: Appeal of an order to suppress evidence gained through an illegal search.

FACT SUMMARY: The Illinois Supreme Court suppressed evidence seized from Lance and Sue Gates (D) holding that the information in an anonymous letter failed to adequately show the reliability of the informant and his basis of knowledge and therefore showed insufficient probable cause to issue the search warrant.

🏛 RULE OF LAW
A magistrate must evaluate the totality of the circumstances presented to him, including, but not limited to, the reliability of an informant and the basis of his knowledge, in determining whether probable cause exists to issue a search warrant.

FACTS: An Illinois (P) magistrate issued a search warrant for the car and residence of Larry and Sue Gates (D) based on an affidavit prepared by Mader, a Bloomingdale police detective, which stated he had initiated an investigation of the Gateses (D) based on information received in an anonymous letter which alleged in some detail the Gateses' (D) drug trafficking activities between Florida and Illinois (P) and said that on a particular date, the Gateses would follow this procedure and pick up over $100,000 in drugs. The affidavit further stated that Mader's investigation had corroborated this information, in that among other things, the Gateses (D) had traveled to Florida on the day predicted, and had left the next morning travelling toward Chicago. Pursuant to the warrant, the Bloomingdale police searched the Gateses' (D) car and residence upon their return and seized drugs, weapons, and other contraband. The trial court suppressed the evidence and the appellate court affirmed. The Illinois Supreme Court affirmed on the basis that probable cause could be found only if sufficient facts were presented to show both the relationship of the informant and the basis of his knowledge. It found the affidavit insufficient in this regard and held there was no probable cause to issue the warrant. Illinois (P) appealed.

ISSUE: Must a magistrate evaluate the totality of the circumstances presented to him, including, but not limited to, the reliability of the informant and the basis of his knowledge, in determining whether probable cause exists to issue a search warrant?

HOLDING AND DECISION: (Rehnquist, J.) Yes. A magistrate must evaluate the totality of the circumstances presented to him, including, but not limited to, the reliability of an informant and his basis of knowledge, in determining whether probable cause exists to issue a search warrant. In determining probable cause, reliability and basis of knowledge are more useful as interacting issues, where a weak showing of one can be compensated for by a strong showing in the other, than as separate requirements. To require strict adherence to the two-pronged test would severely curtail the use of anonymous information essential to effective police investigations. In this case, the affidavit showing corroboration of the letter coupled with the specificity of detail contained in the letter, adequately show the reliability of the informant based on a totality of the circumstances, and, therefore, it was within the power of the issue magistrate to find that probable cause existed and to issue the warrant. Reversed.

CONCURRENCE: (White, J.) The warrant should be upheld, yet on the basis that it meets the two-pronged test of reliability and basis of knowledge and not on the more expansive totality of circumstances test. Instead of adopting an overly expansive test, the two-pronged test should be clarified to avoid undue rigidness.

DISSENT: (Brennan, J.) By rejecting the two-pronged test the Court provides no standards to aid lay magistrates in making probable cause determinations. Further, the totality of circumstances test adopted by the Court opens the door to probable cause determinations made on less-than-reliable information from credible sources.

DISSENT: (Stevens, J.) The facts and circumstances in this case show nothing more than a corroboration of events that are just as easily explainable as innocent travel as they are of criminal activity. Because of the lack of sufficient specificity of detail in the letter, it cannot itself be said to show reliability, and therefore no probable cause existed to issue the warrant using either the two-pronged test or the totality of the circumstances test.

▶ ANALYSIS

This case shows the Court encouraging the issuance of search warrants by lowering the standards required to find probable cause. The two-pronged test derived from the cases of *Aguilar v. Texas*, 378 U.S. 108 (1964), and *Spinelli v. United States*, 393 U.S. 410 (1969), had evolved to the point where the Court felt that effective police functions were being undercut by overly expansive interpretations of Fourth Amendment rights. It is argued that the adoption of the totality of the circumstances test is actually retention of the two-pronged test with recognition of a good-faith exception to the exclusionary rule.

■=■

Continued on next page.

Quicknotes

AFFIDAVIT A declaration of facts written and affirmed before a witness.

PROBABLE CAUSE A reasonable basis for believing that a crime has been committed.

TOTALITY OF THE CIRCUMSTANCES TEST Standard that focuses on all the circumstances of a particular case, instead of individual factors.

■▬■

Maryland v. Pringle

State (P) v. Convicted drug possessor (D)

540 U.S. 366 (2003).

NATURE OF CASE: Appeal by state from reversal of conviction for cocaine possession.

FACT SUMMARY: When Pringle (D) was arrested for cocaine possession when he was a front-seat passenger in a vehicle and the cocaine was found in the back seat, he argued that he did not have sufficient possession of the cocaine to show probable cause for his arrest; hence any confession resulting from such arrest would be invalid.

🏛 RULE OF LAW
The passenger of a vehicle, even if separated from the drugs, has sufficient constructive possession of drugs located in the vehicle to give rise to probable cause for the passenger's arrest.

FACTS: A police officer stopped an automobile for speeding. There were three occupants in the car. Pringle (D) was the front-seat passenger. When the driver opened the glove compartment to get the registration, the officer observed a large amount of rolled-up cash. The driver consented to a vehicle search, which yielded $763 from the glove compartment and cocaine from behind the back seat armrest. Pringle (D) and both other occupants were arrested. Pringle (D) waived his *Miranda* rights [*Miranda v. Arizona*, 384 U.S. 436 (1966)] and confessed the cocaine belonged to him. The trial court denied Pringle's (D) motion to suppress the confession as fruit of an illegal arrest, holding the officer had probable cause for the arrest. Pringle (D) was convicted of cocaine possession; however, the Court of Appeals of Maryland reversed, holding that the mere finding of cocaine in the back seat armrest when Pringle (D) was simply a passenger in the front seat failed to establish probable cause to arrest Pringle (D) for possession. Maryland (P) appealed.

ISSUE: Does the passenger of a vehicle, even if separated from the drugs, have sufficient constructive possession of drugs located in the vehicle to give rise to probable cause for the passenger's arrest?

HOLDING AND DECISION: (Rehnquist, C.J.) Yes. The passenger of a vehicle, even if separated from the drugs, has sufficient constructive possession of drugs located in the vehicle to give rise to probable cause for the passenger's arrest. Maryland law authorizes police officers to execute warrantless arrests, inter alia, for felonies committed in an officer's presence or where the officer has probable cause to believe a felony has been, or is being, committed. Here, the officer, upon recovering the plastic bags of cocaine, had probable cause to believe a felony had been committed. As to whether there was probable cause to

believe Pringle (D) had committed that crime, Maryland law defines "possession" as the exercise of actual or constructive dominion over a thing by one or more persons. The probable cause standard is incapable of precise definition or quantification into percentages because it deals with probabilities and depends on the totality of the circumstances. In the instant case, Pringle (D) was one of three men riding in the car in the early morning hours when a large amount of rolled-up cash and five baggies of cocaine were found. The cocaine was "accessible" to all three of the occupants, including Pringle (D). It was an entirely reasonable inference from these facts that any or all three of the occupants had knowledge of, and exercised dominion and control over, the cocaine. Thus, a reasonable officer could conclude there was probable cause to believe Pringle (D) committed the crime of possession of cocaine, either solely or jointly. Reversed and remanded.

▶ ANALYSIS

As the Supreme Court makes clear in *Pringle*, the probable cause standard is a practical, nontechnical conception that deals with the factual and practical considerations of everyday life on which reasonable and prudent persons, "not legal technicians," act. Probable cause is a "fluid concept"—turning on the assessment of probabilities in particular factual contexts, not readily, or even usually, reduced to a neat set of legal rules.

■■■

Quicknotes

FELONY A criminal offense of greater seriousness than a misdemeanor; felonies are generally defined pursuant to statute as any crime that is punishable by death or by a term of imprisonment exceeding one year.

INTER ALIA Among other things.

■■■

United States v. Watson

Federal government (P) v. Credit card thief (D)

423 U.S. 411 (1976).

NATURE OF CASE: Appeal from reversal of a conviction for theft of credit cards from the malls.

FACT SUMMARY: Watson (D) was arrested without a warrant by a Government (P) postal inspector who, on the basis of information from a reliable informant, had time to obtain an arrest warrant for theft of credit cards from the malls.

🏛 RULE OF LAW

A law officer may arrest a suspect without a warrant for a felony committed in his presence as well as for a felony not committed in his presence if he has reasonable grounds for making the arrest.

FACTS: A reliable informant told a Government (P) postal inspector that Watson (D) had supplied him with a stolen credit card and had agreed to furnish more cards later. Subsequently, the informant met with Watson (D) in a restaurant. When Watson (D) indicated that he had the cards, the informant signaled to the inspector, who arrested Watson (D) without a warrant. Watson's (D) conviction was reversed by the court of appeals on the ground that the inspector had time to obtain an arrest warrant but failed to do so. The Government (P) appealed.

ISSUE: May a law officer arrest a suspect without a warrant for a felony committed in his presence as well as for a felony not committed in his presence if he has reasonable grounds for making the arrest?

HOLDING AND DECISION: (White, J.) Yes. Never has any case indicated that an arrest warrant is required under the Fourth Amendment to make an arrest for a felony. At common law, no such warrant was required, and in 1792, the Second Congress saw no inconsistency between the Fourth Amendment and giving federal marshals the same power as state officers to make warrantless arrests. Reversed.

CONCURRENCE: (Powell, J.) The holding creates an anomaly because great discretion is given in making warrantless arrests while rarely can a warrantless search be made even though it would appear that an arrest is a greater personal invasion. "But logic sometimes must defer to history and experience."

DISSENT: (Marshall, J.) The case should have simply been decided on the ground that the inspector had probable cause to believe that an offense was taking place in his presence (at the restaurant), and that the suspect was then in possession of the evidence. The Court need not have gone beyond that; having done so, it must be said that the common-law rule provides no support for the far-reaching modern rule fashioned here. And, as a matter of doctrine, the long-standing existence of a government practice does not immunize it from scrutiny under the Constitution.

▶ ANALYSIS

The ALI Model Code of Pre-Arraignment Procedure (1975) § 120.1 provides that a law officer, if he has reasonable cause, may make warrantless arrests for felonies and, under certain circumstances, for misdemeanors. The commentary to that section states: "This section does not require an officer to arrest under a warrant even if a reasonable opportunity to obtain a warrant exists. As to arrests on the street, such a requirement would be entirely novel."

Quicknotes

FELONY A criminal offense of greater seriousness than a misdemeanor; felonies are generally defined pursuant to statute as any crime that is punishable by death or by a term of imprisonment exceeding one year.

MISDEMEANOR Any offense that does not constitute a felony, which is generally less severe and for which a lesser punishment is imposed.

United States v. Robinson

Federal government (P) v. Heroin possessor (D)

414 U.S. 218 (1973).

NATURE OF CASE: Action against Robinson (D) for possession and facilitation of concealment of heroin.

FACT SUMMARY: A police officer arrested Robinson (D) for a traffic violation. It was conceded that he had probable cause for the arrest. During his search of Robinson (D), the officer found a cigarette package containing heroin.

RULE OF LAW

A full search of a person incident to a lawful arrest is a reasonable search under the Fourth Amendment and need not be limited to a frisk for weapons in cases involving crimes, such as traffic violations, where there would be no further evidence of such crimes.

FACTS: As a result of a previous investigation of Robinson's (D) driver's permit, Officer Jenks decided that there was reason to believe that Robinson (D) was driving without a license. He signaled Robinson (D) to stop his car, and when he did, Jenks arrested him. It was conceded that Jenks had probable cause for the arrest. In accordance with police department procedures, Jenks searched Robinson (D). He felt an object in Robinson's (D) coat, but couldn't tell its size or what it was. He pulled it out and found a crumbled cigarette package. He opened it and found heroin capsules inside. The court of appeals held that since no further evidence could have been obtained from a search in this case, Jenks should have only conducted a search for weapons.

ISSUE: Are there circumstances in which a police officer may not conduct a full search of an arrestee's person following a lawful arrest?

HOLDING AND DECISION: (Rehnquist, J.) No. A search, incident to a lawful arrest, is a traditional exception to the warrant requirement of the Fourth Amendment. The validity of the search of the person of the arrestee is well established and is considered to be a reasonable search under the Fourth Amendment. The court of appeals felt that in a case involving a traffic violation, the principles of *Terry v. Ohio*, 392 U.S. 1 (1968), should be applied and only a search for weapons could be justified. *Terry v. Ohio* held that a frisk incident to an investigative stop based on less than probable cause must be limited to a search for weapons. That decision recognizes a sharp distinction between such frisks and searches incident to arrests for probable cause. That case affords no basis for extending the limitation placed on a stop-and-frisk search without probable cause to a probable cause arrest. The court of

appeals, in effect, determined that the only reason supporting a full search incident to a lawful arrest was the possibility of discovering evidence. However, the reason for a full search rests equally on the need to disarm the arrestee. The danger to the officer is far greater in the case of the extended proximity that follows the custodial arrest of a suspect than in a stop-and-frisk encounter. Further, the danger to the officer flows from the arrest itself, rather than from the grounds for arrest. The search of Robinson's (D) person conducted by Jenks and the seizure of the heroin were permissible under the Fourth Amendment. Officer Jenks was not required to limit the search to a search for weapons. Reversed.

DISSENT: (Marshall, J.) The vast majority of the several state and federal courts which have considered this question have held that absent special circumstances, a police officer has no right to conduct a full search of the person incident to a lawful arrest for violation of a motor vehicle violation. Here, the majority attempts to avoid case-by-case adjudication of Fourth Amendment issues. However, "there is no formula for the determination of reasonable, each case is to be decided on its own facts and circumstances." Further, the powers granted to the police in this case are strong ones, subject to potential abuse. There is always the possibility that a police officer, lacking probable cause to obtain a search warrant, will use a traffic arrest as a pretext to conduct a search. In this case, Jenks's removal of the cigarette package, which he said he did not believe was a weapon, exceeded the limitation of the *Terry* frisk for weapons. May a police officer, when effecting an arrest of a traffic offender, make a fuller search of the person than *Terry* permits? To answer this question, the individual's interest in remaining free from unnecessarily intrusive invasions of privacy must be balanced with society's interest that police officers not take unnecessary risks in performing their duties. It is not necessary to solve this balancing question here, but empirical evidence does support the court of appeals' decision rather than the result reached by the majority. This evidence indicates that "virtually all of the killings of officers in the line of duty are caused by guns and weapons, the very type of weapons which will not go undetected in a properly conducted weapon search. In this case, however, Jenks's search extended beyond Robinson's (D) person to a separate search of effects found on his person. Assuming, arguendo, that it was reasonable for Jenks to remove the cigarette package from Robinson's (D) person, there was no justification

Continued on next page.

consistent with the Fourth Amendment for his looking inside the package. Once in Jenks's hands, even if the package did contain a weapon, it was out of Robinson's (D) reach. Opening the package, therefore, did not further the protective purpose of the search.

▶ *ANALYSIS*

Most courts have upheld inventory of the items found on the arrestee's person as a part of the booking process, on the grounds it is a reasonable means of safeguarding the accused's property while they are in jail, and ensuring weapons and contraband are not introduced into the jail. Some courts have limited the inventory authority somewhat by ruling that evidence found in an inventory must be suppressed if the police conducted the inventory without a correct determination of whether the arrestee would, of necessity, be held in jail. As to an officer's power to seize items uncovered in a search incident to an arrest, in *State v. Elkins*, 245 Ore. 279 (1966), it was held that before an officer can seize implements of a crime other than that for which the arrest was made, he must have reasonable grounds to believe that the article is contraband.

■■■

Quicknotes

CONTRABAND Items that are illegal to have in one's possession or to trade or produce.

INVESTIGATORY STOP A brief, nonintrusive stop, requiring the police officer to have a reasonable suspicion that a crime has been committed based on specific and articulable facts.

PROBABLE CAUSE A reasonable basis for believing that a crime has been committed.

■■■

Maryland v. King

State (P) v. Arrestee (D)

133 S. Ct. 1958 (2013).

NATURE OF CASE: Certiorari review of Fourth Amendment search in appeal of criminal rape conviction.

FACT SUMMARY: Alonzo King (D) was arrested and charged in Maryland (P) with assault. As part of the booking process, King's DNA sample was taken by applying a cotton swab to the inside of his cheek. A later analysis determined King's (D) DNA matched that taken from a rape victim years earlier. King (D) was tried and convicted for the rape, but his conviction was overturned on the basis the DNA sample was an unreasonable search.

RULE OF LAW
It is reasonable under the Fourth Amendment for officers to take and analyze a buccal swab of an arrestee's DNA when the arrest is for a serious offense, supported by probable cause, and the arrestee is brought to the police station for legitimate police booking procedures.

FACTS: Alonzo King (D) was arrested and charged for assault. Police processed King (D) for detention, and, as part of the booking process, conducted a buccal swab to collect King's (D) DNA. The DNA matched that from a rape sample taken six years earlier. King (D) was tried and convicted for the rape. His conviction was later overturned on the grounds obtaining and using the cheek swab during the 2009 booking was an unreasonable search of the person. The United States Supreme court granted certiorari review.

ISSUE: Is it reasonable under the Fourth Amendment for officers to take and analyze a buccal swab of an arrestee's DNA when the arrest is for a serious offense, supported by probable cause, and the arrestee is brought to the police station for legitimate police booking procedures?

HOLDING AND DECISION: (Kennedy, J.) Yes. It is reasonable under the Fourth Amendment for officers to take and analyze a buccal swab of an arrestee's DNA when the arrest is for a serious offense, supported by probable cause, and the arrestee is brought to the police station for legitimate police booking procedures. The Maryland DNA Collection Act (the Act) authorizes law enforcement officials to collect DNA samples. The legitimate government interest accomplished with the DNA swab is the need for law enforcement officers safely and accurately to process and identify those in their custody. A suspect's criminal history is a critical part of his identity and it is common for arrestees to conceal true identity. Police already compare booking photographs and sketches and make computerized comparison of fingerprints. The

use of DNA for identification is no different. Identifying those who have committed prior crimes is important also to ascertain who might be likely to flee if permitted conditional leave from custody. A person with a past criminal action might be more likely to flee to avoid more serious charges. Finally, use of DNA may free an innocent person wrongfully imprisoned for the same offense. DNA identification is superior to fingerprinting and the time to accomplish DNA identification is shrinking. There is little reason to question the government's legitimate interest in knowing for certainty the identity of the person it has arrested. In comparison, the intrusion of a cheek swab is minimal. The privacy concerns of an arrestee also are diminished. Merely being in custody does not make any search of an arrestee a reasonable one, but this is a reasonable search. Reversed.

DISSENT: (Scalia, J.) When the Court has permitted a suspicionless search, it has required a justifying motive apart from the investigation of a crime. No such justifying motive exists here. The Court elaborates on its identification purpose but knowing the facts of the DNA search at issue here instantly disabuses one that identification has anything to do with using King's (D) DNA sample. The docket sheet demonstrates King (D) was identified by full name, race, sex, height, weight, date of birth, and address. The search had nothing to do with establishing his identity but did identify the cold case rape sample by its association with King (D). Cases do not readily answer whether fingerprinting is a search, but officers' post-arrest use of fingerprints is for identification while post-arrest use of DNA is to solve crimes. The suspicionless search here was unnecessary because all parties agree King (D) could have had his DNA sampled after his conviction for second-degree assault. The Court now solely burdens those who have been acquitted of the crime of arrest; that is, it only burdens those who are innocent of the state's accusations.

ANALYSIS

When the United States Supreme Court granted certiorari in *Maryland v. King*, 49 states filed amicus briefs in support of Maryland. The Court noted that 26 states and the federal government take DNA samples upon arrest, and the amicus briefs generally argued that the legitimate government interests outweighed the rights and interests of the arrestees. All 50 states and the federal government take DNA samples from convicted offenders and guidance differs on

Continued on next page.

when an individual's DNA may be entered into databases and acted upon by law enforcement.

∎▬∎

Quicknotes

AMICUS BRIEF A brief submitted by a third party not a party to the action, that contains information for the court's consideration in conformity with its position.

UNREASONABLE SEARCH The Fourth Amendment protects against unreasonable searches and seizures; in order to invoke the Fourth Amendment prohibition, the individual must have a reasonable expectation of privacy in respect to the location searched or thing seized.

∎▬∎

Chimel v. California

Burglary convict (D) v. State (P)

395 U.S. 752 (1969).

NATURE OF CASE: Appeal from burglary conviction.

FACT SUMMARY: Police officers, after lawfully arresting Chimel (D) in his house, conducted a search, over his objections, of his entire house, which produced evidence used to obtain his conviction on two charges of burglary.

🏛 RULE OF LAW
Under the Fourth and Fourteenth Amendments, a warrantless search conducted incident to a lawful arrest may only extend to a search of the arrestee's person and to the area "within his immediate control" (i.e., the area within which he might obtain a weapon or destructible evidence).

FACTS: Late one afternoon, police officers arrived at Chimel's (D) home with a warrant authorizing his arrest for the burglary of a coin shop. Chimel's (D) wife allowed the officers to enter the house and wait for Chimel (D) to return from work. When Chimel (D) entered his home, the officers arrested him and then conducted a search, over his objection, of his entire three-bedroom house, including the attic, the garage, and a small workshop. During this search, the officers seized a number of coins, several medal tokens, and other objects, used subsequently at Chimel's (D) trial to obtain his conviction on two charges of burglary. Upon affirmation of this conviction, Chimel (D) brought a petition for certiorari to this court.

ISSUE: When a suspect is lawfully arrested in one room of his house, can a search of his entire house be constitutionally justified as incident to that arrest?

HOLDING AND DECISION: (Stewart, J.) No. Under the Fourth and Fourteenth Amendments, a warrantless search conducted incident to a lawful arrest may only extend to a search of the arrestee's person and to the area "within his immediate control" (i.e., the area within which he might obtain a weapon for destructible evidence). The past decisions of this Court on such searches have been far from consistent, and this case marks the final determination of which one of two divergent lines of cases applies. On one hand, the *Harris*, 331 U.S. 145 (1947), and *Rabinowitz*, 339 U.S. 56 (1950), line of cases have given a broad scope to warrantless searches conducted incident to arrest. Under these cases, anything within the "possession" of the arrestee (as broadly defined to include a search of the arrestee's entire apartment in *Harris*, and to include a search of the arrestee's one-room business office in *Rabinowitz*) may be searched at the time of his arrest, in order

to seize any evidence connected with his suspected crime. On the other hand, the *Go-Bart*, 282 U.S. 344 (1931), *Lefkowitz*, 285 U.S. 452 (1932), and *Trupiano*, 334 U.S. 699 (1948), line of cases limits warrantless charges incident to arrest. In both *Go-Bart* and *Lefkowitz*, such searches were limited to evidence which was "visible and accessible and in the offender's immediate custody." In *Trupiano*, the Court stated that a search warrant is always required absent some showing of "necessity" and there must be something more of a necessity for a warrantless search than mere arrest. The decision of this Court today is an attempt to define, along the line of the *Trupiano* case, when such necessity exists. As this Court stated in *Trupiano*, the burden is upon those seeking an exemption from the warrant requirement to show that it is justified by necessity. Such justification in the case of warrantless searches incident to arrest may extend no further than the arrestee's person and the area within his immediate control. It is reasonable for an officer to search the arrestee's person for his own safety, since the arrestee may have concealed weapons, and it is reasonable to search the area within the arrestee's control to prevent him from reaching a weapon or destroying evidence. But, any extension beyond such an area would lead to the "evaporation" of the Fourth Amendment's right against unreasonable searches and seizures. Here, the search of Chimel's (D) house was far beyond that area considered reasonable. As such, the judgment is reversed.

▶ ANALYSIS

This case illustrates the limited scope of a warrantless search conducted incident to a lawful arrest. Whenever police take an arrested person into custody, it is "reasonable" to make a "full search" of his person, regardless of the reason for his arrest. But this decision leaves open the question of whether a "full search," or only a limited search for weapons, may be conducted when the person is not taken into custody after his arrest. Note, however, that after a lawful arrest, when the suspect is taken into custody, a warrantless search of his clothing and the property in his immediate possession may be done "after he has been brought to the station house" and "after a substantial period of time during his incarceration"—at least when there is probable cause linking the clothes to his crime.

■▬■

Quicknotes

EXIGENT CIRCUMSTANCES Circumstances requiring an extraordinary or immediate response; an exception to

Continued on next page.

the prohibition on a warrantless arrest or search when police officers believe probable cause to exist and there is no time for obtaining a warrant.

SEARCH INCIDENT TO LAWFUL ARREST EXCEPTION PLAIN VIEW
Exception to the requirement of a valid warrant for a search or seizure so long as the officer is lawfully in the location where the evidence is obtained and it is apparent that the thing seized is evidence.

■━■

Kentucky v. King

State (P) v. Individual (D)

___ U.S. ___, 131 S. Ct. 1849 (2011).

NATURE OF CASE: Appeal from state high court decision in favor of defendant.

FACT SUMMARY: After observing suspect purchase cocaine, police officers followed him to a breezeway in an apartment complex. The officers did not know which apartment the suspect entered. Smelling marijuana from one apartment and hearing things moving around in the apartment, the officers entered that apartment and discovered King (D) with drugs, cash, and other drug paraphernalia.

🏛 RULE OF LAW

The exigent circumstances rule may be used to uphold a warrantless search only if police officers do not gain entry into a residence by an actual or threatened violation of the Fourth Amendment.

FACTS: Police officers were following a suspect involved in a controlled purchase of cocaine. The suspect entered the breezeway of an apartment complex. The officers following the suspect into the breezeway did not know into which apartment he disappeared, the one on the left or the right. The officers smelled the odor of marijuana emanating from the apartment on the left. The officers knocked on the door of that apartment and announced their presence. They then heard things being moved around quickly in the apartment. This led the officers to believe that evidence was about to be destroyed. The officers then entered the apartment and found King (D), who was not the original suspect, with drugs, cash, and other drug paraphernalia. Before trial, King (D) moved to suppress the evidence on the grounds the officers' search was an illegal warrantless search and no exceptions existed to uphold the search. The trial court denied the motion and a jury convicted King (D) on various drug charges. The Kentucky Supreme Court then overturned the decision, holding that the police could not rely upon the exigent circumstances exception when the police themselves created the emergency. The state (P) appealed to the United States Supreme Court.

ISSUE: May the exigent circumstances rule be used to uphold a warrantless search only if police officers do not gain entry into a residence by an actual or threatened violation of the Fourth Amendment?

HOLDING AND DECISION: (Alito, J.) Yes. The exigent circumstances rule may be used to uphold a warrantless search only if police officers do not gain entry into a residence by an actual or threatened violation of the Fourth Amendment. First, the exigent circumstances rule allows officers to conduct a search without a warrant if exigent circumstances exist which precludes officers from first obtaining a warrant. Such circumstances include the imminent destruction of evidence. However, lower federal courts have developed the "police created exigency" doctrine that holds that police may not conduct a search without a warrant if the police themselves create or manufacture the exigent circumstances. This Court now holds that the exigent circumstances exception may still be used as long as the police do not gain entry by an actual or threatened violation of the Fourth Amendment. A review of the officers' actions in exigent circumstance cases must be objective, and the Kentucky Supreme Court's use of a subjective test is inappropriate under the Fourth Amendment. Rather than ruminate whether the officers subjectively created the emergency by loudly knocking on the door of the apartment, the facts must be viewed objectively in light of all circumstances. Another test posited by the lower courts, whether it was reasonably foreseeable that the officers' actions would create the exigent circumstances, is also unworkable. There is always some possibility a suspect in the drug trade may have drugs in the residence. Use of the reasonable foreseeability test would include an analysis of the level of predictability that must be reached before the exigent circumstances rule would apply. Lastly, some courts have faulted police when circumstances supporting probable cause exist but the police fail to stop their activities and obtain a warrant. This approach interferes with law enforcement strategies. The police are under no obligation to halt their activities and obtain a search warrant once the minimum standard for probable cause has been reached. Reversed.

DISSENT: (Ginsburg, J.) The officers had probable cause to obtain a search warrant based upon the suspect's entrance into the breezeway and the smell of marijuana from the apartment. Nothing made it impracticable for the police to obtain the appropriate search warrant at that time prior to their entry into the apartment.

▌ANALYSIS

This decision reaffirms the original exigent circumstances rule and severely limits the "police created exigency" exception to that rule. In essence, as long as police do not gain entry by means of an actual or threatened violation of the Fourth Amendment, the warrantless search may be upheld. Note that here the Supreme Court did not engage

Continued on next page.

in a specific analysis as to whether exigent circumstances were present. It assumed that for the purposes of its review, but remanded the case to the Kentucky Supreme Court for a determination of whether exigent circumstances were actually present.

■■■

Quicknotes

EXIGENT CIRCUMSTANCES Circumstances requiring an extraordinary or immediate response; an exception to the prohibition on a warrantless arrest or search when police officers believe probable cause to exist and there is no time for obtaining a warrant.

■■■

Payton v. New York

Murder convict (D) v. State (P)

445 U.S. 573 (1980).

NATURE OF CASE: Appeal from convictions for murder.

FACT SUMMARY: Without a warrant, the police entered Payton's (D) apartment to arrest him for murder and, even though he was not there, seized a shell casing that was in plain sight and was later admitted into evidence at his trial.

RULE OF LAW
Absent exigent circumstances, the police may not make a warrantless, nonconsensual entry into a private residence to make a routine felony arrest.

FACTS: Having probable cause to believe Payton (D) had murdered a gas station manager the police entered his apartment to effect a routine felony arrest. Although he was not home, the police found a 30-caliber shell casing in plain sight in the apartment and seized it for ultimate use as evidence at his trial. Payton's (D) motions to suppress the evidence were denied and he was convicted of murder. On appeal, he argued that the statute authorizing warrantless entries to make routine felony arrests violated the Fourth Amendment. The court of appeals affirmed the conviction.

ISSUE: Under normal circumstances, is it constitutional for the police to make a warrantless, nonconsensual entry into a private residence to effect a routine felony arrest?

HOLDING AND DECISION: (Stevens, J.) No. The Fourth Amendment does not permit the police to make a warrantless and nonconsensual entry into a private residence to effect a routine felony arrest in the absence of exigent circumstances. The Fourth Amendment, made applicable to the states by the Fourteenth Amendment, draws a firm line at the entrance to the house. Absent exigent circumstances, that threshold may not reasonably be crossed without a warrant. Inasmuch as no warrant was obtained, the police acted impermissibly in entering Payton's (D) apartment, and the evidence found therein should not have been admitted into evidence at trial. Reversed.

DISSENT: (White, J.) Instead of adopting a rule that will severely hamper effective law enforcement, the Court should embrace a clear and simple rule comporting with the carefully crafted restrictions on the common-law power of arrest entry. That is, after knocking and announcing their presence, police may enter the home to make a daytime arrest without a warrant when there is a probable cause to believe that the person to be arrested committed a felony and is present in the house.

ANALYSIS

At the time this case was decided, some states had already passed laws requiring a warrant as a precondition to a felony arrest in the home. The Court noted that no proof had been offered that such a requirement had caused law enforcement in those states to suffer.

Quicknotes

EXIGENT CIRCUMSTANCES Circumstances requiring an extraordinary or immediate response; an exception to the prohibition on a warrantless arrest or search when police officers believe probable cause to exist and there is no time for obtaining a warrant.

KNOCK AND ANNOUNCE Requirement that a police officer must first knock and announce his intention before he enters an individual's home in the execution of a valid warrant.

California v. Carney

State (P) v. Drug dealer (D)

471 U.S. 386 (1985).

NATURE OF CASE: Appeal from conviction for drug trafficking.

FACT SUMMARY: Carney (D) was accused of trading drugs for sexual favors.

🏛 RULE OF LAW
The "automobile exception" to the warrant requirement applies to motor homes.

FACTS: A Drug Enforcement Agency (DEA) agent placed the motor home of Carney (D) under surveillance. When a youth exited the motor home, he was stopped by Williams, a DEA agent. The youth told Williams that he had received marijuana in return for sexual favors. Williams and other agents searched the motor home and found marijuana and related paraphernalia. Carney (D) was charged with possession for sale. He moved to suppress the evidence as the agents did not have a search warrant. The trial court denied the motion, but the California Supreme Court reversed.

ISSUE: Does the "automobile exception" to the warrant requirement apply to motor homes?

HOLDING AND DECISION: (Burger, C.J.) Yes. The "automobile exception" to the warrant requirement applies to motor homes. The reason for the exception is twofold. Autos are inherently mobile and can be taken away before a warrant is issued. Also, autos, unlike homes, are subject to regulations that lower the owner's expectation of privacy. The motor home here, while having homelike qualities, is also inherently mobile and is subject to the same state licensing as a regular automobile. Therefore, the rationales for the auto exception apply to mobile homes. Reversed.

DISSENT: (Stevens, J.) Where, as here, agents have the element of surprise on their side, and the motor home is parked, the exigencies justifying the auto exception do not apply.

▶ ANALYSIS

While auto searches do not require warrants, probable cause is still necessary. For this reason, the scope of an auto search is limited. It may not be more intrusive than that necessary to obtain the required evidence.

■=■

Quicknotes

AUTOMOBILE EXCEPTION Exception to the requirement of a valid warrant if a police officer has probable cause to believe that a vehicle contains evidence of a crime or contraband; the officer may search the entire vehicle.

EXIGENT CIRCUMSTANCES Circumstances requiring an extraordinary or immediate response; an exception to the prohibition on a warrantless arrest or search when police officers believe probable cause to exist and there is no time for obtaining a warrant.

EXPECTATION OF PRIVACY Requirement that in order to invoke the Fourth Amendment's protection against unreasonable searches and seizures, the individual must have a reasonable expectation of privacy in respect to the location searched or thing seized.

PROBABLE CAUSE A reasonable basis for believing that a crime has been committed.

■=■

California v. Acevedo

State (P) v. Contraband possessor (D)

500 U.S. 565 (1991).

NATURE OF CASE: Appeal from acceptance of motion to suppress evidence.

FACT SUMMARY: In California's (P) criminal action against Acevedo (D) for possession of contraband, the appellate court, reversing the district court's ruling, accepted Acevedo's (D) motion to suppress evidence relating to his contraband possession.

RULE OF LAW
The warrantless search of an automobile or any closed containers within it is reasonable under the Fourth Amendment if there is probable cause for the search.

FACTS: Officers, who had probable cause to believe that contraband was in a residence which they had under surveillance, watched Acevedo (D) enter the address, stay for ten minutes, and reappear carrying a full, brown paper bag. Subsequently, Acevedo (D) placed this bag in the trunk of his car and started to drive away. However, the officers, fearing loss of evidence, stopped him, opened his trunk and the bag without a warrant, and found contraband. At the criminal proceedings brought against Acevedo (D) for possession of contraband, Acevedo (D) moved to suppress the contraband evidence, arguing that since the officers' probable cause was directed specifically at the bag and not at his car, common law dictated that the officers obtain a warrant prior to searching the bag's contents. Notwithstanding Acevedo's (D) argument, the district court denied his motion. On appeal, however, the California Court of Appeal reversed, and the Supreme Court affirmed. California (P) appealed.

ISSUE: Is the warrantless search of an automobile or any closed containers within it reasonable under the Fourth Amendment if there is probable cause for the search?

HOLDING AND DECISION: (Blackmun, J.) Yes. The warrantless search of an automobile or any closed containers within it is reasonable under the Fourth Amendment if there is probable cause for the search. This rule rectifies the two apparently dichotomous common-law rules governing the warrantless search of an automobile and the warrantless search of a closed container within the automobile. The dichotomy dictates that if there is probable cause to search a car, then the entire car—including any closed container found therein—may be searched without a warrant, but if there is probable cause only as to a container in the car, the container may be held but not searched until a warrant is obtained. However, the line between probable cause to search a vehicle and probable cause to search a package in that vehicle is not always clear, and separate rules that govern the two objects to be searched may enable police to broaden their power to make warrantless searches to the detriment of privacy interests. Furthermore, the protection of privacy interests afforded by disallowing the warrantless search of closed container contained within an automobile is minimal since, in an overwhelming majority of cases, a warrant is routinely given after a closed container is seized. Finally, the discrepancy between the two rules has led to confusion for law enforcement officers. Hence, to avoid these anomalous results, necessity dictates that the common-law rule requiring a warrant to search closed containers contained within an automobile be overruled. In the instant case, although the police merely had probable cause as to the contraband, their search of the paper bag was reasonable under the Fourth Amendment. Reversed.

CONCURRENCE: (Scalia, J.) Reversal was proper not because a closed container carried inside a car becomes subject to the "automobile" exception to the general warrant requirement but because the search of a closed container, outside a privately owned building, with probable cause to believe that the container contains contraband, is not one of those searches whose Fourth Amendment reasonableness depends upon a warrant.

DISSENT: (Stevens, J.) It is a cardinal principle that searches conducted outside the judicial process, without prior approval by judge or magistrate, are per se unreasonable under the Fourth Amendment—subject only to a few specifically established and well-delineated exceptions. Moreover, the circumstances in the present case are not so exceptional as to justify invasion of an individual's privacy interest outside the presence of a neutral magistrate.

ANALYSIS

In considering the above rule, the next logical step for the court may be to permit warrantless searches of luggage or personal belongings being transported on foot as opposed to within a motor vehicle since there is a possibility that evidence can be lost, i.e., through the transporter taking flight or through the evidence being hidden, only to be retrieved later. Obviously, the possibility of these two things happening dictates whether such a rule would be adopted. Moreover, a significant increase in drug activity across the country may also make such a rule thinkable.

■■■

Continued on next page.

Quicknotes

AUTOMOBILE EXCEPTION Exception to the requirement of a valid warrant if a police officer has probable cause to believe that a vehicle contains evidence of a crime or contraband; the officer may search the entire vehicle.

CONTRABAND Items that are illegal to have in one's possession or to trade or produce.

PROBABLE CAUSE A reasonable basis for believing that a crime has been committed.

■▬■

Arizona v. Gant

State (P) v. Individual (D)

556 U.S. 332 (2009).

NATURE OF CASE: Appeal from state high court decision in favor of defendant.

FACT SUMMARY: Local police arrested Gant (D) for an outstanding warrant for driving without a license. After the police placed Gant (D) in a police vehicle, a subsequent search of Gant's (D) vehicle revealed cocaine and a handgun.

RULE OF LAW
Police may search the passenger compartment of a vehicle incident to an occupant's arrest only if the occupant may have access to the vehicle or if it is reasonable to believe the vehicle contains evidence of the offense for which the occupant was arrested.

FACTS: After receiving a tip that a house was being use to distribute drugs, Tucson police officers approached the house and spoke to Gant (D). The police then left the house and conducted a records check on Gant (D), which revealed he had an outstanding warrant for driving with a suspended license. The police went back to the house. While they were there, Gant (D) drove into the driveway. Upon recognizing Gant (D), the police immediately arrested him on the outstanding warrant. The arrest took place 10 to 15 feet away from Gant's (D) vehicle. The police then placed Gant (D) in a patrol car and searched his vehicle. The search revealed a handgun and cocaine. At trial, Gant (D) moved to suppress the evidence on the grounds police did not have probable cause for the search. The trial court denied his motion, but the Arizona Supreme Court found the search was unreasonable. The State (P) appealed.

ISSUE: May police search the passenger compartment of a vehicle incident to an occupant's arrest if the occupant may have access to the vehicle or if it is reasonable to believe the vehicle contains evidence of the offense for which the occupant was arrested?

HOLDING AND DECISION: (Stevens, J.) Yes. Police may search the passenger compartment of a vehicle incident to an occupant's arrest only if the occupant may have access to the vehicle or if it is reasonable to believe the vehicle contains evidence of the offense for which the occupant was arrested. In *New York v. Belton*, 453 U.S. 454 (1981), this Court held that searches incident to arrest may include the interior of a vehicle because of the assumption that the interior includes an area that an arrestee may reach, to either destroy evidence or retrieve a weapon. Over the past 28 years, however, *Belton* has been construed to allow all searches of a motor vehicle incident to an arrest, regardless of whether an arrestee may actually have access to the interior of the vehicle. *Belton* should not be interpreted so broadly. Rather, a search of a vehicle may only be conducted where the arrestee has actual access to the vehicle or if there is reason to believe the vehicle contains evidence related to the offense of the arrest. Here, Gant (D) was already handcuffed and in the patrol car at the time of the search. There was no way he could access the vehicle. Second, the police arrested Gant (D) for driving with a suspended license. The vehicle would not contain any additional evidence related to that offense. Accordingly, the search was unreasonable. Affirmed.

CONCURRENCE: (Scalia, J.) This case concerns only those searches conducted after police make an arrest. There is some fear that the Court's abandonment of *Belton's* bright-line rule may actually invite officers to leave a scene unsecured in order to conduct a search. *Belton* should be overruled in its entirety and the following new rule should be followed. Vehicle searches following arrests are reasonable only when the object of the search is evidence of the crime related to the arrest. Because there could be no evidence related to Gant's (D) arrest in the vehicle, the search of his vehicle was unlawful. The majority opinion will also better protect citizens from possible unlawful searches, which would likely occur if the dissent's view of the case was adopted.

DISSENT: (Alito, J.) The *Belton* holding was clear and unequivocal. That case held that whenever an officer makes an arrest of a person from a vehicle, the officer may search the passenger compartment of the arrestee's vehicle. The Court adopted that course because it established a bright-line rule that was easily followed by law enforcement. The Court did not limit its holding with reference to when a search was made. This Court should adhere to *Belton* because of law enforcement's reliance on the rule for the past 28 years. Circumstances have not changed since *Belton* that dictate a change in the law, nor has the *Belton* rule become unworkable. For these reasons, this Court is bound by stare decisis. The Court should have found the search of Gant's (D) vehicle reasonable and consistent with the *Belton* rule.

ANALYSIS

This decision limited *Belton's* holding regarding the ability to search vehicles incident to arrests. However, Justice Scalia's point regarding the limited applicability of the

Continued on next page.

decision is significant. This decision only applies to searches following arrests. It does not apply to those situations where officers ask an occupant to step out of a vehicle and a search is conducted without an arrest being made. Those types of searches are not implicated here.

■═■

Quicknotes

BRIGHT-LINE RULE A legal rule of decision to help resolve ambiguous issues simply and in a straightforward manner, sometimes sacrificing equity for certainty.

PROBABLE CAUSE A reasonable basis for believing that a crime has been committed.

SEARCH INCIDENT TO A LAWFUL ARREST Exception to the requirement of a valid warrant for a search or seizure so long as the officer is lawfully in the location where the evidence is obtained and it is apparent that the thing seized is evidence.

STARE DECISIS Doctrine whereby courts follow legal precedent unless there is good cause for departure.

■═■

Terry v. Ohio

Armed suspect (D) v. State (P)

392 U.S. 1 (1968).

NATURE OF CASE: Certiorari from conviction for carrying a concealed weapon.

FACT SUMMARY: When Officer McFadden became suspicious of the behavior of three men in downtown Cleveland, he stopped them, identified himself, and, believing they were armed and dangerous, frisked them (i.e., patted their outer clothing), finding a concealed weapon on Terry (D).

🏛 RULE OF LAW

Regardless of the existence of probable cause, where a police officer "reasonably" concludes in the light of his experience that criminal activity may be afoot and that the persons with whom he is dealing may be armed and dangerous, he may "stop" such persons; and, if after identifying himself and making reasonable inquiries, his fears are not dispelled, he may conduct a carefully limited search of the outer clothing of such persons for weapons.

FACTS: Officer McFadden, a Cleveland plainclothes detective, became suspicious of two men (one of whom was Terry (D)) who were repeatedly peering into a store down the street and then returning to a corner. When a third man joined these two suspects, Officer McFadden, surmising that the suspects were "casing" a stickup and, therefore, might be armed and dangerous, stopped them. Upon identifying himself as a policeman and receiving only mumbling replies to his questions, McFadden patted (i.e., "frisked") their outer clothing and, upon feeling a pistol under Terry's (D) clothing, removed it. Terry (D) was charged with carrying a concealed weapon. At his trial, Terry (D) moved to suppress the evidence, but the trial court denied his motion and Terry (D) was convicted. Upon affirmation of his conviction by the Ohio Court of Appeals, and dismissal of his appeal by the state supreme court, Terry (D) filed a petition for certiorari with this court.

ISSUE: Is it always unreasonable for a policeman, absent probable cause, to stop a person and subject him to a limited search of his outer clothing for weapons?

HOLDING AND DECISION: (Warren, C.J.) No. Regardless of the existence of probable cause, where a police officer "reasonably" concludes in the light of his experience that criminal activity may be afoot and that the persons with whom he is dealing may be armed and dangerous, he may "stop" such persons and, if after identifying himself and making reasonable inquiries, his fears are not dispelled, he may conduct a carefully limited search of

the outer clothing of such persons for weapons. Stop-and-frisk conduct, although covered by the Fourth Amendment, should not be subjected to the warrant requirement as well. The wide variety of street encounters found by the police requires "necessarily swift action upon on-the-spot observations of the officer on the beat," which historically has not, and practically cannot, be subjected to the warrant requirement. As such, the brief intrusion on the suspect's freedom is more properly tested under the Fourth Amendment's general proscription against "unreasonable" searches and seizures. Under this test of reasonableness, the need to search must be balanced against the invasion involved. In the stop-and-frisk situation, the government has a need to search to promote effective crime control and to protect the police officer's safety. Furthermore, if (1) the stop-and-frisk is based upon "specific inferences" (not on "unparticularized suspicion or hunches"), so that the officer's behavior can later be objectively reviewed, and if (2) the stop-and-frisk is limited to a frisk for weapons, the invasion is justified and reasonable. Here, Officer McFadden legitimately investigated suspicious behavior, acted under "reasonable suspicion" that the suspects might be armed and dangerous, and frisked only their outer garments. As such, the search was reasonable and the evidence is admissible. Judgment affirmed.

CONCURRENCE: (Harlan, J.) There are a few gaps in the decision of the Court, although its ultimate conclusion is sound. If a frisk is to be justified in order to protect the officer, the officer must first have constitutional grounds to make a forcible "stop" (i.e., reasonable suspicion), but a limited frisk incident to such a lawful stop requires no additional justification. There is no reason why an officer should risk a bullet by first questioning the suspect.

CONCURRENCE: (White, J.) There is no need for interrogation during an investigative stop before the officer frisks the suspect. Although an officer may question the suspects briefly, when a temporary detention is justified by a fear for the officer's and others' safety, a protective frisk for weapons is justified regardless of whether or not any questions are asked.

DISSENT: (Douglas, J.) A search and seizure cannot be justified by Fourth Amendment standards unless there is "probable cause" to believe that a crime has been committed or is about to be committed. Here, however, since there was no "probable cause" for the issuance of a warrant, the

Continued on next page.

Court's holding allows police greater freedom to search and seize than even a judge could authorize.

▶ *ANALYSIS*

This case illustrates the less stringent rule applicable to stop-and-frisk than that applicable to arrest and search. This rule was further clarified in *Sibron v. New York*, 392 U.S. 40 (1968), in which the court stated than an officer "must be able to point to particular facts from which he reasonably inferred that the individual was armed and dangerous." However, in *Adams v. Williams*, 407 U.S. 143 (1972), the Court stated that this "reasonable inference" need not be based upon the officer's personal observation. Rather, it may be based upon an unnamed informer's tip that "carries some indicia of reliability," even though the unverified tip is not so reliable as to constitute "probable cause" for an arrest or search warrant.

■═■

Quicknotes

REASONABLE SUSPICION That which would cause an ordinary prudent person under the circumstances to suspect that a crime has been committed based on specific and articulable facts.

STOP AND FRISK A brief, nonintrusive stop, requiring the police officer to have a reasonable suspicion that a crime has been committed based on specific and articulable facts, and involving a search for a concealed weapon that is conducted by patting down the clothes of the person.

■═■

Schneckloth v. Bustamonte

Court (P) v. Car passenger (D)

412 U.S. 218 (1973).

NATURE OF CASE: Petition for writ of habeas corpus, after conviction.

FACT SUMMARY: An officer stopped a car carrying Bustamonte (D) and five other men because it had a burned-out headlight. The one man who had identification said that the car belonged to his brother. When the officer asked if he could search it, the man replied, "Sure." The officer found some stolen checks in the car.

🏛 RULE OF LAW
Whether a consent to a search was, in fact, voluntary is a question of fact to be determined from all of the circumstances, and while the person's knowledge of a right to refuse is a factor to be taken into account, the prosecution is not required to demonstrate such knowledge as a prerequisite to establishing a voluntary consent.

FACTS: Officer Rand stopped an automobile when he observed that its headlight and license plate light were burned out. There were six men, including Bustamonte (D), in the car. Only one of the men had identification, and he said that the car belonged to his brother. When Rand asked if he could search the car, the man replied, "Sure, go ahead," and helped Rand with the search. Rand found some stolen checks in the car. Bustamonte (D), whose motion to suppress was denied, was convicted on the basis of the checks and other evidence. His conviction was affirmed on appeal; the federal district court denied his petition for a writ of habeas corpus. The Ninth Circuit Court of Appeals vacated the order denying the writ and remanded the case for further proceedings, holding that when a prosecutor relies upon consent to justify a search, it is an essential part of the state's burden to prove that the person knew of his/her right to refuse consent. The United States Supreme Court granted certiorari.

ISSUE: Must it be shown by the state that a person who consented to a search knew of his/her right to refuse consent in order for the consent (and the search) to be valid?

HOLDING AND DECISION: (Stewart, J.) No. A search conducted pursuant to a valid consent is constitutionally permissible. But when the state seeks to rely on consent to justify a search, it has the burden of showing that the consent was freely and voluntarily given. Whether consent to a search was voluntary or was the product of duress or coercion is a question of fact to be determined from the totality of all the circumstances. While knowledge

of the right to refuse consent is one factor to be considered, the state need not prove such knowledge in order to prove consent. Searches authorized by consent are of unquestioned benefit to the police. However, such consent must not be coerced. "To approve such searches without the most careful scrutiny would sanction the possibility of official coercion; to place artificial restrictions upon such searches would jeopardize their basic validity;" to require that proof that the person consenting to the search knew of his/her right to refuse consent would seriously impair such searches. In many cases where there was no evidence of coercion, the state would still be unable to show that the person knew of the right to refuse. Likewise, a person who consented to a search could prevent the use of the fruits of the search as evidence by failing to testify to having knowledge of the right to refuse consent. It is suggested that subjects of searches could be advised of their right to refuse. However, "it would be thoroughly impracticable to impose on the informal and unstructured conditions of the normal consent search the detailed requirements of an effecting warning." These conditions are far removed from the structured atmosphere of a trial or even "custodial interrogation." It is contended that consent is a waiver of a person's Fourth and Fourteenth Amendment rights, and that only knowing and intelligent waivers are valid. However, the knowing and intelligent waiver requirement is almost always only applied to those rights guaranteed to a criminal defendant in order to preserve a fair trial, such as rights to counsel, to confrontation, to a jury trial, and to a speedy trial. These rights are aimed at promoting the fair ascertainment of truth at trial. Fourth Amendment rights are quite different and protect one's privacy against arbitrary police intrusion. It would be unrealistic to expect that in the informal, unstructured context of a consent search, an officer could make the detailed type of examination demanded by the intelligent and knowing waiver requirements. Also, a waiver approach to consent searches would be inconsistent with decisions approving third party consents. It is inconceivable that the Constitution could countenance the waiver of a defendant's right to counsel or to confrontation by a third party. Yet, such consents to searches by third parties have been held valid. Here, there was no evidence of any coercive tactics by the police, either from the nature of the police questioning or the environment in which it took place. The court of appeals decision is reversed.

DISSENT: (Marshall, J.) This case deals not with "coercion" but with "consent," a subtly different concept. Freedom

Continued on next page.

from coercion is a substantive right, guaranteed by the Fifth and Fourteenth Amendments. Consent is a mechanism by which substantive requirements are avoided. Consent searches are submitted not because such an exception to the requirements of probable cause and warrant is essential to law enforcement, but because citizens are permitted to choose whether or not they wish to exercise their constitutional rights. Our prior decisions do not support the view that a meaningful choice has been made simply because no coercion was used. Consent means a knowing choice. How can a decision made without knowledge of the available alternatives be called a choice? I would hold that the state may not rely on a purported consent to a search if the subject of the search did not know of his right to refuse consent. The subject's knowledge of this right could be shown by his demonstration of such knowledge at the time of the search, by having him testify under oath (if he is not the defendant), by the subject's prior experience or training, or if the police, at the time of the search, told the subject of his right to refuse consent. There is nothing impractical about this latter method, and the decision to employ it would lie with the officers. "I doubt that a simple statement by an officer of an individuals' right to refuse consent would do much to alter the informality of this exchange, except to alert the subject to a fact that he is entitled to know. For many years, FBI agents have routinely informed subjects of their right to refuse consent. I must conclude, with some reluctance, that when the court speaks of practicality, what it really is talking of is the continued ability of the police to capitalize on the ignorance of citizens so as to accomplish by subterfuge what they could not achieve by relying only on the knowing relinquishment of constitutional rights."

▶ ANALYSIS

A search based upon a valid consent may be conducted without a warrant and without probable cause. Most federal courts have applied the light standards normally applicable to the waiver of constitutional rights to determine the validity of consent to a search. It is said that a consent, in order to be voluntary, must be unequivocal, specific, and intelligently given, uncontaminated by any duress or coercion, and is not lightly to be inferred. In *Bumper v. North Carolina*, 391 U.S. 543 (1968), consent for a search was given after the officer had stated that he had a search warrant. The Court held that the consent was not valid, since the officer's claim of authority was, in effect, an announcement that the occupant had no right to resist the search. Under such circumstances, acquiescence could not be construed as consent.

■■■

Quicknotes

CONSENT A voluntary and willful agreement by an individual possessing sufficient mental capacity to undertake an action suggested by another.

DURESS Unlawful threats or other coercive behavior by one person that causes another to commit acts he would not otherwise do.

PROBABLE CAUSE A reasonable basis for believing that a crime has been committed.

■■■

Illinois v. Rodriguez

State (P) v. Drug possessor (D)

497 U.S. 177 (1990).

NATURE OF CASE: Appeal from acceptance of motion to suppress evidence.

FACT SUMMARY: In Illinois's (P) criminal action against Rodriguez (D) for possession of a controlled substance with intent to deliver, the trial court accepted Rodriguez's (D) motion to suppress evidence relating to his controlled substance possession.

🏛 RULE OF LAW
Where a third party agrees to allow officers to search certain premises over which the officers reasonably believe that the third party has common authority, their subsequent warrantless search of the premises is reasonable under the Fourth Amendment.

FACTS: Fischer, Rodriguez's (D) former girlfriend, authorized the police to conduct a warrantless search of Rodriguez's (D) apartment after he had apparently assaulted her. Prior to entering the apartment, Fischer had referred to it as "our" apartment, and she had told police that she had personal belongings there. Subsequently, after Fischer opened the apartment with a key and gave the police permission to search it, the police found drugs and related paraphernalia, whereupon Rodriguez (D) was arrested. At the criminal proceedings Illinois (P) brought against Rodriguez (D) for possession of a controlled substance with intent to deliver, Rodriguez (D) moved to suppress all evidence seized at the time of his arrest, claiming that Fischer had vacated the apartment several weeks earlier and had no authority to consent to the entry. On the other hand, Illinois (P) argued that even if Fischer had no authority to consent to the entry, since the police reasonably believed that she did, then their entry was permissible. Notwithstanding Illinois' (P) argument, the trial court granted Rodriguez's (D) motion, which was affirmed on appeal to the Illinois Supreme Court. Illinois (P) appealed.

ISSUE: Where a third party agrees to allow officers to search certain premises over which they reasonably believe that the former has common authority, is their subsequent warrantless search of the premises reasonable under the Fourth Amendment?

HOLDING AND DECISION: (Scalia, J.) Yes. When a third party agrees to allow officers to search certain premises over which they reasonably believe that the former has common authority, their subsequent warrantless search of the premises is reasonable under the Fourth Amendment. This rule is derived from examining various common-law requirements, such as warrant and probable cause requirements, which govern the execution of a gov- ernment agent's constitutional authority to intrude on individual liberty. Although unapparent on their face, these requirements have a built-in reasonable standard that allows an agent to exercise reasonable judgment in determining the requirement's scope. Hence, if an agent, in view of the facts and circumstances, is reasonably mistaken as to an applicable requirement's scope, then even though the agent's intrusion on individual liberty is not constitutionally authorized, his conduct is deemed permissible. Since these requirements possess a built-in reasonable standard, then this standard should likewise be deemed applicable to facts bearing upon the authority of consent to a search. In the instant case, although the officers were mistaken as to the authority Fischer apparently had in authorizing the search of Rodriguez's (D) premises, since they, under the circumstances, reasonably believed that she possessed such authority, then evidence of the drugs and related paraphernalia was legitimately found. Hence, Rodriguez's (D) motion to suppress evidence of the drugs' seizure should have been denied. Reversed and remanded.

▶ ANALYSIS

In *State v. Leach*, 782 P.2d 1035 (Wash. 1989), the court ruled that the co-owner's prior consent to the search of a travel agency was not effective against the defendant, who was arrested there but remained present during the search. The court stated as where "the police have obtained consent to search from an individual possessing, at best, equal control over the premises, that consent remains valid against a cohabitant, who also possesses equal control, only while the cohabitant is absent," and "should the cohabitant be present and able to object, the police must also obtain the cohabitant's consent."

■■■

CHAPTER 7

Undercover Investigations

Quick Reference Rules of Law

Hoffa v. United States

Teamster (D) v. Federal government (P)

385 U.S. 293 (1966).

NATURE OF CASE: Appeal from a criminal conviction based on a Fourth Amendment violation.

FACT SUMMARY: While Hoffa (D) was on trial in Tennessee, the Government (P) sent a paid, undercover informant to gather information about Hoffa (D) and report to the Government (P).

🏛 RULE OF LAW
The government's use of an undercover informant without a warrant is not a violation of the Fourth Amendment.

FACTS: Jimmy Hoffa (D) was on trial in Nashville, Tennessee. During the two-month trial, Edward Partin was a constant companion of Hoffa (D), visiting Hoffa (D) repeatedly at his suite in the Andrew Jackson Hotel. Partin was also frequently in the company of Hoffa's (D) associates at the hotel, around town and in the courthouse. Also during this time, Partin was a paid Government (P) informant. Hoffa (D) argues that Partin's failure to disclose his role as an informant vitiated the consent that Hoffa (D) gave Partin to repeatedly enter the hotel suite, and the information given to the Government (P) as a result of Hoffa's (D) confidence was, therefore, a violation of the Fourth Amendment.

ISSUE: Is the government's use of an undercover informant without a warrant a violation of the Fourth Amendment?

HOLDING AND DECISION: (Stewart, J.) No. The government's use of an undercover informant without a warrant is not a violation of the Fourth Amendment. Hoffa (D) was not relying on the safety of his hotel room when Hoffa (D) made incriminating statements. Rather, he relied on a misplaced confidence in an informant. Affirmed.

DISSENT: (Warren, C.J.) Whether the government's use of an undercover agent violates the Constitution must be determined on a case-by-case basis. Here, Partin was a "jailbird" who had serious federal charges pending against him, so that his motives for becoming an informant are suspect. This type of informer and the way the Government (P) used him present a serious potential for undermining the integrity of the truth-finding process. Given his incentives and background, no conviction should be allowed to stand if it is based heavily on his testimony. Here, but for Partin's testimony, it is unlikely Hoffa (D) would have been convicted. Thus, the Fourth Amendment issues should not even have been reached; instead, the testimony should have been discredited as an affront to the quality and fairness of federal law enforcement, which is subject to the Court's supervisory powers. If a criminal defendant had in a similar fashion planted an informer in the prosecution's camp, he would be guilty of obstructing justice. Therefore, the conviction cannot stand.

▶ ANALYSIS

In the companion case of *Osborn v. United States*, 385 U.S. 323 (1996), according to Justice Douglas, the Fourth Amendment issue should turn on whether the informant was a "turncoat friend" or a "government spy." Justice Douglas stressed that a person taking the risk that a friend will turn on him and report to the police is far different from a government plant.

Quicknotes

FOURTH AMENDMENT Provides that persons be secure as to their person and private belongings against unreasonable searches and seizures.

Sherman v. United States

Convicted drug dealer (D) v. Federal government (P)

356 U.S. 369 (1958).

NATURE OF CASE: On certiorari from appellate court judgment upholding narcotics conviction.

FACT SUMMARY: Sherman (D), upon the repeated entreaties of a Government (P) informant, supplied the informer with narcotics.

🏛 RULE OF LAW
The government may not originate a criminal design and implant it in the mind of an innocent person so that the government may prosecute that person.

FACTS: Sherman (D) met another man at a doctor's office where apparently both were seeking treatment of a narcotics addiction. Sherman's (D) acquaintance informed him that he was not responding to treatment and that he was suffering greatly, and asked Sherman (D) if he knew a source of narcotics. Sherman (D) tried to avoid the issue, but the acquaintance repeatedly prevailed on Sherman's (D) sympathy. Sherman (D) finally obtained a quantity of narcotics, which he shared with his acquaintance. The acquaintance, who turned out to be a Government (P) informant, then advised police that Sherman (D) had sold him drugs. Sherman (D) was arrested and convicted, and the court of appeals affirmed. The United States Supreme Court granted certiorari.

ISSUE: May the government originate a criminal design and implant it in the mind of an innocent person so that the government may prosecute that person?

HOLDING AND DECISION: (Warren, C.J.) No. The government may not originate a criminal design and implant it in the mind of an innocent person so that the government may prosecute him. In considering whether entrapment has occurred, we look not only to the conduct of government agents, but to the subjective willingness of the defendant to commit the crime. If a person is predisposed to commit an offense, and the government merely affords him an opportunity to do that wrong which he was ready and willing to do, then the conduct of the government does not constitute entrapment. However, in this case, the testimony of the prosecution's witnesses indicate that Sherman (D) was anything but ready and willing, and that only repeated entreaties by the informer, who claimed to be in great suffering, caused Sherman (D) to supply him with narcotics. Reversed and remanded.

CONCURRENCE: (Frankfurter, J.) Conduct is not less criminal because it is the result of temptation. The better test for entrapment would focus solely on the conduct of the police. As Justice Holmes wrote, "[F]or my part

I think it a less evil that some criminals should escape than that the government should play an ignoble part."

▶ ANALYSIS

In addition to disagreeing with the majority over whether the predisposition of the defendant should be considered in evaluating an entrapment defense, Justice Frankfurter argued that entrapment should be a question of law for the judge, not a jury issue. "It is the province of the court and the court alone," he wrote, "to protect itself and the government from such prostitution of the criminal law."

Quicknotes

ENTRAPMENT An act by public officers that induces a defendant into committing a criminal act.

Jacobson v. United States

Pornography buyer (D) v. Federal government (P)

503 U.S. 540 (1992).

NATURE OF CASE: Appeal of conviction for receiving child pornography.

FACT SUMMARY: Jacobson (D) claimed the Government (P) had entrapped him into violating a child pornography law.

RULE OF LAW
Where government actions create a person's disposition to commit a crime, and then government suggests the crime that the person commits, it is entrapment.

FACTS: At a time when it was legal, Jacobson (D) ordered from an adult bookstore two magazines picturing nude boys, though he later testified he thought he was ordering photos of young men over 17. Congress subsequently passed the Child Protection Act of 1984, criminalizing receipt by mail of sexually explicit depictions of children. The Postal Service found Jacobson's (D) name on the store's mailing list and began mailing Jacobson (D) letters and questionnaires from fictitious research and lobbying organizations and a fake pen pal. The mailings discussed and asked about Jacobson's (D) tastes in pornography and views on censorship. Each time he answered, the next mailing was fit more to his tastes. After two years, the Customs Service, through a fake company, sent Jacobson (D) a child pornography brochure. He placed an order, but it was never filled. The Postal Service, using a fake company, sent Jacobson (D) a letter decrying censorship and claiming the media and government were trying to keep its material out of the country. Jacobson (D) requested a catalogue, from which he later ordered child pornography. Jacobson (D) was arrested upon controlled delivery of the magazine. He unsuccessfully raised an entrapment defense and was convicted under the 1984 Act. The court of appeals affirmed, and Jacobson (D) appealed.

ISSUE: Where government actions create a person's disposition to commit a crime, and then government suggests the crime that the person commits, is it entrapment?

HOLDING AND DECISION: (White, J.) Yes. Where government acts create a person's disposition to commit a crime, and then government suggests the crime that the person commits, it is entrapment. Jacobson (D) had become predisposed to break the law by the time he ordered a magazine from the Government (P). However, the Government (P) did not prove this disposition was not the product of years of Government (P) targeting. The magazines Jacobson (D) ordered from the bookstore were legal when bought. Evidence of predisposition to do what was once legal is not sufficient to show predisposition to do what now is illegal, since most people obey laws with which they disagree. Jacobson's (D) claim that he did not know he was ordering photos of minors from the bookstore was unchallenged. His answers to Government (P) mailings showed predisposition to view child pornography and to support a given agenda through lobbying groups but did not support an inference of predisposition to commit the alleged crime. The strong arguable inference is that by waving the banner of individual rights and disparaging efforts to restrict pornography, the Government (P) excited Jacobson's (D) interest in banned materials and exerted substantial pressure on him to fight censorship by obtaining such materials. The government may not play on an innocent man's weaknesses and beguile him into committing crimes he would not otherwise commit. Reversed.

DISSENT: (O'Connor, J.) Both times the Government (P) offered Jacobson (D) a chance to buy pornography he responded enthusiastically. Thus, a reasonable jury could find a predisposition to commit the crime. Predisposition should be assessed as of the time the government suggested the crime, not when the government first became involved; the government does not need a reasonable suspicion before it can investigate. Moreover, the two-year investigation of Jacobson (D) involved no threats, coercion, or "substantial pressure" to commit the crime. Finally, the Government (P) did not have to prove Jacobson (D) was predisposed to break the law, only that he was predisposed to receive child pornography. The 1984 Act does not require specific intent to break the law, only knowing receipt. Since the requirement of predisposition is designed to eliminate the entrapment defense for those who would have committed the crime absent government inducement, the elements of predisposition should track the elements of the crime.

ANALYSIS

The Court follows the subjective test for entrapment, i.e., whether the defendant was predisposed to commit the crime, as opposed to the objective test, i.e., whether police conduct created a substantial risk that an innocent person would commit the crime. However, as the dissent points out, the Court's main concern "is that the Government (P) went too far and 'abused' the 'processes of detection and enforcement' by luring an innocent person to violate the law." *Jacobson* illustrates how the subjective and objective tests are blurred in application. In analyzing an entrapment

Continued on next page.

claim, courts must look to the conduct of both the defendant and the police.

■■■■

Quicknotes

ENTRAPMENT An act by public officers that induces a defendant into committing a criminal act.

PREDISPOSITION Defendant's inclination to engage in the illegal activity, for which he has been charged.

■■■■

Network Surveillance

Quick Reference Rules of Law

United States v. Warshak

Federal government (P) v. Individual (D)

631 F.3d 266 (6th Cir. 2010).

NATURE OF CASE: Appeal from lower court decision convicting defendants.

FACT SUMMARY: The Government (P) suspected that Warshak (D) and others in his company were defrauding their customers. The Government (P) obtained court orders for copies of 27,000 emails from Warshak's (D) email provider without Warshak's (D) knowledge or consent.

🏛 RULE OF LAW
An email subscriber has a reasonable expectation of privacy in the contents of his or her emails that are stored and retained on the servers of his or her email provider company.

FACTS: Warshak (D) owned Berkeley Premium Nutraceuticals, a company that sold an herbal supplement allegedly used to increase the size of the male erection. The company began operations in 2001, and due to demand for the herbal supplement, it increased the number of employees to 1,500. The Government (P) initiated an investigation that included a request to NuVox Communications, Berkeley's email provider company, to start saving all of Warshak's (D) emails, sent and received. In 2005, the Government (P) issued a subpoena to NuVox to turn over all of Warshak's (D) emails. The Government (P) also obtained an ex parte court order later in the year for any additional emails from Warshak's (D) account. The jury eventually convicted Warshak (D) and others in the company on various charges relating to the defrauding of the company's customers. Warshak (D) appealed on the grounds the Government's (P) actions in obtaining his emails without his consent or a valid warrant violated the Fourth Amendment.

ISSUE: Does an email subscriber have a reasonable expectation of privacy in the contents of his or her emails that are stored and retained on the servers of his or her email provider company?

HOLDING AND DECISION: (Boggs, J.) Yes. An email subscriber has a reasonable expectation of privacy in the contents of his or her emails that are stored and retained on the servers of his or her email provider company. To determine whether a search occurred worthy of Fourth Amendment protection, the court must determine if the individual has a subjective expectation of privacy in the object of the search and if society recognizes that expectation as reasonable. Clearly, Warshak (D) himself expected that his emails, stored on the servers of NuVox, would not be revealed to the Government (P) without his consent. The larger issue is whether that expectation is reasonable. Prior Supreme Court decisions have given the telephone call and the letter substantial Fourth Amendment protections. In both situations, a third party has control over the call (the telephone company) or the letter (the post office employees). However, the Supreme Court has found that individuals have a reasonable expectation of privacy in both their home phone calls and their letters, even though third parties have custody of both at various times. An individual or company's email service provider is the functional equivalent to the telephone company or the post office. Accordingly, when government agents seek to obtain emails from that service provider, they must obtain a valid warrant. Here, the Government (P) failed to obtain the warrant. Reversed.

▶ ANALYSIS

The text notes that another circuit court decision, *Rehberg v. Paulk*, 598 F.3d. 1268 (11th Cir. 2010), essentially held the opposite: that individuals do not have a reasonable expectation of privacy in emails stored on the servers of their email provider company. That decision called the defendant's use of the email provider company a voluntary relinquishment of his right to privacy for any information contained in the emails. Separately, the Supreme Court held in *City of Ontario v. Quon*, 560 U.S. ___ (2010) that an employee does not have a reasonable expectation of privacy in texts and emails sent or received using an employer-provided smart phone.

Quicknotes

EXPECTATION OF PRIVACY Requirement that in order to invoke the Fourth Amendment's protection against unreasonable searches and seizures, the individual must have a reasonable expectation of privacy in respect to the location searched or thing seized.

SEARCH AND SEIZURE An inspection conducted in order to obtain evidence to be utilized for the prosecution of a crime and the subsequent taking of such evidence.

Smith v. Maryland

Convicted robber (D) v. State (P)

442 U.S. 735 (1979).

NATURE OF CASE: Appeal from affirmance of robbery conviction.

FACT SUMMARY: Smith (D) contended that the installation and use of a pen register constitutes a "search" under the Fourth Amendment, so that the police must obtain a warrant before evidence obtained from such use may be admissible.

RULE OF LAW

The installation and use of a pen register does not constitute a "search" under the Fourth Amendment.

FACTS: McDonough was robbed and then harassed by the robber who called her on the phone. Based on a description of the robber and his car, and by tracing the car's license plate, the police identified Smith (D) as the likely robber. At the police's request, and without a warrant, the telephone company installed at its central offices a pen register to record the numbers dialed from the telephone at Smith's (D) home. The register revealed that a call had been placed from Smith's (D) home to McDonough's phone, and on the basis of this and other evidence, the police obtained a warrant to search Smith's (D) residence. The search revealed that a page in his phone book was turned down to McDonough's name and number, and the phone book was seized. Smith (D) was arrested, and McDonough identified him as the man who had robbed her. Smith (D) moved to suppress the evidence obtained from the pen register, which he argued was an unconstitutional warrantless search, but the trial court denied his motion. Smith (D) was convicted, and the state's highest court affirmed. The United States Supreme Court granted certiorari.

ISSUE: Does the installation and use of a pen register constitute a "search" under the Fourth Amendment?

HOLDING AND DECISION: (Blackmun, J.) No. The installation and use of a pen register does not constitute a "search" under the Fourth Amendment. Application of the Fourth Amendment depends on whether the person invoking its protection can claim a "legitimate expectation of privacy" that has been invaded by government action. This inquiry normally embraces two questions: first, whether the individual has exhibited an actual (subjective) expectation of privacy; and second, whether his expectation is one that society is prepared to recognize as "reasonable." Here, since the pen register was installed at the phone company, there was no physical intrusion into Smith's (D) property. Also, a pen register does not record or

transmit the contents of a phone conversation, but only tracks phone numbers dialed. Smith (D) in all probability entertained no actual expectation of privacy in the phone numbers he dialed, and even if he did, his expectation was not "legitimate." First, it is doubtful that telephone users in general have any expectation of privacy regarding the numbers they dial, since they typically know that they must convey phone numbers to the telephone company and that the company has facilities for recording this information and does in fact record it for various legitimate business purposes, including billing them for the calls they make. Smith (D) also did not demonstrate an expectation of privacy merely by using his home phone rather than some other phone, since his conduct, although perhaps calculated to keep the contents of his conversation private, was not calculated to preserve the privacy of the number he dialed. Second, even if Smith (D) did harbor some subjective expectation of privacy, this expectation was not one that society is prepared to recognize as "reasonable." When Smith (D) voluntarily conveyed numerical information to the phone company and "exposed" that information to its equipment in the normal course of business, he assumed the risk that the company would reveal the information to the police. Affirmed.

DISSENT: (Marshall, J.) The majority's premise, that individuals who convey information to third parties assume the risk of disclosure of that information to the government, is misconceived. First, in the context of telephone use—which is a necessity for most—a defendant has relatively no choice in assuming whatever risk might arise from telephone use, since as a practical matter there is no realistic alternative. Because the concept of assumption of risk implies a degree of choice, it is inappropriate to use a risk analysis where such choice is lacking. By making risk analysis dispositive in assessing the reasonableness of privacy expectations, the majority permits the government to define the cope of Fourth Amendment protections, since by announcing what searches it will conduct, the government can force the public to assume the risks of those searches. Instead, the analysis of whether privacy expectations are legitimate should depend not on the risks an individual can be presumed to accept when imparting information to third parties, but on the risks he should be forced to assume in a free and open society. The public should not be forced to accept the risk of pen registers, which are, in a society dependent on telephonic communication, an extensive intrusion. Many members of the public, including members of unpopular political organizations or

Continued on next page.

journalists with confidential sources, might legitimately wish to avoid disclosure of their personal contacts to the government. Permitting governmental access to telephone records on less than probable cause may thus impede certain forms of political affiliation and journalistic endeavor that are the hallmark of a truly free society, and would violate not only the Fourth Amendment, but also the First Amendment. The use of pen registers should therefore not be insulated from independent judicial review, given that most individuals when they dial telephone numbers from the privacy of their homes expect that those numbers will be recorded, if at all, solely for the phone company's business purposes. Accordingly, law enforcement officials should be required to obtain a warrant before they get telephone companies to use pen registers and thereby secure information otherwise beyond the government's reach.

▶ *ANALYSIS*

The USA Patriot Act, 50 U.S.C. § 1842(a)(1), allows the Attorney General to obtain authority for a pen register from the Foreign Intelligence Surveillance Court "for any investigation to obtain foreign intelligence information not concerning a United States person or to protect against international terrorism or clandestine intelligence activities, provided that such investigation of a United States person is not conducted solely upon the basis of activities protected by the First Amendment to the Constitution." Otherwise, the installation and use of pen registers without court order for other than electronic communication service maintenance and operation is prohibited by federal statute. See 18 U.S.C. § 2131.

■■■

Quicknotes

ASSUMPTION OF RISK DOCTRINE An affirmative defense to a negligence suit contending that the plaintiff knowingly and voluntarily subjected himself to a hazardous condition absolving the defendant of liability for injuries incurred.

EXPECTATION OF PRIVACY Requirement that in order to invoke the Fourth Amendment's protection against unreasonable searches and seizures, the individual must have a reasonable expectation of privacy in respect to the location searched or thing seized.

■■■

United States v. Turk

Federal government (P) v. Convicted perjurer (D)

526 F.2d 654 (5th Cir. 1976).

NATURE OF CASE: Appeal from perjury conviction.

FACT SUMMARY: Turk (D) contended that the replaying of a telephone conversation recorded by Kabbaby on tape constituted an illegal interception under the Omnibus Crime Control and Safe Streets Act, 18 U.S.C. §§ 2510-2520, so that the playing of the tape at his perjury trial should have been barred and his perjury conviction overturned.

🏛 RULE OF LAW
The proscribed interception of wire or oral communications does not occur when the contents of an oral communication are revealed through the replaying of a previous recording of that communication.

FACTS: After receiving a tip, the police arrested Kabbaby and Roblin in their car, where they found, among other things, cocaine and a cassette tape. The police played the tape and discovered that it was a recording of a conversation related to drug trafficking that Kabbaby had had with Turk (D). At a federal grand jury hearing, Turk (D) lied about not ever having been involved with drug trafficking, and he was indicted on several counts, including perjury. At trial, and over his objections, the tape was played and the jury found him guilty. He contended that the police action of listening to the tape seized from Kabbaby's car constituted an impermissible "interception" of his oral communication, in contravention of § 2510(4) of the Omnibus Crime Control and Safe Streets Act, 18 U.S.C. §§ 2510-2520, so that this evidence should have been excluded. The Act proscribes generally the interception or disclosure of wire or oral communications, and provides a procedure through which law enforcement officials can be authorized to intercept such communications in certain limited circumstances. Section 2510(4) provides that "'intercept' means the aural acquisition of the contents of any wire or oral communication through the use of any electronic, mechanical, or other device." The Fifth Circuit Court of Appeals granted review.

ISSUE: Does the proscribed interception of wire or oral communications occur when the contents of an oral communication are revealed through the replaying of a previous recording of that communication?

HOLDING AND DECISION: (Goldberg, J.) No. The proscribed interception of wire or oral communications does not occur when the contents of an oral communication are revealed through the replaying of a previous recording of that communication. Kabbaby's recording of the telephone conversation was an interception as defined by § 2510(4). However, the Act exempts situations in which one party to the conversation is himself the interceptor. Whether the police officers' action was an interception depends on how "aural acquisition" is defined. A broad interpretation, which is rejected, is that "aural acquisition" encompasses any physical hearing of the contents of a communication. A better interpretation, more consistent with the purpose of § 2510(4) to limit wiretapping and electronic surveillance, is that "aural acquisition" is concerned primarily with the activity engaged in at the time of the oral communication that causes such communication to be overheard by uninvited listeners. Such an interpretation excludes from the definition of "intercept" the replaying of a previously recorded communication, because if it did not, innumerable "interceptions," and thus violations of the Act, could flow from a single recording. Moreover, the legislative history supports such an interpretation, since although Congress was concerned with protecting individuals' privacy rights against unjustified intrusions it did not attempt to deal with all such intrusions in the Act, but limited the Act to aural acquisitions made by electronic, mechanical, or other devices. Other forms of surveillance are not covered by the Act. Congress was primarily concerned with the act of surveillance, not the literal "aural acquisition" (i.e., the hearing—either contemporaneously with the communication or thereafter) of the communication. Affirmed.

▶ ANALYSIS

The statute involved here is also known as the Wiretap Act, and is actually the third title of the Omnibus Crime Control and Safe Streets Act. As the court in this case indicated, the Act is primarily concerned with the use of secret recording devices (i.e., "bugging") and the interception of private telephone conversations ("wiretapping"). It applies to interceptions made by both government and private actors. The Electronic Communications Privacy Act (ECPA) expanded the Wiretap Act to cover computer communications and data.

■■■

Deal v. Spears

Terminated employee (P) v. Former employer (D)

980 F.2d 1153 (8th Cir. 1992).

NATURE OF CASE: Appeal from judgment for plaintiffs in civil action brought under Title III of the Omnibus Crime Control and Safe Streets Act, 18 U.S.C. §§ 2510-2520, for illegally intercepting and disclosing telephone communications.

FACT SUMMARY: The Spearses (D), who formerly employed Deal (P), contended that they were not civilly liable under Title III of the Omnibus Crime Control and Safe Streets Act, 18 U.S.C. §§ 2510-2520, for illegally intercepting and disclosing 22 hours of telephone communications made by Deal (P) while at work because Deal (P) had consented to the interceptions of the calls and because their conduct came within the telephone extension/business use exemption of Title III.

RULE OF LAW

(1) For purposes of Title III of the Omnibus Crime Control and Safe Streets Act, 18 U.S.C. §§ 2510-2520, an individual does not give consent to the interception of her phone calls where the individual has not been informed that phone monitoring is occurring and where express consent has not otherwise been given.

(2) For purposes of Title III of the Omnibus Crime Control and Safe Streets Act, 18 U.S.C. §§ 2510-2520, a business owner does not come within the Title's telephone extension/business use exemption where the business owner's interception of phone calls made on the business's telephone and extension thereto goes beyond the boundaries of the ordinary course of business.

FACTS: The Spearses (D) operated a store and lived next to it in a mobile home. The telephone in the store had an extension in the home and was the only phone line for both locations. Deal (P) was employed at the store, and during this time was having an extramarital affair with Calvin Lucas (P). Deal (P) was married. At some point, the store was robbed. The Spearses (D) suspected it was an inside job involving Deal (P) and installed a recording device on the extension phone in the hope of catching her in an unguarded admission. They did not inform Deal (P) that all her phone conversations would be recorded. The Spearses (D) recorded about 22 hours of Deal's (P) conversations, which were mostly with Lucas (P) and of a sexually provocative nature. Deal (P) also made and received numerous other personal phone calls during her workday. Even before installing the recording device, the Spearses (D) had directed Deal (P) to cut down

on her personal phone calls, and had warned her that they might resort to monitoring the calls or installing a pay phone to cut down on this abuse. The Spearses (D) listened to all 22 hours of the tapes, and while not finding anything on them related to the burglary, they did discover that Deal (P) had sold a keg of beer to Lucas (P) in violation of store policy, and terminated her for this infraction. They also informed Deal's (P) husband and Lucas's (P) wife of the general nature of the tapes. Deal (P) and Lucas (P) brought suit under Title III of the Omnibus Crime Control and Safe Streets Act, 18 U.S.C. §§ 2510-2520, for civil damages arising out of the Spearses' (P) recording of their personal phone conversations. Title III makes the intentional interception and disclosure of wire and electronic communications a criminal offense and provides for civil damages for such conduct. [Damages were awarded to Deal (P) and Lucas (P).] The Spearses (D) appealed, claiming that they were exempt from liability because Deal (P) had consented to the interception of the calls and because their conduct came within one of Title III's exemptions known as the business use of a telephone exemption. The Eighth Circuit Court of Appeals granted review.

ISSUE:

(1) For purposes of Title III of the Omnibus Crime Control and Safe Streets Act, 18 U.S.C. §§ 2510-2520, does an individual give consent to the interception of her phone calls where the individual has not been informed that phone monitoring is occurring and where express consent has not otherwise been given?

(2) For purposes of Title III of the Omnibus Crime Control and Safe Streets Act, 18 U.S.C. §§ 2510-2520, does a business owner come within the Title's telephone extension/business use exemption where the business owner's interception of phone calls made on the business's telephone and extension thereto goes beyond the boundaries of the ordinary course of business?

HOLDING AND DECISION: (Bowman, J.)

(1) No. For purposes of Title III of the Omnibus Crime Control and Safe Streets Act, 18 U.S.C. §§ 2510-2520, an individual does not give consent to the interception of her phone calls where the individual has not been informed that phone monitoring is occurring and where express consent has not otherwise been given. Constructive consent is insufficient, and express consent may be implied from the circumstances. Here, however, the fact that the Spearses (D) informed Deal (P) that her calls might be monitored in the future to

Continued on next page.

cut down on her calls and the fact that the phone extension in their home meant that her calls could be overheard are not enough to indicate Deal's (P) express consent. First, the Spearses (D) did not tell Deal (P) that all her calls would in fact be recorded; knowledge of the capability of monitoring alone is not implied consent. Second, as to the extension, Deal (P) testified that she could tell when the extension in the residence was being used because there was an audible "click" on the line. Thus, as a matter of law, the Spearses (D) failed to prove Deal's (P) express consent. Affirmed as to this issue.

(2) No. For purposes of Title III of the Omnibus Crime Control and Safe Streets Act, 18 U.S.C. §§ 2510-2520, a business owner does not come within the Title's telephone extension/business use exemption where the business owner's interception of phone calls made on the business's telephone and extension thereto goes beyond the boundaries of the ordinary course of business. The exemption at issue is actually a restrictive definition, which excludes from the definition of "device" used for the unlawful interception of wire and electronic communications a business phone or extension thereto that is used in the ordinary course of its business. Here, the Spearses (D) had a legitimate business reason for listening in on Deal's (P) phone conversations, both to determine if she had participated in the burglary and to deter her personal use of the business phone. However, they could have achieved these goals by listening to the extent necessary to determine that the calls were personal and made or received in violation of store policy. Listening to all 22 hours of her conversations, without regard to their relation to the Spearses' (D) legitimate business interests, was an extensive intrusion that was not justified by those business interests; the scope of the interception went well beyond the boundaries of the ordinary course of business. Affirmed as to this issue.

▶ ANALYSIS

Title III of the Omnibus Crime Control and Safe Streets Act, 18 U.S.C. §§ 2510-2520, also known as the Wiretap Act, provides that a party to the communication being intercepted may intercept, or give permission for a third-party to intercept, the communication. Thus, the consent of one party to the communication will be enough to exempt the interception from the Act's liability provisions. However, some state wiretapping statutes go farther and require the consent of all parties to the communication before the exception will be effective, even where the secretly recorded party is engaged in wrongdoing.

Police Interrogation and Confessions

Quick Reference Rules of Law

Miranda v. Arizona (No. 759) (Together with Vignera v. New York, Westover v. United States, and California v. Stewart)

Interrogated suspect (D) v. State (P)

384 U.S. 436 (1966).

NATURE OF CASE: Certiorari from various convictions, and from the reversal of one.

FACT SUMMARY: Convictions resulted in several cases from confessions obtained through incommunicado-interrogation in a police-dominated atmosphere, without full warnings of constitutional rights.

🏛 RULE OF LAW
When a person has been taken into police custody or otherwise deprived of his freedom of action in any significant way, the following warnings must be given prior to questioning: (1) that he has the right to remain silent; (2) that any statement he does make may be used as evidence against him; (3) that he has the right to have an attorney present; and (4) that if he cannot afford an attorney, one will be appointed for him.

FACTS: Convictions in the cases of *Miranda v. Arizona*, *Vignera v. New York*, *Westover v. United States*, and *California v. Stewart* are brought before this Court through petitions of certiorari. In each of these cases, confessions resulted after incommunicado-interrogation in a police-dominated atmosphere, without full warning of constitutional rights (or without any indication in the police records that such warnings were given). And in each of these cases, the confessions obtained from such interrogation were used as the basis for the resulting convictions. Only in the case of *Stewart* was the conviction reversed by the Supreme Court of California, on the basis that Stewart (D) had not been informed of his rights. Because of the related nature of these cases, the United States Supreme Court granted certiorari to determine the central issue involved.

ISSUE: When a person is taken into custody, is it necessary that his constitutional rights to remain silent and to have an attorney present be explained to him before questioning?

HOLDING AND DECISION: (Warren, C.J.) Yes. "[T]he prosecution may not use statements, whether exculpatory or inculpatory, stemming from custodial interrogation of the defendant unless it demonstrates the use of procedural safeguards effective to secure the privilege against self-incrimination. By custodial interrogation, we mean questioning initiated by law enforcement officers after a person has been taken into custody or otherwise deprived of his freedom of action in any significant way. As for the procedural safeguards to be employed, unless other full effective means are devised to inform accused persons of their right to silence and to assure a continuous opportunity to exercise it, the following measures are required. Prior to any questioning, the person must be warned that he has a right to remain silent, that any statement he does make may be used against him as evidence, and that he has the right to the presence of an attorney, either retained or appointed (if he cannot afford). The defendant may waive effectuation of these rights, provided the waiver is made voluntarily, knowingly, and intelligently. If, however, he indicates in any manner and at any stage of the process that he wishes to consult with an attorney before speaking, there can be no questioning. Likewise, if the individual is alone and indicates in any manner that he does not wish to be interrogated, the police may not question him. The mere fact that he may have answered some questions or volunteered some statements on his own does not deprive him of the right to refrain from answering any further inquiries until he has consulted with an attorney and thereafter consents to be questioned." The rationale for this decision is based upon the nature of custodial interrogation and its relationship to the Fifth Amendment's Self-Incrimination Clause. The true nature of custodial interrogation clearly is described in standard police manuals and texts, which teach "psychologically oriented coercive techniques" (e.g., incommunicado detention, prolonged questioning). Such practices are inherently contrary to the principle that an individual may not be compelled to incriminate himself. And freedom from self-incrimination is "one of our nation's most cherished principles," based upon our accusatory system of justice which protects the "dignity and integrity of its citizens" by requiring that government may only produce incriminating evidence "by its own independent labors." It is elementary that, unless there are sufficient safeguards (i.e., those announced in this decision) to ensure the right against self-incrimination in custodial interrogation, its recognition at trial is meaningless. Here, in each case, the accused was put through custodial interrogations without the appropriate safeguards, and the prosecution has not demonstrated any "knowing and intelligent waiver" of rights in any of the cases. It is true that Westover (D) was informed of his rights by the FBI before his statement, but he had been subjected to police interrogation for over 14 hours prior to that time (i.e., before he was handed over to the FBI). Since the FBI questioning immediately followed the police interrogation, from Westover's (D) point of view at least, there

Continued on next page.

had, in fact, been one continuous period of questioning with the warning of his rights only at the end of the process. Convictions reversed in *Miranda*, in *Vignera*, and in *Westover*; and the reversal of the conviction in *Stewart* affirmed.

DISSENT AND CONCURRENCE: (Clark, J.)

(Dissent in the cases of *Vignera, Westover,* and *Miranda*; concurrence in the case of *Stewart*.) The Court should have been more restrained in these cases. There is a decided lack of information and empirical data on the practical operation of requirements comparable to those announced today. Furthermore, custodial interrogation has long been recognized as an "essential tool in effective law enforcement," and the rule, prior to today, recognized this fact by judging the voluntariness from the "totality of all the circumstances" (including whether an accused had been advised of his rights). The rule today, however, is too rigid.

DISSENT: (Harlan, J.) The decision of the Court

today in abandoning its historical case-by-case approach represents poor constitutional law. The Court's new rules are designed to "ultimately discourage any confession at all." Such an approach cannot be sustained by constitutional or policy considerations. First, constitutionally, there is no basis for extending the Fifth Amendment to the police station. Historically, the ban against self-incrimination has applied only in criminal proceedings, not in "extra-legal" situations, such as interrogations. Furthermore, even if it can be applied to custodial interrogations, it has never been held to forbid all pressures on an accused, as the Court today attempts to do. Similarly, there is no constitutional basis for applying the right to counsel to custodial interrogations. The danger of injustice by allowing an untrained person to defend himself in a technical court situation is the basis for this right, and that rationale is not applicable to custodial situations. Second, in considering policy issues, although it is true that police questioning will inherently entail some pressure on the suspect, until today the role of the Constitution has been to "sift out" only "undue pressure." The inflexible rules today, however, ignore this. Those who use coercive tactics may simply lie in court about having given the required warnings. Nothing is gained and many voluntary confessions will be lost. In conclusion, neither the constitutional interpretations nor the consequence of today's ruling is justifiable.

DISSENT: (White, J.) First, the Fifth Amendment for-

bids self-incrimination only if it is "compelled." Yet, the Court today has no factual basis for concluding that custodial interrogations are so inherently coercive, as to make any statements arising from them, if there is no warning of rights, compelled. In fact, the Court has not examined a single transcript of any police interrogation. Furthermore, even if it is assumed that "all" such interrogations are coercive, the rule adopted today is irrational. If such interrogations are so "coercive," how can a suspect ever voluntarily waive his rights as the Court indicates he can?

Second, and more importantly, the Court overlooks the ominous consequences of its decision. Although the Court states that the rule adopted is necessary to preserve the "integrity" of the individual, it overlooks the fact that without effective prevention of crime (or personal violence) there can be no human dignity. The most basic function of any government is to provide for the security of an individual and his property, but after today's decision, effective law enforcement will be impaired, both by the fact that more who are guilty may go free and many who could easily explain their innocence will waste police time while waiting for their attorneys.

▶ ANALYSIS

Miranda illustrates the rule applicable to evidence sought to be admitted against an accused as "part of the prosecution's case," but a statement obtained in violation of the *Miranda* rule "may be used to impeach" an accused's testimony if he takes the stand at trial and if the statement is otherwise "voluntary and trustworthy." *Miranda* also does not apply to mere on-the-scene questioning, general fact-finding inquiries of citizens, or spontaneous admissions volunteered before the police began interrogation. Furthermore, it must be noted that several issues or problems have been raised in the wake of *Miranda*. First, while a waiver of rights will not be inferred from silence, the type of expression required still remains open to question. However, the lower courts are in general agreement that a warning of rights need not be repeated at the beginning of each successive interrogation for a valid waiver to occur. Second, the Supreme Court has not addressed itself to the question of whether automatic reversal of a conviction, based upon a confession obtained in violation of *Miranda*, is required. Third, the Supreme Court has also left open the question of whether the "fruits" (*Wong Sun*, 371 U.S. 471 (1963)) derived from statements obtained in violation of *Miranda* are admissible. Finally, fourth, although the Court in *Miranda* states that the warnings are necessary "unless other full effective means are devised to inform accused persons" of their rights, it is questionable what would be considered "effective." The Crime Control Act of 1968, applicable to federal criminal trials, seeks to substitute for the *Miranda* warnings a test of "voluntariness" based upon the totality of circumstances. However, the Court in *Miranda* does seem to indicate that something more than test of voluntariness is required, although the constitutionality of this legislation is presently undetermined.

■━■

Continued on next page.

Quicknotes

CERTIORARI A discretionary writ issued by a superior court to an inferior court in order to review the lower court's decisions; the Supreme Court's writ ordering such review.

COERCION The overcoming of a person's free will as a result of threats, promises, or undue influence.

CUSTODIAL INTERROGATION The questioning of a suspect by police while in custody.

EMPIRICAL EVIDENCE Evidence based on observation or experimentation.

EXCULPATORY EVIDENCE A statement or other evidence that tends to excuse, justify, or absolve the defendant from alleged fault or guilt.

FIFTH AMENDMENT Provides that no person shall be compelled to serve as a witness against himself, or be subject to trial for the same offense twice, or be deprived of life, liberty, or property without due process of law.

INCULPATORY Evidence tending to show a person's guilt in committing a criminal act.

UNDUE INFLUENCE Improper persuasion that deprives an individual of freedom of choice.

J.D.B. v. North Carolina
Individual (D) v. State (P)
564 U.S. ___, 131 S. Ct. 2394 (2011).

NATURE OF CASE: Appeal from state high court decision in favor of the state.

FACT SUMMARY: Police suspected J.D.B. (D), a 13-year-old seventh grade student, of breaking into two homes. Police questioned him at his school without informing him of his *Miranda* (1966) rights [*Miranda v. Arizona*, 384 U.S. 436 (1966)].

🏛 RULE OF LAW
When determining whether a suspect is in custody, thus requiring the police to inform the suspect of his *Miranda* rights, police must take into account the age of the suspect.

FACTS: Police suspected J.D.B. (D), a 13-year-old seventh grade student, of breaking into two homes. Two police officers questioned him in a room at his school in the presence of other school officials. The questioning lasted from 30-45 minutes and the police did not read J.D.B. (D) his *Miranda* rights prior to the questioning. The police officers also did not inform J.D.B. (D) he was free to leave. J.D.B. (D) confessed to the crimes. A trial court judge later found J.D.B. (D) delinquent. J.D.B. (D) appealed on the ground his statements were made while he was in custody and he was not given his *Miranda* rights. The North Carolina Supreme Court rejected his appeal on the grounds he was not in custody at the time of the questioning. His statements therefore could be used against him. J.D.B. (D) appealed to the United States Supreme Court.

ISSUE: When determining whether a suspect is in custody, thus requiring the police to inform the suspect of his *Miranda* rights, must the police take into account the age of the suspect?

HOLDING AND DECISION: (Sotomayor, J.) Yes. When determining whether a suspect is in custody, thus requiring the police to inform the suspect of his *Miranda* rights, police must take into account the age of the suspect. Whether a suspect is in custody deserving of his *Miranda* rights is an objective inquiry. The inquiry typically is whether a reasonable person in the suspect's position would understand his or her freedom to terminate the inquiry. Here, a child may sometimes feel pressured to submit to questioning when an adult would not. Also, other areas of the law, such as tort law, account for distinctions between adults and children. When reviewing one's tort liability, whether the person is an adult or a child will change the outcome of that determination. Officers are competent enough to account for a child's age when making their determination whether or not to give

a suspect his or her *Miranda* rights. On remand, the state courts should determine whether or not J.D.B. (D) was in custody at the time of the questioning in light of this decision. Remanded.

DISSENT: (Alito, J.) The strength of the *Miranda* rule is that it created an objective, reasonable person test for determining custody that could be applied to everyone. The whole purpose of the test was to avoid subjective considerations of a suspect's characteristics and provide law enforcement with a clear rule to follow. Now, the majority's decision may eventually force police officers to make independent, fact intensive inquiries for each suspect based upon the suspect's age, education, employment or prior involvement with the police. The majority also improperly relies upon tort law for support. In negligence cases, the liability determination is completed long after an incident occurred, with a thorough review of the facts by a judge or jury. In contrast, police must make their determination whether to provide *Miranda* rights quickly during an ongoing investigation.

▶ ANALYSIS

This was a five to four Supreme Court decision, with Justice Kennedy joining Justices Sotomayor, Ginsburg, Breyer, and Kagan to reverse the state court decision. There is an ongoing confrontation within the Supreme Court over the scope of *Miranda*, with the more conservative justices seeking to limit *Miranda's* scope and the liberal members of the Court seeking to broaden its application.

Quicknotes

MIRANDA RULE A required warning given before any questioning by law enforcement authorities can take place. Individuals in custody receive warnings regarding their privilege against self-incrimination, right to remain silent, and right to be represented by an attorney.

Rhode Island v. Innis

State (P) v. Convict with a conscience (D)

446 U.S. 291 (1980).

NATURE OF CASE: Appeal from a murder conviction.

FACT SUMMARY: On the way to the police station in a police car after his arrest, Innis (D) overheard remarks between the officers expressing concern that handicapped children in the area might find the hidden shotgun, whereupon Innis (D) told them to turn around so he could show them where he had hidden it.

🏛 RULE OF LAW
Any words or actions on the part of the police that they should know are reasonably likely to elicit an incriminating response from the suspect constitute "interrogation" under *Miranda* and bring the *Miranda* safeguards into play.

FACTS: After being arrested for murder, Innis (D) received the *Miranda* warnings [*Miranda v. Arizona*, 384 U.S. 436 (1966)] and said he wanted to speak with an attorney. While being taken to the station in a police car, he overheard a conversation between the officers. "God forbid," one officer said, "that one of the students at the school for the handicapped finds a gun and hurt himself." At that point, Innis (D) told the officers to turn the car around so that he could show them where he had hidden the gun used in the murder. The gun, which was thus found, was used in evidence when Innis (D) was later convicted of murder. The Rhode Island Supreme Court reversed the conviction, holding that the officers had engaged in "interrogation" in violation of *Miranda*.

ISSUE: If the police should know that their words or actions are reasonably likely to elicit an incriminating response from the suspect, do such words or actions constitute "interrogation"?

HOLDING AND DECISION: (Stewart, J.) Yes. Any words or actions on the part of the police that the police should know are reasonably likely to elicit an incriminating response from the suspect constitute "interrogation" under *Miranda*. That is, the term "interrogation" as used in *Miranda* covers express questioning or its functional equivalent. In this particular case, the facts are that the officers engaged in an entire conversation that consisted of no more than a few offhand remarks. The Court cannot say, on that basis, that the officers should have known it was reasonably likely that Innis (D) would suddenly be moved to make a self-incriminating response to this overheard conversation. Therefore, whatever "subtle

compulsion" Innis (D) experienced cannot be equated with "interrogation" bringing *Miranda* into play. Reversed.

CONCURRENCE: (Burger, C.J.) The test adopted in this case introduces new elements of uncertainty. It requires a police officer, in the brief time available, to evaluate the suggestibility and susceptibility of an accused. Even psychiatrists would normally have to employ extensive questioning and observation to make the judgment now charged to police officers. However, I concur in the result in this case because it is not inconsistent with *Miranda*.

DISSENT: (Marshall, J.) As I read the Court's definition of "interrogation" for *Miranda* purposes, I find it equivalent, for practical purpose, to my own formulation. I view the *Miranda* safeguards as applying whenever police conduct is intended or likely to produce a response from a suspect in custody. I am, however, utterly at a loss to understand how the objective standard adopted by the Court, when applied to this case, can rationally lead to the conclusion that there was no interrogation. One can scarcely imagine a stronger appeal to the conscience of a suspect than the assertion that if the weapon is not found an innocent, handicapped child will be hurt or killed.

DISSENT: (Stevens, J.) In my view, any statement that would normally be understood by the average listener as calling for a response is the functional equivalent of a direct question, whether or not it is punctuated by a question mark. The Court takes a narrower view in defining "interrogation" for *Miranda* purposes in a holding that represents a plain departure from the principles set forth in *Miranda*. It prohibits only those relatively few statements or actions that a police officer should know are likely to elicit an incriminating response, when statements that appear to call for a response from the suspect, as well as those that are designed to do so, should be considered interrogation. What the Court does in this decision is to narrow the scope of protection afforded a suspect. However, even if the Court's definition of "interrogation" is assumed to be the proper standard, the officers should have known that their appeal to the conscience of the suspect was likely to elicit an incriminating response. Thus, under either definition of the term, "interrogation" occurred in violation of *Miranda*.

Continued on next page.

▶ *ANALYSIS*

In *Harryman v. Estelle*, 616 F.2d 879 (5th Cir. 1980), Harryman was arrested as a burglary suspect. A search of his person revealed a condom containing white powder tucked under the waistband of his trousers. The officer, who later claimed he spoke out of shock and surprise, asked, "What is this?" to which Harryman answered: "Oh, you know what it is. It is heroin." Noting that the rigidity of the *Miranda* rules and the way they are to be applied is recognized as the decision's greatest strength, the court of appeals found *Miranda* had been violated by this interchange between officer and suspect. In its opinion, the court stated "it is enough to decide that what the officer said could reasonably have had the force of a question on the accused."

■■■

Quicknotes

CUSTODIAL INTERROGATION   The questioning of a suspect by police while in custody.

PRIVILEGE AGAINST SELF-INCRIMINATION A privilege guaranteed by the Fifth Amendment to the federal Constitution in a criminal proceeding for communications made by an accused and protecting an accused or witness from having to give testimony that may incriminate himself.

■■■

Maryland v. Shatzer

State (P) v. Individual (D)

559 U.S. 98, 130 S. Ct. 1213 (2010).

NATURE OF CASE: Appeal from state high court decision in favor of the state.

FACT SUMMARY: Police suspected that Shatzer (D), an inmate at a state correctional facility, had sexually abused his own son. Police questioned him but ended the inquiry when Shatzer (D) invoked his right to an attorney. Two and a half years later, police questioned him again and Shatzer (D), after waiving his right to an attorney, made incriminating statements.

RULE OF LAW
When a criminal suspect, who had previously invoked his right to an attorney, is then released from custody for a period of 14 days, his subsequent waiver of his right to an attorney at a follow up interrogation shall be deemed valid.

FACTS: Police suspected that Shatzer (D), an inmate at a state correctional facility, had sexually abused his own son. Police questioned him but ended the inquiry when Shatzer (D) invoked his right to an attorney. Two and a half years later, police questioned him again and Shatzer (D), after waiving his right to an attorney, made incriminating statements. Police questioned him again a few days later. Shatzer (D) again waived his right to counsel, agreed to take a polygraph test and then failed the test. After conviction at the state trial court level for various charges relating to sexual abuse, the Maryland Supreme Court eventually overturned Schatzer's (D) conviction. It did so on the grounds that no break in custody occurred between the original questioning and the follow up questioning. Accordingly, once Shatzer (D) had invoked his right to an attorney, the police were not allowed to continue asking him on multiple occasions whether he would decline to invoke that right. The state appealed.

ISSUE: When a criminal suspect, who had previously invoked his right to an attorney, is then released from custody for a period of 14 days, shall his subsequent waiver of his right to an attorney at a follow up interrogation be deemed valid?

HOLDING AND DECISION: (Scalia, J.) Yes. When a criminal suspect, who had previously invoked his right to an attorney, is then released from custody for a period of fourteen days, his subsequent waiver of his right to an attorney at a follow up interrogation shall be deemed valid. Under prior case law, police have been prevented from constantly questioning a criminal suspect whether he had decided to forego his right to an attorney. However, when a suspect has been released from custody for a long enough period of time, there is little reason to believe his change of heart regarding his right to counsel is due to police coercion. The suspect has been given time to consult with his attorney or his friends and family. Accordingly, the suspect's decision to waive his right to an attorney is likely due to his understanding that cooperation would be more beneficial. The Court also now holds that the appropriate length of time between such custodial interrogations is 14 days. This two week period will allow the defendant time to get reacclimated to life, consult with an attorney or family members, and make further deliberations as how to proceed. Reversed.

CONCURRENCE: (Thomas, J.) The majority is correct that in this case, Shatzer's (D) release back into prison for two and a half years between interrogations certainly constituted a break in custody. However, the Court's arbitrary decision to apply a 14-day rule finds no basis in this Court's prior Fifth Amendment jurisprudence.

CONCURRENCE: (Stevens, J.) The majority correctly found that a break in custody occurred in this case, allowing Shatzer (D) to validly waive his right to an attorney at the subsequent interrogation. The problem with the new 14-day rule is that when the police fail to provide indigent defendants with counsel after an initial request, those defendants may ultimately believe the police lied to them and that they really have no right to an attorney.

ANALYSIS

A constant refrain in search and seizure law or the law regarding custodial inquiries is the goal of providing clear guidelines to law enforcement. This goal was clearly the main reason behind the judicially created 14-day period between interrogations. Opponents of the rule favor individual, case-by-case review of such incidents.

Quicknotes

CUSTODIAL INTERROGATION The questioning of a suspect by police while in custody.

Berghuis v. Thompkins

State (D) v. Convicted criminal (P)

560 U.S. 370 (2010).

NATURE OF CASE: Appeal from reversal of denial of habeas corpus request.

FACT SUMMARY: After Thompkins (P) was advised of his *Miranda* rights, Thompkins (P) did not expressly say he wanted to remain silent, did not want to talk with the police, or wanted an attorney. Eventually, toward the end of a three-hour interrogation during which Thompkins (P) was largely silent, he answered "yes" when asked if he prayed to God to forgive him for the shooting of victim who had died. Thompkins (P) was found guilty of murder and sentenced to life without parole. In his habeas corpus petition, Thompkins (P) argued that he had invoked his Fifth Amendment right to remain silent, that he had not waived that right, and that his inculpatory statements were involuntary.

🏛 RULE OF LAW

(1) A criminal suspect's silence during an interrogation does not invoke his right to remain silent.

(2) A criminal suspect waives his right to remain silent when he knowingly and voluntarily makes a statement to the police.

(3) The police are not required to obtain a waiver of a criminal suspect's *Miranda* rights before interrogating him.

FACTS: After advising respondent Thompkins (P) of his rights, in full compliance with *Miranda v. Arizona*, 384 U.S. 436 (1966), detective Helgert and another officer interrogated him about a shooting in which one victim died. At no point did Thompkins (P) say that he wanted to remain silent, that he did not want to speak with the police or that he wanted an attorney. He refused, however, to sign a written acknowledgment that he had been advised of or understood his *Miranda* rights. He was largely silent during the three-hour interrogation, but near the end, he answered "yes" when asked if he prayed to God to forgive him for the shooting. He moved to suppress his statements, claiming that he had invoked his Fifth Amendment right to remain silent, that he had not waived that right, and that his inculpatory statements were involuntary. The trial court denied the motion, the state's intermediate court affirmed, and the state's highest court denied review. The jury found Thompkins (P) guilty, and he was sentenced to life in prison without parole. The district court denied his subsequent habeas request, reasoning that Thompkins (P) did not invoke his right to remain silent and was not coerced into making statements during the interrogation, and that it was not unreasonable for the state's intermediate appel-

late court to determine that he had waived his right to remain silent. The court of appeals reversed, holding that the state court was unreasonable in finding an implied waiver of Thompkins' (P) right to remain silent. The United States Supreme Court granted certiorari.

ISSUE:

(1) Does a criminal suspect's silence during an interrogation invoke his right to remain silent?

(2) Does a criminal suspect waive his right to remain silent when he knowingly and voluntarily makes a statement to the police?

(3) Are the police required to obtain a waiver of a criminal suspect's *Miranda* rights before interrogating him?

HOLDING AND DECISION: (Kennedy, J.)

(1) No. A criminal suspect's silence during an interrogation does not invoke his right to remain silent. Thompkins' (P) silence during the interrogation did not invoke his right to remain silent. A suspect's *Miranda* right to counsel must be invoked "unambiguously." If the accused makes an "ambiguous or equivocal" statement or no statement, the police are not required to end the interrogation, or ask questions to clarify the accused's intent. There is no principled reason to adopt different standards for determining when an accused has invoked the *Miranda* right to remain silent and the *Miranda* right to counsel. Both protect the privilege against compulsory self-incrimination by requiring an interrogation to cease when either right is invoked. The unambiguous invocation requirement results in an objective inquiry that "avoid[s] difficulties of proof and . . . provide[s] guidance to officers" on how to proceed in the face of ambiguity. Had Thompkins (P) said that he wanted to remain silent or that he did not want to talk, he would have invoked his right to end the questioning. He did neither, and therefore did not invoke his right to remain silent.

(2) Yes. A criminal suspect waives his right to remain silent when he knowingly and voluntarily makes a statement to the police. Thompkins (P) waived his right to remain silent when he knowingly and voluntarily made a statement to police. A waiver must be "the product of a free and deliberate choice rather than intimidation, coercion, or deception" and "made with a full awareness of both the nature of the right being abandoned and the consequences of the decision to abandon it." Such a waiver may be "implied" through a "defendant's silence, coupled with an understanding of his rights

Continued on next page.

and a course of conduct indicating waiver." If the State (D) establishes that a *Miranda* warning was given and that it was understood by the accused, an accused's uncoerced statement establishes an implied waiver. The record here shows that Thompkins (P) waived his right to remain silent. First, the lack of any contention that he did not understand his rights indicates that he knew what he gave up when he spoke. Second, his answer to the question about God is a "course of conduct indicating waiver" of that right. Had he wanted to remain silent, he could have said nothing in response or unambiguously invoked his *Miranda* rights, ending the interrogation. That he made a statement nearly three hours after receiving a *Miranda* warning does not overcome the fact that he engaged in a course of conduct indicating waiver. Third, there is no evidence that his statement was coerced. He does not claim that police threatened or injured him or that he was fearful. The interrogation took place in a standard-sized room in the middle of the day, and there is no authority for the proposition that a three-hour interrogation is inherently coercive. The fact that the question referred to religious beliefs also does not render his statement involuntary.

(3) No. The police are not required to obtain a waiver of a criminal suspect's *Miranda* rights before interrogating him. Thompkins (P) argues that, even if his answer to Helgert could constitute a waiver of his right to remain silent, the police were not allowed to question him until they first obtained a waiver. However, a rule requiring a waiver at the outset would be inconsistent with precedent holding that courts can infer a waiver "from the actions and words of the person interrogated." Any waiver, express or implied, may be contradicted by an invocation at any time, terminating further interrogation. When the suspect knows that *Miranda* rights can be invoked at any time, he or she can reassess his or her immediate and long-term interests as the interrogation progresses. After giving a *Miranda* warning, police may interrogate a suspect who has neither invoked nor waived *Miranda* rights. Thus, the police were not required to obtain a waiver of Thompkins's (P) *Miranda* rights before interrogating him. Reversed.

DISSENT: (Sotomayor, J.) Under the majority's decisions, criminal suspects must now unambiguously invoke their right to remain silent—which, counterintuitively, requires them to speak. At the same time, suspects will be legally presumed to have waived their rights even if they have given no clear expression of their intent to do so. Those results are not supported by *Miranda* or subsequent precedent and are inconsistent with the fair-trial principles on which those precedents are grounded. The question whether a suspect has validly waived his right is "entirely distinct" as a matter of law from whether he invoked that right. The questions are related, however, in terms of the practical effect on the exercise of a suspect's rights. A suspect may at any time revoke his prior waiver of rights, or guard against the possibility of a future finding that he implicitly waived his rights, by invoking the rights and thereby requiring the police to cease questioning. Thus, analytically, the first question should be whether Thompkins (P) waived his right to remain silent. Precedent places a heavy burden on the prosecution to show waiver, and the presumption is that the suspect did not waive his rights. Waiver may not be presumed merely because a confession was eventually obtained. Here, the circumstances of the interrogation show that Thompkins (P) never waived his right to remain silent. He never expressly waived that right, and his refusal to sign even an acknowledgment that he understood his *Miranda* rights evinces, if anything, intent not to waive those rights. So does his silence during the interrogation for nearly three hours. Essentially, his course of conduct did not manifest waiver. Thus, it is objectively unreasonable to conclude the prosecution met its "heavy burden" of proof on a record "consisting of three one-word answers, following two hours and 45 minutes of silence punctuated by a few largely nonverbal responses to unidentified questions." By so concluding, however, the majority turns long-standing *Miranda* precedent on its head and significantly dilutes its protections and lowers the prosecution's hitherto high burden of proof. Because *Miranda* and its precedents perceive custodial interrogation to be inherently coercive, requiring proof of a course of conduct beyond the inculpatory statements themselves is critical to ensuring that those statements are voluntary admissions and not the dubious product of an overborne will. Because Thompkins (P) should prevail on his waiver argument, the issue of whether he invoked his right to remain silent should not have been reached, as it was by the majority. Nonetheless, even as to Thompkins' (P) argument that in any event his conduct invoked his right to remain silent, the majority is wrong in holding that a suspect must expressly invoke that right by speaking. Such a novel clear-statement rule for invocation invites police to question a suspect at length—notwithstanding his persistent refusal to answer questions—in the hope of eventually obtaining a single inculpatory response which will suffice to prove waiver of rights. Contrary to the majority's reasoning, there has been a precedential distinction between protections involving the right to counsel and the right to remain silent. The appropriate rule is that when a suspect's conduct is sufficiently unambiguous as to invocation, the police must scrupulously honor that conduct. While this does not provide a bright-line rule, as does the majority's clear-statement rule, the police nonetheless have been following the prior fact-specific rule for over three decades and no evidence has been presented that the status quo has proved unworkable. The clear-statement rule is also a poor fit for the right to silence, since advising a

Continued on next page.

suspect that he has a "right to remain silent" is unlikely to convey that he must speak (and must do so in some particular fashion) to ensure the right will be protected. By contrast, telling a suspect "he has the right to the presence of an attorney, and that if he cannot afford an attorney one will be appointed for him prior to any questioning if he so desires," implies the need for speech to exercise that right. Moreover, if a suspect's statements or conduct is ambiguous, it is not an undue burden to have the police ask questions clarifying the suspect's intent, such as "Do you want to talk to us?" Such an approach is a more faithful application of precedents than the majority's clear-statement approach.

▶ *ANALYSIS*

Prior to this decision, courts had to grapple with doctrinal questions of what it took to make a legally valid invocation of, or waiver of, *Miranda* rights. If a suspect's conduct fell between these extremes, there was also the issue of what was acceptable police conduct. The *Thompkins* decision has seemingly done away with those issues. Now, where the police have given the suspect the proper *Miranda* warnings and the suspect understands those warnings and has not been coerced, until the moment when the suspect clearly invokes one of his *Miranda* rights, the police may continue to seek a waiver of those rights, and, even absent a clear waiver, as soon as the suspect says anything to the police he will be held to have impliedly waived his rights.

■══■

Quicknotes

FIFTH AMENDMENT Provides that no person shall be compelled to serve as a witness against himself, or be subject to trial for the same offense twice, or be deprived of life, liberty, or property without due process of law.

HABEAS CORPUS A proceeding in which a defendant brings a writ to compel a judicial determination of whether he is lawfully being held in custody.

INCULPATORY Evidence tending to show a person's guilt in committing a criminal act.

MIRANDA RULE A required warning given before any questioning by law enforcement authorities can take place. Individuals in custody receive warnings regarding their privilege against self-incrimination, right to remain silent, and right to be represented by an attorney.

MIRANDA WARNINGS Specified warnings that must be communicated to a person prior to a custodial interrogation; in the absence of the communication of such warnings, any communications made during the interrogation are inadmissible at trial.

■══■

Salinas v. Texas

Suspect (D) v. State (P)

133 S. Ct. 2174 (2013).

NATURE OF CASE: Certiorari review to resolve lower courts division on prosecution's use of privilege assertion

FACT SUMMARY: Salinas (D) voluntarily arrived at the police station for questioning in a homicide. He was aware he was a suspect. He was not in custody and was not given the *Miranda* warnings [*Miranda v. Arizona*, 384 U.S. 436 (1966)]. Prosecutors later used his silence in response to a particular question as indication of his guilt.

RULE OF LAW

A witness must expressly claim the Fifth Amendment privilege against self-incrimination during noncustodial police questioning.

FACTS: The police requested Salinas (D) come to the station for questioning as a suspect in a homicide. Salinas (D) voluntarily went to the station and was free to leave at any time. He was not given any *Miranda* warnings. Salinas (D) answered questions until the police asked if his shotgun would match the shells recovered at the scene. Salinas (D) looked down and did not answer the question. The prosecutor later used Salinas's (D) silence as evidence of his guilt. The United States Supreme Court granted certiorari review to resolve split in the lower courts on the issue of prosecution's use of defendant's assertion of privilege during noncustodial police questioning as part of its case-in-chief. Salinas (D) did not invoke privilege during his questioning, so the Court does not reach that issue.

ISSUE: Must a witness expressly claim the Fifth Amendment privilege against self-incrimination during noncustodial police questioning?

HOLDING AND DECISION: (Alito, J.) Yes. A witness must expressly claim the Fifth Amendment privilege against self-incrimination during noncustodial police questioning. The privilege is an exception to the government's right to everyone's testimony. Express invocation is not required at a criminal defendant's own trial when the defendant refuses to take the stand or if government coercion makes the forfeiture of the privilege involuntary. Neither exception applies here. Salinas (D) seeks a new exception for silent witnesses facing official suspicions. In *Berghuis v. Thompkins*, 560 U.S. 370 (2010), this Court held the defendant failed to invoke the privilege when, post-*Miranda* warnings, he remained silent for two hours and 45 minutes. Salinas (D) only was momentarily silent. Silence is insufficient to put police on notice of the witness's reliance on Fifth Amendment privilege. Salinas (D) argues it would be unfair to require an unschooled witness to understand the legal technicalities of invoking the Fifth Amendment privilege. The Fifth Amendment, however, does not permit an unqualified right to remain silent and the courts are permitted to evaluate the reasons for the silence. Establishing Salinas's (D) proposed rule would require officers to ascertain when silence became expressive conduct and that is unworkable. [Decision not stated in casebook excerpt.]

CONCURRENCE: (Thomas, J.) The prosecutor's comments regarding Salinas's (D) silence did not compel Salinas (D) to give self-incriminating testimony, so his claim would fail even if he had invoked the privilege. This Court decided in *Griffin v. California*, 380 U.S. 609 (1965), the prosecutor could not comment on a defendant's refusal to testify. That decision lacked foundation and should not be extended here to apply to comments on silence.

DISSENT: (Breyer, J.) The Fifth Amendment prohibits the prosecutor from commenting on the witness's silence during police questioning. To allow comment on silence directly or indirectly puts the witness in an impossible predicament. If the witness remains silent, that might be used as evidence of consciousness of guilt. If the witness answers, he might provide incriminatory information. *Berghuis* is beside the point. In that case, the Court held he waived his privilege as to the later statements, not as to his silence. The circumstances surrounding Salinas's (D) silence indicated Salinas (D) was invoking the privilege. The plurality struggles because the "explicit statement" rule is a serious obstacle to those unaware of such linguistic detail. The right question is whether the circumstances and the individual's silence indicate an exercise of the Fifth Amendment privilege. Here, the answer is yes.

ANALYSIS

Salinas was a closely watched case because it may have added to the instructions law enforcement are required to provide to suspects facing questioning. It instead confirmed a suspect's silence may be used as evidence of consciousness of guilt at trial unless the suspect expressly invoked the privilege. The burden remains on the suspect to know what words to say to fully protect himself against self-incrimination.

■▬≡▬■

Continued on next page.

Quicknotes

CASE-IN-CHIEF The portion of a proceeding where the party with the burden of proof presents evidence to support his case.

FIFTH AMENDMENT Provides that no person shall be compelled to serve as a witness against himself, or be subject to trial for the same offense twice, or be deprived of life, liberty, or property without due process of law.

***MIRANDA* WARNINGS** Specified warnings that must be communicated to a person prior to a custodial interrogation; in the absence of the communication of such warnings, any communications made during the interrogation is inadmissible at trial.

■══■

Montejo v. Louisiana

Individual (D) v. State (P)

556 U.S. 778 (2009).

NATURE OF CASE: Appeal from a state high court decision in favor of the state.

FACT SUMMARY: At his arraignment on murder charges, the court appointed Montejo (D) counsel, although he did not specifically request it. Later that day, after police informed him of his *Miranda* rights [*Miranda v. Arizona*, 384 U.S. 436 (1966)], without the presence of his counsel, Montejo (D) wrote a letter of apology to the murder victim's wife. Prosecutors successfully used the letter against Montejo (D) at trial.

🏛 RULE OF LAW
When a court automatically appoints counsel for an indigent defendant or the defendant has requested counsel, there is no longer a presumption that any subsequent waiver of the defendant's right to counsel will be involuntary.

FACTS: At his arraignment for murder charges, the court appointed Montejo (D) with counsel. He did not specifically request counsel at the hearing, but instead remained silent. Later that day and without the presence of his counsel, two police detectives asked if Montejo (D) would help them locate the murder weapon. The officers read Montejo (D) his *Miranda* rights and Montejo (D) agreed to join the officers. On the trip, Montejo (D) wrote an apology letter to the victim's wife. At trial, prosecutors successfully used the letter against Montejo (D). The court then sentenced Montejo (D) to death. The Louisiana Supreme Court upheld the conviction on the ground Montejo (D), informed of his *Miranda* rights, validly waived his right to an attorney before drafting the apology letter. Montejo (D) appealed to the United States Supreme Court.

ISSUE: When a court automatically appoints counsel for an indigent defendant or the defendant has requested counsel, is there any longer a presumption that any subsequent waiver of the defendant's right to counsel will be involuntary?

HOLDING AND DECISION: (Scalia, J.) No. When a court automatically appoints counsel for an indigent defendant or the defendant has requested counsel, there is no longer a presumption that any subsequent waiver of defendant's right to counsel will be involuntary. A prior decision from this court, *Michigan v. Jackson*, 475 U.S. 625 (1986), held that police could not initiate interrogation of a criminal defendant once he has requested an attorney. The Court now overrules that decision as unworkable. Many states, such as Louisiana, automatically appoint counsel for indigent defendants without even giving them to the opportunity to request counsel. Therefore, the *Jackson* rule does not even apply in those states. Rather than confuse the issue, it is better to do away with the decision and rely upon other decisions that already provide criminal defendants with protection from coerced interrogations. Under prior case law, any suspect subject to a custodial interrogation must be advised of his right to have a lawyer present and may request one. Also, once a suspect invokes his right to an attorney, the interrogation must cease. No subsequent interrogation may commence until an attorney is present. While these decisions rely upon the Fifth Amendment right to counsel as opposed to the Sixth Amendment right, the justifications supporting them apply equally once a suspect is charged with a crime. A waiver of these rights is valid both for Fifth and Sixth Amendment purposes. The case is remanded to the state courts for a determination of whether Montejo (D) requested counsel when the officers approached him to accompany them on their search for the murder weapon. Reversed and remanded.

DISSENT: (Stevens, J.) The *Jackson* rule was not founded upon Fifth Amendment considerations. It rested instead upon the Sixth Amendment right to counsel that is granted to all indicted defendants. The commencement of a criminal proceeding, changing a suspect into a criminal defendant, is a significant moment. Defendants must be fully aware of the ramifications of a waiver of the right to counsel at that stage. Here, the record is not clear that Montejo (D) validly waived his right to counsel.

▶ ANALYSIS

The Fifth Amendment right to counsel applies to suspects in custody prior to indictment. The Sixth Amendment right arises once judicial proceedings have begun against a defendant. This decision essentially does away with the bright line rule of *Jackson* which held that any waiver by a charged defendant of the right to counsel after one requests it must be involuntary and thus invalid.

■=■

Quicknotes

FIFTH AMENDMENT Provides that no person shall be compelled to serve as a witness against himself, or be subject to trial for the same offense twice, or be deprived of life, liberty, or property without due process of law.

Continued on next page.

SIXTH AMENDMENT Provides the right to a speedy and public trial by impartial jury, the right to be informed of the accusation, the right to confront witnesses, and the right to have the assistance of counsel in all criminal prosecutions.

■▬■

Moran v. Burbine

Court (P) v. Murder convict (D)

475 U.S. 412 (1986).

NATURE OF CASE: Appeal from reversal of denial of habeas corpus in state criminal proceeding.

FACT SUMMARY: While being interrogated by police, an attorney wishing to represent Burbine (D) called the police, a fact not conveyed to Burbine (D) by the police.

🏛 RULE OF LAW
A voluntary confession obtained by police, who fail to inform a defendant that an attorney attempted to contact him, is not an invalid intrusion upon the defendant's *Miranda* rights.

FACTS: Burbine (D) was arrested on suspicion of breaking and entering, and murder. Burbine (D) did not request an attorney. His sister obtained one to represent him, and the attorney called the police station, informing the police that she wished to represent him. The police informed the attorney that Burbine (D) was not to be further questioned that night. Nonetheless, Burbine (D) was later interrogated, after having expressly waived his *Miranda* rights [*Miranda v. Arizona*, 384 U.S. 436 (1966)] following a proper warning. Burbine (D) confessed to the murder. The confession was admitted at trial, and Burbine (D) was convicted. After exhausting state appeals, Burbine (D) petitioned for federal habeas corpus. The district court declined to grant habeas corpus, but the court of appeals reversed.

ISSUE: Is a voluntary confession obtained by police, who fail to inform a defendant that an attorney attempted to contact him, an invalid intrusion upon the defendant's *Miranda* rights?

HOLDING AND DECISION: (O'Connor, J.) No. A voluntary confession obtained by police, who fail to inform a defendant that an attorney attempted to contact him, is not an invalid intrusion upon the defendant's *Miranda* rights. A *Miranda* waiver is valid if it is voluntary and intelligently made. A failure to be informed of an attorney's attempts at contact in no way diminishes one's ability to knowingly waive a right, which Burbine (D) did. Had Burbine (D) requested an attorney, matters would be different, but Burbine (D) never did so. Police are not under a duty to provide a defendant with a steady stream of information not requested. The benefits of burdening the police with such a duty would be minimal and would come at the cost of making it much harder to obtain confessions, something in which society has a strong interest. Since no constitutional right was violated, the conduct

of the police, while not exemplary, did not call for reversal of the conviction. Reversed.

DISSENT: (Stevens, J.) As the attorney was, in effect, an agent of Burbine (D), the deception practiced upon her was in fact a deception upon Burbine (D), which necessarily invalidated the "intelligent" and "knowing" aspect of the waiver of his rights.

▶ ANALYSIS

Besides the Fifth Amendment issue, the Court also discussed Sixth and Fourteenth Amendment concerns. The Sixth Amendment argument was dismissed because Burbine (D) had not yet been formally charged. With regard to the Fourteenth Amendment, the Court concluded that the police conduct was not fundamentally unfair, a conclusion with which the dissent took issue.

■▬■

Quicknotes

FIFTH AMENDMENT Provides that no person shall be compelled to serve as a witness against himself, or be subject to trial for the same offense twice, or be deprived of life, liberty, or property without due process of law.

FOURTEENTH AMENDMENT Declares that no state shall make or enforce any law that shall abridge the privileges and immunities of citizens of the United States. No state shall deny to any person within its jurisdiction the equal protection of the laws.

HABEAS CORPUS A proceeding in which a defendant brings a writ to compel a judicial determination of whether he is lawfully being held in custody.

MIRANDA RULE A required warning given before any questioning by law enforcement authorities can take place. Individuals receive warnings regarding their privilege against self-incrimination, right to remain silent, and right to be represented by an attorney.

SIXTH AMENDMENT Provides the right to a speedy trial by impartial jury, the right to be informed of the accusation, to confront witnesses and to have the assistance of counsel in all criminal prosecutions.

■▬■

Dickerson v. United States

Bank robber (D) v. Federal government (P)

530 U.S. 428 (2000).

NATURE OF CASE: Appeal from denial of motion to suppress statement based on *Miranda* violation.

FACT SUMMARY: Dickerson (D) sought to suppress a statement he made while in an FBI field office prior to being given his *Miranda* warnings.

🏛 RULE OF LAW
When a decision of the court involves interpretation and application of the Constitution, Congress may not legislatively supersede such decision.

FACTS: Dickerson (D) was indicted for bank robbery and conspiracy to commit bank robbery. Before trial he moved to suppress a statement he made at an FBI field office, on the grounds that he had not received *Miranda* warnings [*Miranda v. Arizona*, 384 U.S. 436 (1966)] before being interrogated. The district court granted the motion, and the Government (P) took an interlocutory appeal to the court of appeals, which reversed, stating that § 3501 was satisfied since the statement was made voluntarily. Dickerson (D) appealed.

ISSUE: Where a decision of the court involves interpretation and application of the Constitution may Congress legislatively supersede such decision?

HOLDING AND DECISION: (Rehnquist, C.J.) No. Where a decision of the court involves interpretation and application of the Constitution, Congress may not legislatively supersede such decision. *Miranda* and its progeny govern the admissibility of statements made during custodial interrogation in both state and federal courts. Section 3501 provides that the admissibility of a custodial suspect's statements should depend on whether they are voluntarily made. Prior to *Miranda*, the admissibility of a suspect's confession was evaluated under a voluntariness test. The requirement of voluntariness was based on the Fifth Amendment right against self-incrimination and the Due Process Clause of the Fourteenth Amendment. The Court's decisions in *Miranda* and *Malloy* changed the focus of the due process inquiry. In *Malloy v. Hog*an, 378 U.S. 1 (1964), the Court held that the Fifth Amendment's self-incrimination clause is incorporated into the Due Process Clause of the Fourteenth Amendment and this applies to the states. In *Miranda*, the Court recognized that the coercion inherent in custodial interrogation makes it difficult to determine whether a statement is voluntary or involuntary and heightens the risk of self-incrimination. Section 3501 was enacted two years after the decision in *Miranda* and was intended by Congress to overrule the Court's decision in that case. The issue is whether Congress has

the constitutional authority to do so. While Congress retains the ultimate authority to modify or set aside any judicially created rules of evidence and procedure that are not required by the Constitution, it may not legislatively supersede the Court's decisions that interpret and apply the Constitution. *Miranda* is a constitutional decision. The Court specifically stated that it was intended "to explore some facets of the problems of applying the privilege against self-incrimination to in-custody interrogation and to give concrete constitutional guidelines for law enforcement agencies and courts to follow." The decision is otherwise replete with references to constitutional rules and standards. *Miranda* announced a constitutional rule that Congress may not supersede legislatively. Reversed.

DISSENT: (Scalia, J.) *Marbury v. Madison*, 1 Cranch 137 (1803), held that an Act of Congress will not be enforced if what it prescribes violates the Constitution. The majority opinion fails to state, however, that what § 3501 prescribes, the use of a voluntary confession at trial, violates the Constitution.

▶ ANALYSIS

The Court also relies on the principle of stare decisis as weighing heavily against overruling *Miranda*, since *Miranda* warnings have become "embedded in routine police practice to the point where the warnings have become part of our national culture." Justice Scalia rejects such rationale on the basis that the court rules are both "mutable and modifiable" and that they "must make sense."

Quicknotes

CUSTODIAL INTERROGATION The questioning of a suspect by police while in custody.

INTERLOCUTORY APPEAL The appeal of an issue that does not resolve the disposition of the case but is essential to a determination of the parties' legal rights.

STARE DECISIS Doctrine whereby courts follow legal precedent unless there is good cause for departure.

Chavez v. Martinez

Police officer (D) v. Initiator of § 1983 suit (P)

538 U.S. 760 (2003).

NATURE OF CASE: Appeal from refusal of federal court of appeals to grant qualified immunity to police officer in a § 1983 suit against him.

FACT SUMMARY: Martinez (P) brought a § 1983 suit against Chavez (D), a patrol officer, for interrogating him in the hospital during emergency medical treatment for life-threatening gunshot wounds, arguing that such conduct violated his Fifth Amendment protection against self-incrimination.

RULE OF LAW
The Fifth Amendment protection against self-incrimination applies only in criminal cases.

FACTS: During a police altercation, an officer shot Martinez (P) five times, causing life-endangering injuries. Chavez (D), a patrol officer, arrived on the scene and accompanied Martinez (P) to the hospital where he continuously interrogated Martinez (P) during medical treatment, despite Martinez's (P) statements to the officer, "I don't know," "I am choking," "I am dying, please," and "I don't want to die." Although Martinez (P) was never charged with a crime and his answers were never used against him in any criminal prosecution, he brought a § 1983 suit, arguing, inter alia, that Chavez (D) had violated his Fifth Amendment privilege against self-incrimination. The federal court of appeals held that Chavez (D) was not entitled to a defense of qualified immunity because he violated Martinez's (P) clearly established constitutional rights. Chavez (D) appealed.

ISSUE: Does the Fifth Amendment protection against self-incrimination apply only in criminal cases?

HOLDING AND DECISION: (Thomas, J.) Yes. The Fifth Amendment protection against self-incrimination applies only in criminal cases. The Fifth Amendment requires that no person shall be compelled "in any criminal case" to be a witness against himself. This Court fails to see how Martinez (P) can allege a violation of this right since he was never prosecuted for a crime, let alone compelled to be a witness in a criminal case. A "criminal case" at the very least requires the initiation of criminal proceedings. Although conduct by law enforcement officials prior to trial may ultimately impair that right, a constitutional violation occurs only at trial. Here, Martinez (P) was never made to be a "witness" against himself because his statements were never admitted as testimony against him in a criminal case. Nor was he ever placed under oath and exposed to the cruel trilemma of self-accusation, perjury, or contempt. Rules designed to safeguard a constitutional right do not extend the scope of the constitutional right itself, just as violations of judicially crafted prophylactic rules do not violate the constitutional rights of any person. Even assuming, arguendo, that the persistent questioning of Martinez (P) somehow deprived him of a liberty interest, this Court cannot agree with Martinez's (P) characterization of Chavez's (D) behavior as "egregious" or "conscience shocking" since medical personnel were able to treat Martinez (P) throughout the interrogation and Chavez (D) did not interfere with the medical treatment. Reversed.

CONCURRENCE: (Souter, J.) Martinez (P) has not here been able to make the "powerful showing," subject to a realistic assessment of costs and risks, necessary to expand protection of the privilege against compelled self-incrimination to the point of the civil liability he asks this Court to recognize.

CONCURRENCE: (Scalia, J.) Without violation of the actual right protected by the text of the Self-Incrimination Clause, the § 1983 action is doomed.

CONCURRENCE AND DISSENT: (Stevens, J.) The interrogation was the functional equivalent of an attempt to obtain an involuntary confession from a prisoner by torturous methods. As a matter of law, that type of brutal police conduct constitutes an immediate deprivation of the prisoner's constitutionally protected interest in liberty.

CONCURRENCE AND DISSENT: (Kennedy, J.) A constitutional right arises the moment torture or its close equivalents are brought to bear. Constitutional protection for a tortured suspect is not held in abeyance until some later criminal proceeding takes place.

CONCURRENCE AND DISSENT: (Ginsburg, J.) The Self-Incrimination Clause applies at the time and place police use severe compulsion to extract a statement from a suspect.

ANALYSIS

As the *Chavez* decision makes clear, the text of the Self-Incrimination Clause cannot support a view that the mere use of compulsive questioning, without more, violates the Constitution.

Continued on next page.

Quicknotes

INTER ALIA Among other things.

LIBERTY INTEREST A right conferred by the Due Process Clauses of the state and federal constitutions.

QUALIFIED IMMUNITY An affirmative defense relieving officials from civil liability for the performance of activities within their discretion so long as such conduct is not in violation of an individual's rights pursuant to law as determined by a reasonable person standard.

■━■

United States v. Patane

Federal government (P) v. Possessor of illegal firearm (D)

542 U.S. 630 (2004).

NATURE OF CASE: Appeal from suppression of physical evidence in criminal case.

FACT SUMMARY: When a police officer seized Samuel Patane's (D) pistol from his bedroom during an arrest, after being given Patane's (D) permission to do so, Patane (D) was subsequently indicted for possession of an illegal firearm. Pantane (D) argued that since he was not given full *Miranda* warnings, the pistol should be suppressed as a "physical fruit" of the poisonous tree.

🏛 RULE OF LAW
The Self-Incrimination Clause is not violated by the admission into evidence of the physical fruit of a voluntary statement.

FACTS: Upon arresting Samuel Patane (D) at his residence for violating a restraining order, a police officer attempted to advise Patane (D) of his *Miranda* rights [*Miranda v. Arizona*, 384 U.S. 436 (1966)] but got no further than the right to remain silent. At that point, Patane (D) interrupted, asserting that he knew his rights, whereupon the warnings were not completed. The police officer asked Patane (D) about an illegal Glock pistol he believed Patane (D) possessed. Pantane (D) told the police officer the pistol was in his bedroom and gave permission to seize it. Pantane (D) was indicted for possession of the pistol. The court of appeals affirmed the district court's suppression of the pistol, and the Government (P) appealed.

ISSUE: Is the Self-Incrimination Clause violated by the admission into evidence of the physical fruit of a voluntary statement?

HOLDING AND DECISION: (Thomas, J.) No. The Self-Incrimination Clause is not violated by the admission into evidence of the physical fruit of a voluntary statement. The police do not necessarily violate *Miranda* rights by negligent or even deliberate failures to provide a suspect with the full panoply of *Miranda* warnings. Potential violations occur, if at all, only upon the admission of unwarned statements into evidence at trial. At that point, the exclusion of unwarned statements is a complete and sufficient remedy for any perceived *Miranda* violation. Thus, unlike unreasonable searches under the Fourth Amendment or actual violations of the Due Process Clause or the Self-Incrimination Clause, there is, with respect to mere failures to warn, nothing to deter. There is therefore no reason to apply the "fruit of the poisonous tree" doctrine. It is not for this Court to impose its proffered police practices on either federal law enforcement officials or their state counterparts. Characterization of *Miranda* as a constitutional rule does not lessen the need to maintain the closest possible fit between the Self-Incrimination Clause and any judge-made rule designed to protect it. Here, there is no such fit because the introduction of the nontestimonial fruit of a voluntary statement (the pistol) does not implicate the Self-Incrimination Clause. The admission of such fruit presents no risk that a defendant's coerced statements will be used against him or her at a criminal trial. There is simply no need to extend (and therefore no justification for extending) the prophylactic rule of *Miranda* to this context. Reversed.

CONCURRENCE: (Kennedy, J.) In light of the important probative value of reliable physical evidence, it is doubtful that exclusion can be justified by a deterrence rationale sensitive to both law enforcement interests and a suspect's rights during an in-custody interrogation.

DISSENT: (Souter, J.) In closing their eyes to the consequences of giving an evidentiary advantage to those who ignore *Miranda*, the majority adds an important inducement for interrogators to ignore the rule in that case. While there is a price for excluding evidence, the Fifth Amendment is worth a price.

DISSENT: (Breyer, J.) The "fruit of the poisonous tree" doctrine should be extended to cases such as this.

▶ ANALYSIS

As *Patane* makes clear, the *Miranda* rule is not a code of police conduct, and police do not necessarily violate the Constitution (or even the *Miranda* rule, for that matter) by mere failures to warn. Because various prophylactic rules (including the *Miranda* rule) necessarily sweep beyond the actual protections of the Self-Incrimination Clause, the Supreme Court has consistently taken the position that any further extension of these rules must be justified by its necessity for the protection of the actual right against compelled self-incrimination. It is for this reason, for example, that statements taken without *Miranda* warnings (though not actually compelled) can be used to impeach a defendant's testimony at trial.

■=■

Quicknotes

CUSTODIAL INTERROGATION The questioning of a suspect by police while in custody.

Continued on next page.

FRUIT OF POISONOUS TREE Doctrine that evidence obtained as a result of illegal procedures is tainted and is usually inadmissible at trial.

MIRANDA **RULE** A required warning given before any questioning by law enforcement authorities can take place. Individuals in custody receive warnings regarding their privilege against self-incrimination, right to remain silent, and right to be represented by an attorney.

MIRANDA **WARNINGS** Specified warnings that must be communicated to a person prior to a custodial interrogation; in the absence of the communication of such warnings, any communications made during the interrogation are inadmissible at trial.

■=■

Missouri v. Seibert

State (P) v. Murder suspect (D)

542 U.S. 600 (2004).

NATURE OF CASE: Appeal from reversal of a murder conviction.

FACT SUMMARY: Patrice Seibert (D) argued that since her murder confession was obtained by the police technique of interrogating in successive, unwarned and warned phases, known as "question-first," the requirements of *Miranda* [*Miranda v. Arizona*, 384 U.S. 436 (1966)] were violated.

🏛 RULE OF LAW
The police technique of interrogating in successive, unwarned and warned phases violates the requirements of *Miranda*.

FACTS: In questioning Patrice Seibert (D), a murder suspect, the police interrogator employed a widely used interrogation technique known as "question-first" in which the interrogator questions the suspect first, then gives the *Miranda* warnings, and then repeats the questioning until the interrogator obtains the confession or incriminating statement which the suspect has already previously provided. After employing this technique of interrogating in successive, unwarned and warned phases, Seibert (D) confessed to murder prior to her warnings and then again after being given the warnings. The trial court suppressed Seibert's (D) pre-warning confession but admitted her post-warning confession. She was convicted of murder. The Missouri Supreme Court reversed, holding that here where the interrogation was "nearly continuous," the second statement was clearly "the product of the invalid first statement" and should have been suppressed. Missouri (P) appealed.

ISSUE: Does the police technique of interrogating in successive, unwarned and warned phases violate the requirements of *Miranda*?

HOLDING AND DECISION: (Souter, J.) Yes. The police technique of interrogating in successive, unwarned and warned phases violates the requirements of *Miranda*. *Miranda* addressed interrogation practices likely to disable an individual from making a free and rational choice about speaking and held that a suspect must be "adequately and effectively" advised of the choice the Constitution guarantees. The object of the "question-first" technique here utilized against Seibert (D) was to render *Miranda* warnings ineffective by waiting for a particularly opportune time to give them, after the suspect had already confessed. Just as no talismanic incantation is required to satisfy *Miranda*'s strictures, it would be absurd to think that mere recitation of the litany suffices to satisfy *Miranda*

in every conceivable circumstance. The issue when interrogators question first and warn later is thus whether the warnings reasonably convey to a suspect his *Miranda* rights. Unless the warnings could place a suspect who has just been interrogated in a position to make an informed choice as to whether to speak, there is no practical justification for accepting the formal warnings as compliance with *Miranda*, or for treating the second stage of interrogation as distinct from the first, unwarned and inadmissible segment. By any objective measure, applied to circumstances exemplified here, it is likely that if the interrogators employ the technique of withholding warnings until after interrogation succeeds in eliciting a confession, the warnings will be ineffective in preparing the suspect for successive interrogation, close in time and similar in content. Accordingly, the question-first tactic effectively threatens to thwart *Miranda*'s purpose of reducing the risk that a coerced confession would be admitted. Affirmed.

CONCURRENCE: (Breyer, J.) Courts should exclude the "fruits" of the initial unwarned questioning unless the failure to warn was in good faith.

CONCURRENCE: (Kennedy, J.) Not every violation of *Miranda* requires suppression of the evidence obtained. The scope of the *Miranda* suppression remedy depends on a consideration of whether admission of the evidence under the circumstances would frustrate *Miranda*'s "central concerns and objectives."

DISSENT: (O'Connor, J.) Because here the isolated fact of the interrogating officer's intent could not have had any bearing on Seibert's (D) capacity to comprehend and knowingly relinquish her right to remain silent, it could not by itself affect the voluntariness of her confession.

▶ ANALYSIS

As the Supreme Court makes clear in *Seibert*, the reason for the increased popularity of the question-first method of interrogation is to obtain a confession the suspect would not make if he understood his rights at the outset. The underlying police assumption, which is accurate, is that with one confession in hand before the warnings, the interrogator can usually count on getting a duplicate. It is unrealistic, explained the Court, to treat two bouts of integrated and proximately conducted questioning as independent interrogations subject to independent evaluation

Continued on next page.

simply because *Miranda* warnings formally punctuate them in the middle.

$\blacksquare\equiv\blacksquare$

Quicknotes

CUSTODIAL INTERROGATION The questioning of a suspect by police while in custody.

***MIRANDA* RULE** A required warning given before any questioning by law enforcement authorities can take place. Individuals in custody receive warnings regarding their privilege against self-incrimination, right to remain silent, and right to be represented by an attorney.

***MIRANDA* WARNINGS** Specified warnings that must be communicated to a person prior to a custodial interrogation; in the absence of the communication of such warnings, any communications made during the interrogation are inadmissible at trial.

$\blacksquare\equiv\blacksquare$

Brewer v. Williams (Williams I)

Court (P) v. Mental patient (D)

430 U.S. 387 (1977).

NATURE OF CASE: Appeal from a conviction of murder.

FACT SUMMARY: Williams (D) was convicted of murder based on a confession obtained during a custodial trip.

🏛 RULE OF LAW
The police cannot interrogate a defendant represented by known counsel after a refusal to speak without the presence of his attorney.

FACTS: Williams (D), an escaped mental patient, killed a 10-year-old girl. Williams (D) subsequently contacted a lawyer in Des Moines, informed him that he was in Davenport, and was willing to surrender to the police in Des Moines who were searching for him. The attorney informed the police and they sent a car to Waterloo to return him to Des Moines under a warrant issued for his arrest. The attorney informed both the police and his client that under no circumstances was Williams (D) to say anything. Williams (D), in the meantime, had been arrested in Davenport and hired counsel there to represent him at the arraignment on the murder charge. His attorney requested permission to accompany Williams (D) on the trip to Des Moines, but was refused. The attorney warned both Williams (D) and the police that there was to be no conversation during the trip concerning the crime as Williams (D) was represented by counsel who had informed him to remain silent. During the first part of the trip, Williams (D) repeatedly refused to speak unless counsel was present. One of the detectives then began to play on Williams's (D) religious beliefs, pleading with him to reveal the dead girl's whereabouts so that she could obtain a Christian burial. Williams (D) finally revealed the whereabouts of the body after confessing to the crime. Williams (D) appealed the admissibility of his confession after conviction. Williams (D) alleged, among other things, that the tactics used to obtain the confession violated his right to counsel.

ISSUE: Is questioning without the presence of known counsel during a critical stage of the proceedings violative of the Sixth and Fourteenth Amendments?

HOLDING AND DECISION: (Stewart, J.) Yes. The Sixth and Fourteenth Amendments grant an accused the right to the presence of counsel during all critical stages of proceedings. First, this was a critical stage. Williams (D) had a warrant issued for his arrest and had already been arraigned in Davenport on the charge. The police officers knew he was represented by counsel; that he had been informed not to speak; that Williams (D) told them he would not speak without counsel present. Williams (D)

had pleaded not guilty to the charge. There are no grounds present herein that establish that Williams (D) knowingly, intelligently and voluntarily waived his rights. The state bears the heavy burden of establishing that once rights have been invoked by the defendant/accused, that they have been waived. No clear and convincing evidence of such a waiver is present herein. While the crime is abhorrent, we must reverse the conviction and remand for a new trial. The judgment of the court of appeals is affirmed.

DISSENT: (Burger, C.J.) After at least five warnings from two attorneys, Williams (D) voluntarily lead the police to where the body was buried. There was no coercion or threats. Williams (D) was prompted solely on the simple statement by the detective. In my mind, this would constitute a voluntary waiver of known rights. The exclusionary rule should not be arbitrarily applied to nonegregious police conduct.

DISSENT: (White, J.) The voluntary confession of Williams (D), made without threats or coercions of a known right, is conclusive evidence of a waiver.

DISSENT: (Blackmun, J.) This was not an example of purposeful police conduct. The trip was necessary to transport Williams (D) to Des Moines. Merely making a Christian plea on behalf of the family seems to me not unreasonable and is simply not the type of coercion for which a reversal should be granted.

▶ ANALYSIS

The *Brewer* decision follows the rationale of *Rhode Island v. Innis*, 446 U.S. 291 (1980), in which the Court "focuses primarily on the perceptions of the suspect" as to whether the suspect is being held for custodial interrogation. *Brewer* added that any information the officer has regarding the suspect's peculiar susceptibilities to a certain kind of persuasion is relevant in determining what the officer should have known was likely to occur. *Brewer* could probably have been reversed on *Miranda* grounds [*Miranda v. Arizona*, 384 U.S. 436 (1966)] on a showing that the confession was involuntary, due to the suspect's known susceptibility to religion-based questioning.

■=■

Quicknotes

CUSTODIAL INTERROGATION The questioning of a suspect by police while in custody.

■=■

Texas v. Cobb

State (P) v. Convicted murderer (D)

532 U.S. 162 (2001).

NATURE OF CASE: Murder case.

FACT SUMMARY: Cobb (D) argued that his conviction for capital murder should be reversed on the basis that his confession should have been suppressed since it was elicited in violation of his Sixth Amendment right to counsel.

🏛 **RULE OF LAW**
The Sixth Amendment right to counsel does not extend to crimes that are "factually related" to those that have actually been charged.

FACTS: Cobb (D) gave a written statement confessing to the burglary of his neighbor's house and was indicted. He later confessed to the killing of his neighbor's wife and daughter, which he had previously denied. He was convicted of capital murder for the murder of more than one person in the course of a criminal transaction and sentenced to death. He appealed, contending that his confession should be suppressed because it was obtained in violation of his Sixth Amendment right to counsel. The court of criminal appeals reversed and remanded, concluding that the right to counsel had attached on the capital murder charge when Cobb (D) was charged with the burglary because the two crimes were "factually interwoven," even though he had not yet been charged with murder.

ISSUE: Does the Sixth Amendment right to counsel extend to crimes that are "factually related" to those that have actually been charged?

HOLDING AND DECISION: (Rehnquist, C.J.) No. The Sixth Amendment right to counsel does not extend to crimes that are "factually related" to those that have actually been charged. The Sixth Amendment right of counsel is offense-specific and cannot be invoked once for all future prosecutions since it does not attach until a prosecution has been commenced. This Court has held that a defendant's statements regarding offenses for which he had not been charged were admissible notwithstanding the attachment of his Sixth Amendment right to counsel on other charged offenses. Some courts, however, had craved an exception for crimes that are "factually related" to a charged offense. We decline to support this view. However, we do hold that the Sixth Amendment right to counsel, when it attaches, does encompass offenses that even if not formally charged would be considered the same offense under the *Blockburger* test [*Blockburger v. United States*, 284 U.S. 299 (1932)]. The test to be applied to determine whether there is more than one offense is whether each provision requires proof of a fact that the other does not.

As defined by Texas law, capital murder and burglary are not the same offense under *Blockburger*. Thus, the police were not barred from interrogating Cobb (D) regarding the murders and his confession was admissible. Reversed.

CONCURRENCE: (Kennedy, J.) Note that the court reached its conclusion without approving of the decision in *Michigan v. Jackson*, 475 U.S. 625 (1986). This is wise since I believe the reasoning in that case was questionable. It is difficult to see the utility of a rule that invalidates a confession obtained after a voluntary waiver of the suspect's *Miranda* rights [*Miranda v. Arizona*, 384 U.S. 436 (1966)].

DISSENT: (Breyer, J.) This case focuses on the meaning of the word "offense." The Court's definition undermines Sixth Amendment protections while doing nothing to further effective law enforcement. The majority's rule permits law enforcement to question those charged with a crime without first approaching counsel, by asking questions about any other related crime not charged in the indictment.

▶ *ANALYSIS*

The *Blockburger* test adopted here has also been applied to determine the scope of the Fifth Amendment's double jeopardy clause, prohibiting multiple or successive prosecutions for the same "offense." The Court extends such test to the Sixth Amendment's "offense" reasoning that there is no constitutional difference between the meanings of the term in either context.

■▬■

Quicknotes

BURGLARY Unlawful entry of a building at night with the intent to commit a felony therein.

FIFTH AMENDMENT Provides that no person shall be compelled to serve as a witness against himself, or be subject to trial for the same offense twice, or be deprived of life, liberty, or property without due process of law.

MIRANDA RULE A required warning given before any questioning by law enforcement authorities can take place. Individuals receive warnings regarding their privilege against self-incrimination, right to remain silent, and right to be represented by an attorney.

MURDER Unlawful killing of another person either with deliberation and premeditation or by conduct demonstrating a reckless disregard for human life.

Continued on next page.

SIXTH AMENDMENT Provides the right to a speedy trial by impartial jury, the right to be informed of the accusation, to confront witnesses, and to have the assistance of counsel in all criminal prosecutions.

■▬■

CHAPTER 10

Lineups, Showups, and Other Pre-Trial Identification Procedures

Quick Reference Rules of Law

Manson v. Brathwaite

Court (P) v. Heroin dealer (D)

432 U.S. 98 (1977).

NATURE OF CASE: Appeal from the reversal of a conviction for the sale of narcotics.

FACT SUMMARY: Glover, a police officer, after describing the man who had sold him heroin, was given a photograph of the suspect for identification purposes.

RULE OF LAW

If identification is independently reliable, it will not be excluded solely because police identification techniques were suggestive.

FACTS: Glover, an undercover policeman, purchased heroin from Brathwaite (D). During the purchase, which took several minutes, Glover was no more than two or three feet from him. Glover returned to headquarters and described the individual whom he had seen in great detail. From the description, another officer pulled a picture of Brathwaite (D) from their files. Glover saw the photograph two days later and promptly identified Brathwaite (D) as the seller. The photograph and identification were subsequently admitted at trial without objection. Brathwaite (D) was found guilty and was sentenced to prison. Fourteen months later, Brathwaite (D) challenged the photographic identification on the grounds that it was too suggestive, thereby rendering the identification itself per se excludable. The court of appeals reversed the conviction holding that independent indicia of reliability could not overcome the suggestibility of the identification technique.

ISSUE: Will independent indicia of reliability allow admissibility of a witness whose original police identification was based on suggestive identification techniques?

HOLDING AND DECISION: (Blackmun, J.) Yes. The circuits have split over whether a per se rule should apply to excluding identification based on suggestive identification procedures. Some favor per se exclusion. Others take each case separately in order to determine if the identification would be otherwise reliable, and, if so, allowing it in evidence. We think the latter theory is correct. To hold otherwise would exclude relevant information from the jury merely because of improper police procedure. The case-by-case approach will be a deterrent to the police and will prevent the guilty from being freed. The linchpin in this area is the independent reliability of the identification. Here, we have a trained police officer who viewed Brathwaite (D) closely for two to three minutes from a short distance. Glover then described Brathwaite (D) in detail shortly thereafter. The pictorial identification was two days later. All of this indicates independent reliability based on a trained observer, a prompt identification, and a reasonable opportunity to view the suspect. Independently reliable identifications need not be excluded to satisfy due process requirements. Reversed.

DISSENT: (Marshall, J.) In this case, the Court disregards distinctions in analysis developed in previous decisions and fashions a rule that is not supported by precedent. The use of a single picture on the presentation of a single suspect is inherently suggestive.

ANALYSIS

The per se rule is used to discourage police abuses. The majority appears to indicate that nonpolice witnesses will be less likely to survive an ad hoc, case-by-case, approach because they are more prone to misidentification since they are not trained observers. The stress on them is also deemed greater, which may cause faulty identifications. No hard and fast rules can be developed in this area, but the Court apparently focuses on: (1) the length of time in which the accused was viewed; (2) the nature of the witness; (3) the circumstances; (4) the length of time between the incident and the identification; and (5) the ability to give an initial description of the accused.

Quicknotes

PRIVILEGE AGAINST SELF-INCRIMINATION A privilege guaranteed by the Fifth Amendment to the federal Constitution in a criminal proceeding for communications made by an accused and protecting an accused or witness from having to give testimony that may incriminate himself.

PROCEDURAL DUE PROCESS The constitutional mandate that if the state or federal government acts so as to deny a citizen of a life, liberty or property interest the individual is first entitled to notice and the right to be heard.

CHAPTER 11

Grand Jury Investigations

Quick Reference Rules of Law

Boyd v. United States

Illegal importer (D) v. Federal government (P)

116 U.S. 616 (1886).

NATURE OF CASE: Appeal of forfeiture action.

FACT SUMMARY: Using evidence secured through force from Boyd (D), the Government (P) seized property illegally imported.

🏛 RULE OF LAW
A defendant cannot be compelled to produce incriminating documents.

FACTS: Using a statute validating the practice, a government attorney obtained an order mandating that Boyd (D) produce an invoice covering certain imported glass, which the Government (P) suspected had been illegally imported. Using the invoice as evidence, the Government (P) seized the glass and confiscated it. Boyd (D) appealed, contending the production order was unconstitutional.

ISSUE: Can a defendant be compelled to produce incriminating documents?

HOLDING AND DECISION: (Bradley, J.) No. A defendant cannot be compelled to produce incriminating documents. The Fourth Amendment protects citizens against unreasonable searches and seizures. The forcible production of one's papers is much like forced testimony, which is clearly prohibited by the Fifth Amendment. In either case, such governmental conduct constitutes an excessive intrusion of the Government (P) into an individual's realm of protected liberty and cannot be permitted. Reversed.

CONCURRENCE: (Miller, J.) The Fourth Amendment is not involved here, as no search or seizure occurs. However, forced document production is tantamount to self-incrimination.

▶ ANALYSIS

Both in its application of the Fourth and Fifth Amendments, *Boyd* is no longer good law. Compelled document production has long since ceased to be considered a Fourth Amendment issue. As far as the Fifth Amendment is concerned, document production is no longer equated with compelled testimony.

■■■

Quicknotes

FORFEITURE The loss of a right or interest as a penalty for failing to fulfill an obligation.

PRIVILEGE AGAINST SELF-INCRIMINATION A privilege guaranteed by the Fifth Amendment to the federal Constitution in a criminal proceeding for communications made by an accused and protecting an accused or witness from having to give testimony that may incriminate himself.

■■■

United States v. Dionisio

Federal government (P) v. Subpoenaed defendant (D)

410 U.S. 1 (1973).

NATURE OF CASE: Appeal from judgment for civil contempt.

FACT SUMMARY: Dionisio (D) refused to give voice exemplars to the grand jury.

🏛 RULE OF LAW
Both the initial compulsion of a person to appear before a grand jury and a subsequent directive to make a voice recording are not unreasonable seizures within the meaning of the Fourth Amendment.

FACTS: Approximately 20 persons, including Dionisio (D), were subpoenaed before the grand jury to give voice exemplars for comparison with recorded conversations taken pursuant to a court-ordered surveillance. Dionisio (D) refused to give a voice exemplar, claiming protection under the Fourth and Fifth Amendments. The district judge ordered Dionisio (D) to give a voice exemplar. When Dionisio (D) refused, he was held in civil contempt and was committed to custody until he obeyed the order or until the expiration of 18 months.

ISSUE: Do voice exemplars, required to be given to a grand jury to be used for comparison with recorded conversations, violate a defendant's Fourth Amendment rights?

HOLDING AND DECISION: (Stewart, J.) No. Voice exemplars, required to be given to a grand jury to be used for comparison with recorded conversations, do not violate a defendant's Fourth Amendment rights. First, a subpoena to appear before a grand jury is not a seizure of the person. It is the obligation of every person to appear and give evidence before the grand jury. It is an orderly, lawful process without social stigma and under the supervision of a judge. The fact that 20 persons were subpoenaed for the same reason is constitutionally irrelevant. Second, the order to give a voice exemplar was not a seizure under the meaning of the Fourth Amendment. What a person knowingly exposes to the public is not protected. Physical characteristics of voice, as opposed to content of conversations, are not reasonably expected to be private. Therefore, there is no need for the grand jury to determine reasonableness prior to ordering the exemplar where there is no other Fourth Amendment violation. To so require would impede the grand jury's proper function. Reversed.

DISSENT: (Marshall, J.) The only recognized exception in prior cases from Fourth Amendment coverage involved grand jury subpoenas requiring individuals to appear and testify. There is no basis for extending that exception when we move beyond the realm of grand jury investigations limited to testimonial inquiries, as in this case. The danger that law enforcement officials may seek to usurp the grand jury process to secure incriminating evidence from a suspect through the simple expedient of a subpoena arises and would, if the Fourth Amendment was held inapplicable here, allow law enforcement to accomplish indirectly what it would not be able to constitutionally accomplish directly.

▶ ANALYSIS

In *Davis v. Mississippi*, 394 U.S. 721 (1969), the Court held that an unlawful seizure could not be used to obtain fingerprints to be used to determine whether a person is the suspected criminal. *Dionisio* allows the grand jury to do exactly that on the rationale that subpoena is not a seizure and that voice prints are not a seizure. The grand jury is thus in a position to gain real evidence from a potential defendant prior to any finding of probable cause.

■▬■

Quicknotes

CIVIL CONTEMPT CITATION One party's failure to comply with a court order requiring that party to undertake an action for the benefit of another party to the action.

EXPECTATION OF PRIVACY Requirement that in order to invoke the Fourth Amendment's protection against unreasonable searches and seizures, the individual must have a reasonable expectation of privacy in respect to the location searched or thing seized.

GRAND JURY A group summoned to investigate, inform, and accuse persons of crimes when sufficient evidence exists to do so.

SUBPOENA A mandate issued by court to compel a witness to appear at trial.

■▬■

United States v. R. Enterprises, Inc.

Federal government (P) v. Pornography company (D)

498 U.S. 292 (1991).

NATURE OF CASE: Appeal from a partial grant of motions to quash subpoenas by a grand jury investigating interstate transportation of obscene materials.

FACT SUMMARY: After R. Enterprises, Inc. (D) and two other companies were served with subpoenas duces tecum in connection with a grand jury investigation they moved to quash the subpoenas on the grounds that the materials sought were irrelevant to the grand jury's investigation.

🏛 RULE OF LAW

Where a subpoena is challenged on relevancy grounds, a motion to quash must be denied unless there is no reasonable possibility that the materials being sought will produce information relevant to the general subject of the grand jury's investigation.

FACTS: Three companies, including R. Enterprises, Inc., (D) that distributed adult and sexually oriented materials were served with subpoenas duces tecum in connection with a grand jury investigation into allegations of interstate transportation of obscene materials. The grand jury sought a variety of corporate books and records and, from one company, videotapes which had been shipped to retailers. All three companies moved to quash the subpoenas, arguing that the materials requested were irrelevant to the investigation. The district court denied the motions. The court of appeals, however, quashed the business records subpoenas issued to R. Enterprises (D) and one other company. The Government (P) appealed.

ISSUE: Where a subpoena is challenged on relevancy grounds, must a motion to quash be denied unless there is no reasonable possibility that the materials being sought will produce information relevant to the general subject of the grand jury's investigation?

HOLDING AND DECISION: (O'Connor, J.) Yes. Where a subpoena is challenged on relevancy grounds, a motion to quash must be denied unless there is no reasonable possibility that the materials being sought will produce information relevant to the general subject of the grand jury's investigation. The burden of showing unreasonableness must be on the recipient who seeks to avoid compliance. Where a challenging party does not know the general subject of the investigation, a court may be justified in requiring the Government (P) to reveal that information before requiring the party to carry its burden of persuasion. Here, however, there is no doubt that R. Enterprises (D) knew the subject of the grand jury investigation. Because the district court could have concluded on the facts that there was a reasonable possibility that the information requested was relevant to the investigation, it correctly denied the motions to quash. Thus, the judgment of the court of appeals is reversed.

CONCURRENCE: (Stevens, J.) The trial court needs only inquire into the relevance of subpoenaed materials after the moving party has initially demonstrated to the court that he has some valid objection to compliance. In the grand jury context, the law enforcement interest will almost always prevail, and the documents must be produced. However, it should not be suggested that the deferential relevance standard formulated here will govern decisions in every case, no matter how intrusive or burdensome the request.

▶ ANALYSIS

Many of the rules and restrictions that apply at a trial do not apply in grand jury proceedings. This is especially true of evidentiary restrictions. The Court rejected the use of the standard applied by the court of appeals, set out by the Supreme Court in *United States v. Nixon*, 418 U.S. 683 (1974), since that standard of relevancy, admissibility, and specificity was established in the trial context. In announcing the instant rule, the Court referred to Federal Rule of Criminal Procedure 17(c), which governs subpoenas duces tecum issued in federal criminal proceedings.

Quicknotes

GRAND JURY A group summoned to investigate, inform, and accuse persons of crimes when sufficient evidence exists to do so.

MOTION TO QUASH To vacate, annul, void.

SUBPOENA DUCES TECUM A subpoena compelling a witness to bring specified documents to court or to deposition.

Fisher v. United States

Income tax violator (D) v. Federal government (P)

425 U.S. 391 (1976).

NATURE OF CASE: Action to enforce an Internal Revenue Service summons.

FACT SUMMARY: The Internal Revenue Service sought to compel Fisher's (D) attorney to turn over accountant's worksheets, tax returns, and accountant-client correspondence Fisher (D) had obtained from his accountant and turned over to his attorney when it looked as if an income tax case against Fisher (D) might arise.

🏛 **RULE OF LAW**
The Fifth Amendment does not protect against compelled production of a taxpayer's papers if such production would not involve testimonial self-incrimination.

FACTS: The Internal Revenue Service (IRS) was investigating Fisher (D) for possible civil or criminal liability under the federal income tax laws. Thus, Fisher (D) went to his accountant and recovered the accountant's worksheets, and retained copies of the tax returns and the accountant's copies of correspondence between the accounting firm and Fisher (D). Fisher (D) turned them over to his attorney, but the IRS issued a summons directing the attorney to produce those documents. The attorney refused, and the Government (P) began enforcement actions. Fisher's (D) attorney basically argued that the Fifth Amendment's protection against self-incrimination precluded forced production of these documents.

ISSUE: Does the Fifth Amendment protect against compelled production of a taxpayer's papers if such production would not involve testimonial self-incrimination?

HOLDING AND DECISION: (White, J.) No. The Fifth Amendment protects against compelled production of a taxpayer's papers only if such production would involve testimonial self-incrimination, which it would not under the circumstances of this particular case. It protects against "compelled self-incrimination," not the disclosure of private information. The attorney-client privilege applies only to documents in the hands of an attorney that would have been privileged in the hands of the client by reason of the Fifth Amendment, and the documents sought would not have been privileged in Fisher's (D) hands under the Fifth Amendment. Thus, they must be produced.

CONCURRENCE: (Brennan, J.) While I agree the privilege against compelled self-incrimination did not protect the papers in this case, I feel the court's opinion does not adequately stress the protection secured by the privilege against compelled production of one's private books and papers.

CONCURRENCE: (Marshall, J.) The proper focus is, in cases like this, upon the private nature of the papers subpoenaed and not whether the act of production involves testimonial self-incrimination.

▶ *ANALYSIS*

One law review note takes a similar position to that expressed by Justice Marshall. It argues that this case and another similar one mean that "no zone of privacy now exists that the government cannot enter to take an individual's property for the purpose of obtaining criminal information." Note, 76 *Mich. L. Rev.* 184, 209-11 (1977).

■=■

Quicknotes

ATTORNEY-CLIENT PRIVILEGE A doctrine precluding the admission into evidence of confidential communications between an attorney and his client made in the course of obtaining professional assistance.

PRIVILEGE AGAINST SELF-INCRIMINATION A privilege guaranteed by the Fifth Amendment to the federal Constitution in a criminal proceeding for communications made by an accused and protecting an accused or witness from having to give testimony that may incriminate himself.

■=■

United States v. Hubbell

Federal government (P) v. Criminal (D)

530 U.S. 27 (2000).

NATURE OF CASE: Grant of writ of certiorari to review conditional plea agreement and court of appeals decision.

FACT SUMMARY: Pursuant to a subpoena and a grant of immunity from prosecution, Hubbell (D) produced documents to the Independent Counsel (P). A grand jury later returned an indictment against Hubbell (D) after the Government (P) presented evidence based on the same documents Hubbell (D) produced.

🏛 RULE OF LAW
The Fifth Amendment prevents the government from compelling a suspect to produce incriminating documents under a grant of immunity and then prosecuting that suspect using information gained from those incriminating documents.

FACTS: Hubbell (D) pled guilty and was sentenced to prison. In the plea agreement, Hubbell (D) agreed to provide information about matters related to the Whitewater investigation. While Hubbell (D) was serving his sentence, the Independent Counsel (P) served him (D) with a subpoena requesting the production of certain documents. Hubbell (D) refused, invoking his Fifth Amendment right against self-incrimination. The Government (P) obtained a court order directing Hubbell (D) to produce the documents under a grant of immunity. The documents were then produced. A second prosecution arose out of information gained from these documents. The district court dismissed the indictment, holding that the evidence was derived from the testimonial aspects of the immunized act of producing documents. The court of appeals vacated that judgment and remanded for the lower court to hold a hearing to establish the extent of the Government's (P) independent knowledge of the documents. On remand, the Government (P) entered into a conditional plea bargain with Hubbell (D) and the United States Supreme Court granted the Government's (P) request for a writ of certiorari.

ISSUE: Does the Fifth Amendment protect a witness from being compelled to disclose the existence of incriminating documents that the government is unable to describe with reasonable particularity and can the government prosecute that witness if he or she produces such documents under a grant of immunity?

HOLDING AND DECISION: (Stevens, J.) No. There is a difference between the use of compulsion to extort communications from a defendant and compelling a person to engage in conduct that may be incriminating.

Thus, criminal suspects may be compelled to provide blood or handwriting samples. This act of exhibiting physical characteristics is not the same as a sworn communication by a witness that relates either express or implied assertions of fact or belief. Thus, although a person may be compelled to provide documents, even though they may contain incriminating evidence, the Fifth Amendment protects a witness from prosecution using this incriminating information, whether it was derived directly or indirectly from the compelled production of documents. Hubbell's (D) action of producing hundreds of documents was a first step in a chain of evidence that led to his own prosecution. The documents were produced only under a grant of immunity and a district court order. Compliance under these circumstances cannot then be turned against him (D). The indictment against Hubbell (D) must be dismissed. Affirmed.

DISSENT: (Rehnquist, C.J.) The judgment of the court of appeals should be reversed in part, for the reasons given by Judge Williams in his dissenting opinion in that court, 167 F.3d 552 (C.A.D.C. 1999).

CONCURRENCE: (Thomas, J.) This decision involves the act-of-production doctrine that provides that those who are compelled to produce incriminating physical evidence pursuant to a subpoena may invoke the Fifth Amendment privilege as a bar to production when the act of producing the evidence would contain testimonial features. The Fifth Amendment may be broader than this doctrine, however, and protect against compelled production of any incriminating evidence. The Fifth Amendment provides that no person shall be compelled in any criminal case to be a witness against himself. Witness has been defined as "a person who provides testimony." This definition restricts the Fifth Amendment. Witness also means a person who gives or furnishes evidence. Therefore, a person who responds to a subpoena by producing documentation is also a witness. I remain open to a reconsideration of this definition.

▌ ANALYSIS

In its holding, the court of appeals likened the use of the contents of the produced documents to the use of data drawn from a forced blood draw or compelled handwriting exemplar. The difference, however, may be that the forced blood draws or the giving of handwriting samples are usually not done under grants of immunity.

■■■

Continued on next page.

Quicknotes

CERTIORARI A discretionary writ issued by a superior court to an inferior court in order to review the lower court's decisions; the Supreme Court's writ ordering such review.

IMMUNITY FROM PROSECUTION Statutory protection from prosecution afforded to a witness in exchange for his testimony.

CHAPTER 12

The Scope of the Exclusionary Rules

Quick Reference Rules of Law

Rakas v. Illinois

Auto passenger (D) v. State (P)

439 U.S. 128 (1978).

NATURE OF CASE: Appeal of criminal convictions.

FACT SUMMARY: Various defendants sought to suppress evidence in which they had no proprietary interest seized from a vehicle in which they were passengers.

> ## RULE OF LAW
> A person may not move to suppress evidence in which he had no proprietary interest or expectation of privacy.

FACTS: Police stopped a vehicle that matched the description of a getaway car. After a search, a shotgun and shotgun shells were found. These belonged to the owner of the vehicle, who was also the driver. Charged with various crimes [not specified in the casebook excerpt], the passengers (D) moved to suppress the gun and shells. This was denied, and the passengers (D) were convicted, along with the driver. The Illinois appellate courts affirmed. The United States Supreme Court accepted the passengers' (D) writ for certiorari.

ISSUE: May a person move to suppress evidence in which he has no proprietary interest or expectation of privacy?

HOLDING AND DECISION: (Rehnquist, J.) No. A person may not move to suppress evidence in which he has no proprietary interest or expectation of privacy. The rights secured by the Fourth Amendment are personal; a person cannot move to suppress evidence seized in violation of another's rights. For a person to have a personal interest in the evidence sufficient to confer a right to seek suppression, one of two things must occur. One, the movant may have some sort of ownership or possessory interest in the evidence; such a seizure would violate a personal interest. In the alternative, the party seeking suppression must demonstrate that the items were seized from some sort of area in which he had a legitimate expectation of privacy. Absent these circumstances, a person cannot make a Fourth Amendment claim. Here, the passengers (D) had no proprietary interest in the seized articles. Further, they had no expectation of privacy in the interior of another person's vehicle. Consequently, they suffered no Fourth Amendment violation. Affirmed.

DISSENT: (White, J.) The majority holds that the Fourth Amendment protects property, not people. The ruling undercuts the force of the exclusionary rule in its deterrence of bad-faith Fourth Amendment violations. The police are now invited to engage in patently unreasonable searches every time an automobile contains more than one person.

ANALYSIS

Prior to this case, the Court considered the type of analysis made here to be one of standing. The Court believed this to be an inappropriate focus on procedure. In the opinion, the Court takes pains to point out that it was dealing with substantive Fourth Amendment law, not procedure.

■=■

Quicknotes

EXPECTATION OF PRIVACY Requirement that in order to invoke the Fourth Amendment's protection against unreasonable searches and seizures, the individual must have a reasonable expectation of privacy in respect to the location searched or thing seized.

FOURTH AMENDMENT Provides that persons be secure as to their person and private belongings against unreasonable searches and seizures.

■=■

Minnesota v. Carter

State (P) v. Accused (D)

525 U.S. 83 (1998).

NATURE OF CASE: Appeal from an order holding that an illegal search had occurred.

FACT SUMMARY: When a police officer saw people packaging cocaine through a window and later arrested the occupants of the apartment, they alleged that their Fourth Amendment rights had been violated, and sought to have the evidence excluded.

🏛 **RULE OF LAW**
An overnight guest in a home may claim the protection of the Fourth Amendment, but one who is merely present with the consent of the householder may not.

FACTS: A confidential informant told the police that when walking by the window of a ground floor apartment, he had seen people putting a white powder into bags. The police officer looked through the same window and saw the men, and notified headquarters to prepare affidavits for a search warrant. When Carter (D) and Johns (D) left the building, they were arrested while in a motor vehicle, and cocaine was later found in the vehicle and in the apartment. Carter (D) and Johns (D) had never been in that apartment before and had been there for two hours to package the cocaine. Carter (D) and Johns (D) were convicted of state drug offenses. The trial court held that since they were only temporary out-of-state visitors, they could not challenge the legality of the government intrusion into the apartment, and that the police officer's observation through the window was not a "search" within the meaning of the Fourth Amendment. The Minnesota Supreme Court reversed, holding that Carter (D) and Johns (D) did have "standing" because they had a legitimate expectation of privacy in the invaded place, and that the officer's observation constituted an unreasonable "search" of the apartment. Minnesota (P) appealed.

ISSUE: If an overnight guest in a home may claim the protection of the Fourth Amendment, may one who is merely present with the consent of the householder also do so?

HOLDING AND DECISION: (Rehnquist, C.J.) No. An overnight guest in a home may claim the protection of the Fourth Amendment, but one who is merely present with the consent of the householder may not. The purely commercial nature of the transaction engaged in here, the relatively short time on the premises, and the lack of any previous connection between Carter (D) and the householder, all lead to the conclusion that their situation is closer to that of one simply permitted on the premises, rather than that of an overnight guest. Therefore, any search that may have occurred did not violate their Fourth Amendment rights. Reversed.

CONCURRENCE: (Scalia, J.) Whereas it is plausible to regard a person's overnight lodging as at least his "temporary" residence, it is entirely impossible to give that characterization to an apartment that he uses to package cocaine.

CONCURRENCE: (Kennedy, J.) Almost all social guests have a legitimate expectation of privacy, and hence protection against unreasonable searches, in their host's home. In this case, Carter (D) and Johns (D) have established nothing more than a fleeting and insubstantial connection with Thompson's home.

DISSENT: (Ginsberg, J.) The Court's decision undermines not only the security of short-term guests but also the security of the home resident herself. When a homeowner chooses to share the privacy of her home and her company with a short-term guest, both host and guest have exhibited an actual (subjective) expectation of privacy, and that expectation is one that our society is prepared to recognize as reasonable.

▶ *ANALYSIS*

Property used for commercial purposes is treated differently for Fourth Amendment purposes than residential property. While Carter (D) and Johns (D) were present in a "home," it was not their home. Only the Dissent argued that a short-term guest in a home should share his host's shelter against unreasonable searches and seizures. Since there was no violation of the Fourth Amendment, the evidence seized by the police was used against Carter (D) and Johns (D).

◼▬◼

Quicknotes

EXPECTATION OF PRIVACY Requirement that in order to invoke the Fourth Amendment's protection against unreasonable searches and seizures, the individual must have a reasonable expectation of privacy in respect to the location searched or thing seized.

FOURTH AMENDMENT Provides that persons be secure as to their person and private belongings against unreasonable searches and seizures.

Continued on next page.

SEARCH An inspection conducted in order to obtain evidence to be utilized for the prosecution of a crime.

SEIZURE The removal of property from one's possession due to unlawful activity or in satisfaction of a judgment entered by the court.

■═■

Wong Sun v. United States

Drug dealer (D) v. Federal government (P)

371 U.S. 471 (1963).

NATURE OF CASE: On certiorari from appellate court judgment upholding conviction for dealing in heroin.

FACT SUMMARY: Wong Sun's (D) co-defendant was unlawfully arrested and made incriminating statements to police.

🏛 **RULE OF LAW**
Statements made by a defendant directly as the result of lawless police conduct are inadmissible against the defendant.

FACTS: Federal agents went to the Chinese laundry operated by Wong Sun's (D) co-defendant, James Wah Toy. Toy told the agent that he was not open for business and to come back. The agent identified himself as a narcotics agent, and Toy ran into his living quarters at the back of the laundry. The agents broke open the door, followed Toy into his bedroom, and arrested him. A search of the premises revealed no narcotics. Toy told the agents that he and another man had been smoking the drug the night before, and told him where the other man lived. Toy and two others were indicted on drug charges, and his statements to the agents in his bedroom were admitted against him.

ISSUE: May statements made by a defendant directly as the result of lawless police conduct be admitted against the defendant?

HOLDING AND DECISION: (Brennan, J.) No. Statements made by a defendant directly as the result of lawless police conduct are inadmissible against the defendant. The court of appeals held that there was neither reasonable grounds nor probable cause for Toy's arrest. We have held that physical evidence obtained during an unlawful invasion must be excluded. Today we hold that verbal evidence that derives so immediately from an unlawful entry is no less the fruit of official illegality than the more tangible fruits of the unwarranted intrusion. There was no intervening independent act to purge the illegality of its taint; therefore the judgment of the court of appeals is reversed.

▶ *ANALYSIS*

Wong Sun (D) made a confession as well, but his confession took place when he voluntarily returned several days after being arraigned to make the statement. Given his independent intervening voluntary act, the Court held that the taint of Toy's unlawful arrest was purged as to Wong Sun's (D) confession.

Quicknotes

EXCLUSIONARY RULE A rule precluding the introduction at trial of evidence unlawfully obtained in violation of the federal constitutional safeguards against unreasonable searches and seizures.

Murray v. United States

Convicted drug possessor (D) v. Federal government (P)

487 U.S. 533 (1988).

NATURE OF CASE: Appeal from conviction for marijuana possession.

FACT SUMMARY: Agents saw marijuana when they illegally entered a warehouse, then obtained a search warrant without using any information discovered during the illegal entry, reentered the warehouse, and seized the marijuana that was used to convict Murray (D).

🏛 RULE OF LAW
Under the "independent source" doctrine, "evidence initially uncovered, but not seized, during an illegal search will not be suppressed if the police later obtain a search warrant which does not rely on any facts discovered during the illegal search, and then seize the evidence during a second search pursuant to the warrant."

FACTS: Federal agents saw Murray (D) and others driving vehicles in and out of a warehouse which the agents believed contained drugs. Two drivers were lawfully arrested and their vehicles were found to contain marijuana. The agents entered the warehouse illegally and saw bales of marijuana, but without seizing the drugs they left the warehouse and applied for a search warrant. The warrant was issued despite the application making no mention of any information discovered during the illegal entry of the warehouse. The agents reentered the warehouse with the warrant and seized marijuana and other evidence. At trial, Murray (D) moved to suppress the evidence as fruit of the illegal search, the motion was denied, and Murray (D) was convicted. The court of appeals affirmed, and Murray (D) appealed to the United States Supreme Court.

ISSUE: Will evidence initially uncovered, but not seized, during an illegal search be suppressed if the police later obtain a search warrant which does not rely on any facts discovered during the illegal search, and then seize the evidence during a second search pursuant to the warrant?

HOLDING AND DECISION: (Scalia, J.) No. Under the "independent source" doctrine, "evidence initially uncovered, but not seized, during an illegal search will not be suppressed if the police later obtain a search warrant which does not rely on any facts discovered during the illegal search, and then seize the evidence during a second search pursuant to the warrant." Society's interest in deterring unlawful police behavior and society's interest in having juries review all probative evidence of a crime are properly balanced by putting the police in the same position they would have been in but for their illegal conduct.

If, as here, police discover evidence illegally, but later acquire it through a lawful, independent source, suppressing the evidence would put the police in a worse position than they would have been absent the illegal conduct. This rule does not encourage officers to first search unlawfully and then get a warrant because if they already have probable cause they risk suppression of the evidence should they be unable to satisfy the independent source doctrine. If they do not already have probable cause, no information obtained during the illegal search can be used to establish probable cause, and, moreover, if a court does not believe that the officers would have sought a search warrant absent the illegal search, then the evidence will be suppressed. Judgment vacated and remanded for determination of whether the warrant-authorized search was an independent source of the challenged evidence.

DISSENT: (Marshall, J.) Under this ruling officers have an incentive to search illegally first, then seek a warrant. If the illegal search turns up no evidence, the officers have saved the substantial time and inconvenience of obtaining a search warrant. If the illegal search does turn up evidence, it is a simple matter to exclude from the warrant application any information gained from the illegal entry. The defendant then will be reduced to the nearly unwinnable argument that the officers are lying when they testify that they would have sought the warrant absent the illegal search.

▶ ANALYSIS

Closely related to the "independent source" doctrine, and another limit on "fruit of the poisonous tree" analysis, is the "inevitable discovery" doctrine announced in *Nix v. Williams*, 467 U.S. 431 (1984), which is discussed at length in *Murray*. In *Nix*, police learned the whereabouts of the victim's body by questioning the defendant in violation of his Sixth Amendment right to counsel. A search for the body had been under way, but was called off when the defendant revealed the body's location. The Supreme Court, using much the same reasoning it used in *Murray*, held that evidence concerning the body was admissible because it inevitably would have been discovered by the searchers without the unlawful interrogation.

■■■

Continued on next page.

Quicknotes

FRUIT OF POISONOUS TREE Doctrine that evidence obtained as a result of illegal procedures is tainted and is usually inadmissible at trial.

INDEPENDENT SOURCE Pertaining to evidence derived from another source, independent of the evidence obtained with a defective warrant.

■=■

Pretrial Release

Quick Reference Rules of Law

United States v. Salerno

Federal government (P) v. RICO violator (D)

481 U.S. 739 (1987).

NATURE OF CASE: Appeal from denial of bail.

FACT SUMMARY: Salerno (D) contended the Bail Reform Act violated his constitutional rights by allowing a denial of bail based on his potentially dangerous activities.

🏛 RULE OF LAW
The Bail Reform Act, allowing for the denial of bail upon a showing that the defendant presents a risk of danger, is constitutional.

FACTS: Salerno (D) was charged with violation of the Racketeer Influenced and Corrupt Organizations Act (RICO). Salerno (D) was denied bail after a hearing resulted in a finding that no release conditions would reasonably ensure the safety of any person and the community. Salerno (D) appealed, contending the Bail Reform Act allowing for such denial violated due process and excessive bail prohibitions, and was thus unconstitutional on its face. The court of appeals reversed, and the United States Supreme Court granted certiorari.

ISSUE: Is the Bail Reform Act constitutional?

HOLDING AND DECISION: (Rehnquist, C.J.) Yes. The Bail Reform Act is constitutional. Detention is not punishment. This Act is regulatory, not punitive. The regulatory goal was to protect the public and people close to the trial from potentially harmful individuals. Thus, the regulatory goal was directly related to its means. The Government's (P) interest in preserving safety may outweigh an individual's right to freedom. Thus, some circumstances exist wherein application of the Act is constitutional. Thus, it is not invalid on its face. Reversed.

DISSENT: (Marshall, J.) This statute punishes a person for the commission of a perceived future crime. Incarceration is punishment. Thus, the Act is unconstitutional.

DISSENT: (Stevens, J.) Pretrial commission for future dangerousness is unconstitutional.

▶ ANALYSIS

The traditional basis for determining if bail is available is whether there is a risk of flight. That is, whether there is a risk the defendant will not show up for court proceedings: the higher the possibility of flight—usually based on the severity of the crime—the higher the bail. A person is considered innocent until proven guilty; thus, pretrial detention walks a thin constitutional line.

Quicknotes

PROCEDURAL DUE PROCESS The constitutional mandate that if the state or federal government acts so as to deny a citizen of a life, liberty or property interest the individual is first entitled to notice and the right to be heard.

REGULATORY POWER Power granting authority pursuant to statute to a government agency or body to govern a particular area.

RICO Racketeer Influenced and Corrupt Organization laws; federal and state statutes enacted for the purpose of prosecuting organized crime.

The Decision Whether to Prosecute

Quick Reference Rules of Law

United States v. Armstrong

Federal government (P) v. Federal law violator (D)

517 U.S. 456 (1996).

NATURE OF CASE: Review of dismissal of an indictment for possession of crack cocaine and federal firearms offenses.

FACT SUMMARY: After charges were brought against him for violating federal drug laws, Armstrong (D), alleging that he was selected for prosecution because he was black, brought a motion for discovery in support of his selective-prosecution claim or for dismissal of the indictment.

🏛 RULE OF LAW
A criminal defendant bringing a selective-prosecution claim must make a credible showing of different treatment of similarly situated persons in order to obtain discovery in support of the claim.

FACTS: Armstrong (D) was arrested for violation of federal drug and firearms laws. Armstrong (D) alleged that he had been selected for prosecution because he was black, and filed a motion for dismissal of the charges or for discovery of Government (P) documents regarding their prosecution of similar defendants. The district court granted the discovery motion and dismissed the indictment when the Government (P) would not comply with discovery. The court of appeals reversed but then, upon hearing the case en banc, affirmed the district court's order of dismissal. The United States Supreme Court granted certiorari.

ISSUE: Must a criminal defendant bringing a selective-prosecution claim make a credible showing of different treatment of similarly situated persons in order to obtain discovery in support of the claim?

HOLDING AND DECISION: (Rehnquist, C.J.) Yes. A criminal defendant bringing a selective-prosecution claim must make a credible showing of different treatment of similarly situated persons in order to obtain discovery in support of the claim. Under Federal Rule of Civil Procedure 16, which controls discovery in a criminal case, a defendant must show some evidence of disparate treatment—similar to the requirement under equal protection claims. Here, Armstrong (D) did not make such a showing. Thus, the district court's dismissal of the case was improper. Reversed and remanded.

DISSENT: (Stevens, J.) While the defendant did not make a strong enough showing to merit discovery, the district court did not abuse its discretion in requiring some response from the United States (P) Attorney's Office.

▶ ANALYSIS
The Court notes that the test for obtaining discovery for a selective-prosecution claim should be similar to that of an equal protection claim. Recall that to successfully pursue an equal protection claim, the claimant must show both a discriminatory effect and a discriminatory purpose. In order to show a discriminatory effect, the claimant must also show that similarly situated persons (but of a different race or religion) were not prosecuted. From this equal protection language, the Court developed the test in this case.

■■■

Quicknotes

CERTIORARI A discretionary writ issued by a superior court to an inferior court in order to review the lower court's decisions; the Supreme Court's writ ordering such review.

DISCOVERY Pretrial procedure during which one party makes certain information available to the other.

DISCRIMINATORY IMPACT The effect of an action that affects one group of persons more significantly than another; insufficient to prove discriminatory intent on its own.

DISCRIMINATORY PURPOSE Intent to discriminate; must be shown to establish an Equal Protection violation.

EN BANC The hearing of a matter by all the judges of the court, rather than only the necessary quorum.

EQUAL PROTECTION A constitutional guarantee that no person shall be denied the same protection of the laws enjoyed by other persons in similar life circumstances.

■■■

CHAPTER 15

The Preliminary Hearing

Quick Reference Rules of Law

State v. Clark

State (P) v. Alleged forgers (D)

Utah Sup. Ct., 20 P.3d 300 (2001).

NATURE OF CASE: State's appeal from the quashing of a bindover for trial.

FACT SUMMARY: When Clark (D) and Smith (D) were bound over for trial, the district court quashed the binding over.

RULE OF LAW
To support a binding over for trial, the prosecution must present sufficient evidence only to support a reasonable belief that an offense has been committed and that the defendant committed it.

FACTS: Clark (D) and Smith (D) were charged with forgery and bound over for trial by a magistrate. The binding over was quashed by the district court on grounds the state failed to meet its evidentiary burden at the preliminary hearing, and the State (P) appealed.

ISSUE: To support a binding over for trial, must the prosecution present sufficient evidence only to support a reasonable belief that an offense has been committed and that the defendant committed it?

HOLDING AND DECISION: (Durrant, J.) Yes. To support a binding over for trial, the prosecution must present sufficient evidence only to support a reasonable belief that an offense has been committed and that the defendant committed it. Unlike a motion for a directed verdict, this evidence need not be capable of supporting a finding of guilt beyond a reasonable doubt. Instead, the quantum of evidence necessary to support a binding over is less than that necessary to survive a directed verdict motion. Specifically, there is no principled basis for attempting to maintain a distinction between the arrest warrant probable cause standard and the preliminary hearing probable cause standard. The "reasonable belief" standard has the advantage of being more easily understood while still allowing magistrates to fulfill the primary purpose of the preliminary hearing, namely, ferreting out groundless and improvident prosecutions. Here, the district court, by dismissing the forgery charges because the State (P) failed to demonstrate the defendants had acted with the requisite intent, wrongly applied the directed verdict standard. Viewed in the light most favorable to the prosecution, the facts presented here were sufficient to meet the reasonable belief standard since the facts revealed that the defendants attempted to cash a forged check at local banks mere hours after the check was reported stolen. When cashiers told defendants they were seeking approval to cash the check, defendants abandoned the forged check and left the bank. Reversed.

▌ ANALYSIS

As the *Clark* decision notes, notwithstanding that the evidence to a binding over will be viewed in the light most favorable to the prosecution, to prevail at a preliminary hearing the prosecution must still produce believable evidence of all the elements of the crime charged.

■=■

Quicknotes

BINDING OVER The imprisonment of a criminal defendant in order to guarantee the defendant's appearance at a criminal trial.

DIRECTED VERDICT A verdict ordered by the court in a jury trial.

PROBABLE CAUSE A reasonable basis for believing that a crime has been committed.

QUANTUM An essential amount; a modicum of the required degree.

REASONABLE BELIEF A reasonable basis for believing that a crime is being or has been committed.

REASONABLE DOUBT Enough doubt on the part of jurors to acquit a defendant based on the absence of evidence.

■=■

Grand Jury Review

Quick Reference Rules of Law

Costello v. United States

Grand jury indictee (D) v. Federal government (P)

350 U.S. 359 (1956).

NATURE OF CASE: Petition for certiorari after conviction of income tax invasion.

FACT SUMMARY: Three investigating officers were the only witnesses before the grand jury who indicted Costello (D). They had no firsthand knowledge of the transactions upon which their computations were based. Hence, the indictment was based solely on hearsay.

🏛 RULE OF LAW
An indictment returned by a legally constituted and unbiased grand jury, if valid on its face, is enough to call for trial of the charge on the merits, regardless of the fact that the only evidence before the grand jury is hearsay.

FACTS: At Costello's (D) trial, the Government (P) called 144 witnesses and introduced 368 exhibits, all of which related to business transactions and expenditures by the Costellos (D). Three government agents, whose investigations had produced the evidence used against Costello (D) at trial, summarized the evidence already introduced, and introduced computations showing, if correct, that the Costellos (D) had received far greater income than they had reported. The three agents were the only witnesses before the grand jury. Costello (D) moved to dismiss the indictment on the ground that the only evidence before the grand jury was hearsay since the officers had no firsthand knowledge of the transactions upon which their computations were based.

ISSUE: May a defendant be required to stand trial and a conviction be sustained where only hearsay evidence was presented to the grand jury?

HOLDING AND DECISION: (Black, J.) Yes. A defendant may be required to stand trial and a conviction may be sustained where only hearsay evidence was presented to the grand jury. Neither the Fifth Amendment nor any other constitutional provision prescribes the kind of evidence upon which grand juries must act. The grand jury convenes as a body of lay people, free from technical rules. If indictments could be challenged on the ground that there was inadequate or incompetent evidence before the grand jury, a great delay would result, since before a trial on the merits, an accused could insist on a kind of preliminary trial to determine the adequacy and competency of the evidence before the grand jury. Perhaps most important, such a change would run as a body not hampered by rigid procedural or evidential rules. An indictment returned by a legally constituted and unbiased grand jury, if valid on its face, is enough to call for trial of the charge of the merits. The Fifth Amendment requires nothing more. Costello's (D) conviction is affirmed.

CONCURRENCE: (Burton, J.) In this case, substantial and rationally persuasive evidence apparently was presented to the grand jury. Hence, the indictment should be sustained. However, if it is shown that the grand jury had before it no such evidence upon which to base its indictment, that indictment should be quashed.

▶ ANALYSIS

Depending upon its scope, *Costello* may (or may not) reflect the majority position among those states that regularly prosecute by indictment. In many states, courts will dismiss an indictment upon a showing that there was no sworn witness or legal documentary evidence before the grand jury. In several, courts have held an indictment is also subject to attack where based solely on the testimony of an incompetent witness. Most indictment states, however, will go no further. An indictment will not be dismissed even if issued solely upon hearsay testimony, and in some jurisdictions, indictments regularly are based entirely upon a summary of investigative reports presented by a single officer or the prosecuting attorney.

■=■

Quicknotes

GRAND JURY A group summoned to investigate, inform, and accuse persons of crimes when sufficient evidence exists to do so.

HEARSAY An out-of-court statement made by a person other than the witness testifying at trial that is offered in order to prove the truth of the matter asserted.

TRIAL ON THE MERITS A judicial determination of the facts or issues brought before it pursuant to its jurisdictional authorities.

■=■

United States v. Williams

Federal government (P) v. Federal statute violator (D)

504 U.S. 36 (1992).

NATURE OF CASE: Appeal from dismissal of an indictment.

FACT SUMMARY: The court of appeals, agreeing with the district court, dismissed an indictment against Williams (D) since the Government (P) failed to disclose substantial exculpatory evidence in its possession to the grand jury.

> 🏛 **RULE OF LAW**
> A federal court may not dismiss an otherwise valid indictment for failure of the prosecution to disclose substantial exculpatory evidence to the grand jury.

FACTS: After a federal grand jury indicted Williams (D) for violating a federal statute, the Tenth Circuit Court of Appeals, agreeing with the district court, granted Williams's (D) motion to dismiss the indictment on the grounds that the Government (P) failed to disclose to the grand jury substantial exculpatory evidence in its possession. The Government (P) appealed.

ISSUE: May a federal court dismiss an otherwise valid indictment for failure of the prosecution to disclose substantial exculpatory evidence to the grand jury?

HOLDING AND DECISION: (Scalia, J.) No. A federal court may not dismiss an otherwise valid indictment for failure of the prosecution to disclose substantial exculpatory evidence to the grand jury. Federal courts "may, within limits, formulate procedural rules not specifically required by the Constitution or . . . Congress" which deal strictly with their power to control their "own" procedures [see *U.S. v. Hasting*, 461 U.S. 499, 505 (1983)]. Moreover, this "supervisory power" may be used in the grand jury context, but only to proscribe misconduct before the grand jury, which amounts to a violation of one of those carefully drafted and approved rules that ensure the integrity of the grand jury's functions. In the instant case, since failure of the Government (P) to disclose substantial exculpatory evidence before the grand jury does not amount to a violation of one of the above rules, its indictment may not be dismissed. Reversed and remanded.

DISSENT: (Stevens, J.) A United States Attorney is the representative not of an ordinary party but of a sovereign whose obligation to govern impartially is compelling and whose interest in a criminal prosecution is not that it shall win a case, but that justice shall be done. It is as much such attorney's duty to refrain from improper methods calculated to produce a wrongful conviction as it is to use every legitimate means to bring about a just one. A federal prosecutor has this exact same duty to protect fundamental fairness when presenting evidence to a grand jury.

▶ *ANALYSIS*

In *U.S. v. John Doe, Inc. I*, 481 U.S. 102 (1987), the Supreme Court held that a government attorney who was involved in a grand jury proceeding may use information obtained during that proceeding in a subsequent civil proceeding in which he is involved, without a disclosure order under Rule 6(e). The Court also upheld a disclosure order. Discussing the requirement of "particularized need," it said generally that "the question that must be asked is whether the public benefits of the disclosure . . . outweigh the dangers created by the limited disclosure requested." 481 U.S. 102, 113.

Quicknotes

EXCULPATORY EVIDENCE A statement or other evidence which tends to excuse, justify, or absolve the defendant from alleged fault or guilt.

GRAND JURY A group summoned to investigate, inform, and accuse persons of crimes when sufficient evidence exists to do so.

CHAPTER 17

The Charging Instrument

Quick Reference Rules of Law

Russell v. United States

Grand jury indictee (D) v. Federal government (P)

369 U.S. 749 (1962).

NATURE OF CASE: Appeal from conviction under federal law of refusing to answer questions when summoned before a congressional subcommittee.

FACT SUMMARY: A grand jury indictment failed to identify the subject under congressional inquiry at the time Russell (D), a witness, was interrogated.

RULE OF LAW
The sufficiency of an indictment is to be measured by two criteria: (1) whether the indictment contains the elements of the offense intended to be charged so as to sufficiently apprise the defendant of what he must be prepared to defend against, and (2) in case any other proceedings are taken against him for a second offense, whether the record shows with accuracy to what extent he may plead a former conviction or acquittal.

FACTS: Russell (D) and other witnesses were indicted by a grand jury for refusing to answer certain questions when summoned before a congressional subcommittee. The indictments stated only that the questions to which answers were refused "were pertinent to the question then under inquiry" by the subcommittee. Motions to quash the indictments, on the ground they failed to state the subject under investigation, were denied. Russell (D) and the other defendants were convicted under a federal law that stated that prosecutions under it could be initiated only by grand jury indictment.

ISSUE: Where witnesses have been indicted, under federal law, for failure to answer questions when summoned by a congressional investigatory body, must the indictment identify the subject under inquiry at the time of the defendant's alleged default or refusal to answer?

HOLDING AND DECISION: (Stewart, J.) Yes. By invoking the aid of the federal courts in dealing with reluctant witnesses, Congress conferred upon the courts the duty to provide individuals prosecuted for this statutory offense every safeguard accorded other types of criminal defendants. There can be criminality here only if: (1) the witness refused to answer a question that pertained to the subject then under investigation by the body; and (2) the pleadings so showed this. Although convictions will not be overturned because of minor, technical deficiencies in an indictment that does not prejudice the accused, care must still be taken. The indictments involved here satisfied the requirement that Russell (D) and the other defendants would not be re-indicted for the same offense since the precise questions asked them were given. However, the indictments are fatally defective for failing to sufficiently apprise them of what they must be prepared to meet. An indictment must do more than simply repeat the language of the criminal statute. It must, in precise terms, inform the accused with reasonable certainty, of the nature of the accusation against him. A corollary purpose of requiring specificity in the indictment is to inform a court of the facts alleged so as to enable it to decide whether they are sufficient in law to suppose a conviction. A court, or prosecutor, should not have to guess what was in the mind of the grand jury at the time it returned the indictment. Reversed.

ANALYSIS

It has been generally held that a charging instrument indictment, or information must fulfill three functions: (1) notice, to enable the defendant to adequately mount a defense; (2) protection against additional prosecutions stemming from the same defense (double jeopardy); and (3) enable a court to judge whether the government's case is based upon a valid interpretation of the offense charged (judicial review). A court satisfies the judicial review function when it determines that the charging instrument sets out the essential elements of the offense. When the instrument has been found to be defective in not setting out all the requisite elements, the ruling is said to be based on the notice function. Russell suggests, perhaps, a fourth function—that the defendant not be tried upon a theory or evidence different than the one embraced in the charging instrument.

Quicknotes

GRAND JURY A group summoned to investigate, inform, and accuse persons of crimes when sufficient evidence exists to do so.

INDICTMENT A formal written accusation made by the prosecution to the grand jury under oath, charging an individual with a criminal offense.

MOTION TO QUASH To vacate, annul, void.

United States v. Resendiz-Ponce

Federal government (P) v. Illegal alien (D)

549 U.S. 102 (2007).

NATURE OF CASE: Appeal from reversal of conviction of illegally attempting to reenter the United States.

FACT SUMMARY: The United States (P) contended that Resendiz-Ponce's (D) conviction for illegally reentering the country should not have been overturned merely because his indictment failed to allege a specific overt act that he committed in seeking reentry, and that such omission was subject to harmless-error review.

> ## 🏛 RULE OF LAW
> An indictment for an "attempt" crime is not constitutionally defective if it does not specify an overt act that the defendant has taken in furtherance of the defendant's criminal goal.

FACTS: Resendiz-Ponce (D), a Mexican citizen, was charged with the crime of attempting to reenter the United States, in violation of 18 U.S.C. § 1326, after having been twice deported. The district court denied his motion to have the indictment dismissed because it did not allege a specific overt act that he committed in seeking reentry, which he contended was an essential element of the crime of attempting to reenter the United States after deportation. The Government (P) did not disagree that an individual cannot be guilty of attempted reentry under § 1326(a) unless he commits an overt act qualifying as a substantial step toward completing his goal or that an indictment must set forth each element of the crime that it charges. Instead, it contended that the indictment that actually issued implicitly alleged that Resendiz-Ponce (D) engaged in the necessary overt act by alleging that he "attempted" to enter the country. In reversing, the court of appeals held that the indictment's omission of an overt act was a fatal flaw not subject to harmless-error review. The United States Supreme Court granted certiorari.

ISSUE: Is an indictment for an "attempt" crime constitutionally defective if it does not specify an overt act that the defendant has taken in furtherance of the defendant's criminal goal?

HOLDING AND DECISION: (Stevens, J.) No. An indictment for an "attempt" crime is not constitutionally defective if it does not specify an overt act that the defendant has taken in furtherance of the defendant's criminal goal. Resendiz-Ponce's (D) indictment was not defective, and, therefore, the harmless-error issue does not have to be reached. First, not only does "attempt" as used in common parlance connote action rather than mere

intent, but, more importantly, as used in the law for centuries, it encompasses both the overt act and intent elements. Thus, an indictment alleging attempted reentry under § 1326(a) need not specifically allege a particular overt act or any other component part of the offense. It was enough for the indictment to point to the relevant criminal statute and allege that Resendiz-Ponce (D) "intentionally attempted to enter the United States. . . ." An indictment has two constitutional requirements: First, it must contain the elements of the offense charged and fairly inform a defendant of the charge against which he must defend, and, second, it must enable him to plead an acquittal or conviction in bar of future prosecutions for the same offense. Here, the use of the word "attempt," coupled with the specification of the time and place of the alleged reentry, satisfied both. Resendiz-Ponce's (D) argument that the indictment would have been sufficient only if it alleged any of three overt acts performed during his attempted reentry—that he walked into an inspection area; that he presented a misleading identification card; or that he lied to an inspector—is rejected because individually and cumulatively those acts were all part of a single course of conduct constituting "attempt" of reentry. Although it is true that some crimes must be charged with greater specificity than an indictment parroting a federal criminal statute's language, this is not one of those crimes. Therefore, there was no infirmity in the present indictment, which complied with Fed. R. Crim. P. 7(c)(1), which provides that an indictment "must be a plain, concise, and definite written statement of the essential facts constituting the offense charged." Reversed and remanded.

DISSENT: (Scalia, J.) Because an "attempt" to commit a crime involves both intent and an overt act of some kind toward commission of the crime, it logically follows that when the Government (P) indicts for attempt to commit a crime, it must allege both the intent and the action taken. Otherwise, the rule that an indictment must allege all the elements of the charged crime would be violated—as it was here. It is not enough, as the majority indicates, to say that in "common parlance" attempt connotes both intent and action. That is irrelevant, since all elements of a crime must be set forth in an indictment, whether or not they are somehow connoted. Moreover, the majority is probably incorrect that "attempt" conveys with precision what conviction of that crime requires. A jury could misinterpret "attempt" to only require intent plus a small step of action, versus the significant step required by law. The majority's

Continued on next page.

sweeping statement that "attempt" has had a uniform meaning in law for centuries is likewise irrelevant and most likely incorrect because the definition of "attempt" has not been consistent through the ages, and in any event, regardless of how static the elements of a crime have remained, this has not excused the inclusion of all the elements of that crime in an indictment. If the majority's reasoning was followed with respect to all crimes, it would lead to a revolution in the requirements of an indictment. Also, as a matter of logic, attempt is a lesser included crime of a completed crime. Therefore, contrary to the majority's assertion, it is not illogical to dismiss an indictment charging "attempt" because it fails to allege an overt act even though a defendant indicted only for a completed offense can be convicted of attempt without the indictment's ever mentioning an overt act. Attempt does not need to be separately charged when it is part of a charge of a completed offense, but all its elements must be specified when it alone is being charged. Finally, the Government (P) presented no evidence that mere recitation of the word "attempt" in attempt indictments has been the traditional practice. Because the indictment was deficient that goes to the next issued that was raised but avoided by the majority—whether such deficiency was structural error as held by the court of appeals; in short, it was.

▌ *ANALYSIS*

Fed. R. Crim. P. 31(c) provides that a defendant may be found guilty of "an attempt to commit the offense charged; or . . . an attempt to commit an offense necessarily included in the offense charged, if the attempt is an offense in its own right." Fed. R. Crim. P. 31(c)(2)-(3). The majority found that this rule supported its position that if a defendant indicted only for a completed offense can be convicted of attempt under Rule 31(c) without the indictment ever mentioning an overt act, it would be illogical to dismiss an indictment charging "attempt" because it fails to allege such an act. Justice Scalia clearly disagreed.

■══■

Quicknotes

ATTEMPT An effort or try, combined with the act falling short of the goal intended.

HARMLESS ERROR An error taking place during trial, that does not require the reviewing court to overturn or modify the trial court's judgment in that it did not affect the appellant's substantial rights or the disposition of the action.

INTENT The state of mind that exists when one's purpose is to commit a criminal act.

OVERT ACT An open act evidencing an intention to commit a crime.

■══■

CHAPTER 18

The Location of the Prosecution

Quick Reference Rules of Law

United States v. Rodriguez-Moreno

Federal government (P) v. Kidnapper (D)

526 U.S. 275 (1999).

NATURE OF CASE: Appeal from conviction of kidnapping and carrying a firearm during and in relation to a crime of violence under 18 U.S.C. § 924(c)(1).

FACT SUMMARY: The Government (P) appealed from the reversal of a kidnapping conviction by the court of appeals on the basis that § 924(c)(1) was not violated since the defendant only used a firearm in Maryland and the kidnapping occurred in New Jersey.

RULE OF LAW
Venue in a prosecution for using or carrying a firearm during and in relation to any crime of violence in violation of 18 U.S.C. § 924(c)(1) is proper in any district in which the crime was committed, even if the firearm was only carried in a single district.

FACTS: During a drug transaction taking place in Houston, a New York drug dealer stole 30 kilograms of Texas drug distributor's cocaine. The distributor hired Rodriguez-Moreno (D) and others to find the dealer and to hold captive the middleman in the transaction, Avendano. Rodriguez-Moreno (D) and his codefendants were tried jointly and charged with conspiring to kidnap Avendano, kidnapping Avendano, and using a firearm in relation to kidnapping Avendano, in violation of 18 U.S.C. § 924(c)(1). Rodriguez-Moreno (D) moved to dismiss for lack of venue, contending that venue was proper only in Maryland, the only place where the Government (P) had proved that he actually used the gun. The district court denied the motion and convicted defendants and the court of appeals reversed.

ISSUE: Is venue in a prosecution for using or carrying a firearm during and in relation to any crime of violence in violation of 18 U.S.C. § 924(c)(1) proper in any district in which the crime was committed, even if the firearm was only carried in a single district?

HOLDING AND DECISION: (Thomas, J.) Yes. Venue in a prosecution for using or carrying a firearm during and in relation to any crime of violence in violation of 18 U.S.C. § 924(c)(1) is proper in any district in which the crime was committed, even if the firearm was only carried in a single district. Here the statute provides that "Whoever, during and in relation to any crime of violence ... for which he may be prosecuted in a court of the United States, uses or carries a firearm, shall, in addition to the punishment provided for such crime of violence ... be sentenced to imprisonment for five years. ..." The court of appeals looked to the verbs of the statute to determine the nature of the substantive offense. While the verb test has

value as an investigative tool, it cannot be applied to the exclusion of other relevant statutory language. To prove the § 924(c)(1) violation the Government (P) was required to show the defendants used a firearm, committed all acts necessary to be subject to punishment for kidnapping in a court of the United States, and used the gun "during and in relation to" the kidnapping of Avendano. Defendants argue that for venue purposes the New Jersey kidnapping was irrelevant to the Maryland firearm crime since a gun was not used during the New Jersey crime. Several circuits have defined kidnapping as a unitary crime that once began does not end until the victim is free. Section 924(c)(1) does not define a "point-in-time" offense when a firearm is used during and in relation to a continuing crime of violence. Reversed.

DISSENT: (Scalia, J.) The issue here is whether the defendant's alleged act of using a firearm during and in relation to a kidnapping occurred; since it occurred only in Maryland, then venue is only proper there.

ANALYSIS

"The locus delicti of the charged offense must be determined from the nature of the crime alleged and the location of the acts constituting the crime." *United States v. Cabrales*, 524 U.S. 1 (1998). First, the court must identify the conduct.

■=■

Quicknotes

VENUE The specific geographic location over which a court has jurisdiction to hear a suit.

■=■

CHAPTER 19

Joinder and Severance

Quick Reference Rules of Law

People v. Merriman

State (P) v. Convicted murderer (D)

Cal. Sup. Ct., 60 Cal. 4th 1, 177 Cal. Rptr. 3d 1, 332 P.3d 1187 (2014).

NATURE OF CASE: Appeal from conviction for murder and sexual offenses.

FACT SUMMARY: Merriman (D) was charged with sexual assault and murder among many other charges. At trial Merriman (D) sought to sever the murder charge from all other charges, but the trial court denied his motion. Merriman (D) claims the denial was an abuse of discretion.

RULE OF LAW

Joinder of offenses in the same class or connected in the commission of the crime is not an abuse of discretion unless there is a reasonable probability the jury was influenced by the joinder in its verdict of guilt.

FACTS: The grand jury indicted Merriman (D) on 25 counts, including sexual offenses against Robyn G., Billie B. and Katrina, murder of Katrina, resisting arrest, and possessing a controlled substance. Merriman (D) later was indicted on five additional charges related to witness tampering from the first grand jury investigation. The prosecution filed its pretrial motion to consolidate the two indictments and the trial court granted the motion. The defense filed its pretrial motion to sever the murder count from all other charges. The trial court severed trial on drug- and firearm-possession charges and with five charges related to Merriman (D) being under the influence. The rest of the charges remained joined with the murder charge for trial. [Merriman (D) filed for post-conviction relief.]

ISSUE: Is joinder of offenses in the same class or connected in the commission of the crime an abuse of discretion?

HOLDING AND DECISION: (Cantil-Sakauye, C.J.) No. Joinder of offenses in the same class or connected in the commission of the crime is not an abuse of discretion unless there is a reasonable probability the jury was influenced by the joinder in its verdict of guilt. Section 954 authorizes joinder of different offenses if they were connected in their commission or if they are in the same class of offenses. Here, the joinder meets the statutory requirements because the sexual offenses and murder charges are assaultive crimes and in the same class. Evading arrest and witness tampering are connected with defendant's wish to avoid criminal liability for Katrina's murder. The drug offense occurred at the time of the commission. Merriman (D) argues the trial court had discretion to sever the charges even if joinder was statutorily appropriate. The evidence, however, would have been admissible at a separate murder trial, so the

trial court was justified in refusing to sever. The sexual assaults would have been admissible pursuant to Evidence Code § 1108 to show propensity. The probative value of the assaults was substantial. The prejudicial value did not outweigh the probative value. While the sexual assaults were demeaning, they paled in comparison to the horrendous nature of the murder. The fact Merriman (D) had not yet been convicted of the sexual assaults against Robyn G. and Bille B. does not tip the scales in his favor. The circumstances surrounding Merriman's (D) flight from the police and subsequent standoff in a bystander's home demonstrates consciousness of guilt for Katrina's murder. The defense can challenge the inference the evidence suggests but offering other reasons for fleeing from the police does not require the trial court to sever the resisting arrest counts from the murder count. The crime allegedly was committed for the benefit of a criminal street gang and the witness tampering again shows consciousness of guilt. Merriman (D) argues the evidence offered in support of the witness tampering counts included highly inflammatory evidence of his white supremacist gang membership and perverse relationship with his mother. Those facts were developed at trial though and the trial court could not have abused its discretion in failing to sever at pretrial. The court considers whether there was "gross unfairness" as a result of joinder. The crimes would have been admissible at a separate murder trial and the jury was instructed to consider each crime separately. There is no reasonable probability that the joinder of counts tainted the jury's verdicts in this case.

ANALYSIS

Joinder of like crimes and related offenses is a more efficient method of trial, but it does leave open a question of prejudice to the accused. The greater number of charges and the descriptions of multiple crimes may persuade, even unconsciously, a jury to find guilt for at least one of the charges whereas separate trials could have very different outcomes.

■═■

Quicknotes

ABUSE OF DISCRETION A determination by an appellate court that a lower court's decision was based on an error of law.

JOINDER The joining of claims or parties in one lawsuit.

PROBATIVE Tending to establish proof.

■═■

United States v. Dixon

Federal government (P) v. Double jeopardy appellant (D)

509 U.S. 688 (1993).

NATURE OF CASE: Consolidated appeals cases from ruling barring subsequent criminal prosecution in one and allowing it in the other.

FACT SUMMARY: Both Dixon (D) and Foster (D), who were convicted of criminal contempt in connection with alleged underlying criminal conduct, argued that the Double Jeopardy Clause barred any subsequent criminal prosecution on charges arising out of the same criminal conduct.

🏛 RULE OF LAW
The Double Jeopardy Clause does not permit subsequent prosecution of an offense that has already been the basis of criminal contempt proceedings.

FACTS: Dixon (D) had been arrested for second-degree murder. The form by which he was released on bond specified that he was not to commit "any criminal offense," and warned that any violation of the conditions of release would subject him "to revocation of release, an order of detention, and prosecution for contempt of court." While awaiting trial, Dixon (D) was arrested and indicted for possession of cocaine with intent to distribute. He was found guilty of criminal contempt and sentenced to 180 days in jail. The trial court later granted Dixon's (D) motion to dismiss the cocaine indictment on double jeopardy grounds. Foster (D) violated a civil protection order (CPO), requiring that he not "molest, assault, or in any manner threaten or physically abuse" his wife. He was held in contempt for numerous violations of the CPO. The court found Foster (D) guilty beyond a reasonable doubt of four counts of criminal contempt, acquitted him on other counts, and sentenced him to 600 days imprisonment. The U.S. Attorney's office later obtained an indictment charging Foster (D) with simple assault, threatening to injure another, and assault with intent to kill. Foster (D) moved to dismiss, claiming a double jeopardy bar to all counts. The trial court denied the double jeopardy claim. The Government (P) appealed in *Dixon*, while Foster (D) appealed the trial court's denial of his motion. After consolidating the two cases, the court of appeals ruled that both subsequent prosecutions were barred by the Double Jeopardy Clause. The Government (P) appealed.

ISSUE: Does the Double Jeopardy Clause permit subsequent prosecution of an offense that has already been the basis of criminal contempt proceedings?

HOLDING AND DECISION: (Scalia, J.) No. The Double Jeopardy Clause does not permit subsequent prosecution of an offense that has already been the basis of criminal contempt proceedings. This protection applies both to successive punishments and to successive prosecutions for the same criminal offense. This Court has concluded that where the two offenses for which the defendant is punished or tried cannot survive the "same-elements" test, the double jeopardy bar applies. The same-elements test inquires whether each offense contains only elements contained in the other; if so, they are the "same offense" and double jeopardy bars additional punishment and successive prosecution. If not, they are not the same offense, and there is no double jeopardy bar. Dixon's (D) cocaine possession, although an offense under the D.C. Code, was not an offense under the contempt statute until a judge incorporated the statutory drug offense into his release order. Here, where the contempt sanction was imposed for violating the order through commission of the incorporated drug offense, the later attempt to prosecute Dixon (D) for the drug offense resembles the double jeopardy situation. Criminal contempt, at least in its non-summary form, "is a crime in every fundamental respect." Because Dixon's (D) drug offense did not include any element not contained in his previous contempt offense, his subsequent prosecution violated the double jeopardy clause. The foregoing analysis obviously applies to the indictment against charging Foster (D), with assault, based on the same event that was the subject of his prior contempt conviction for violating the provision of the CPO forbidding him to commit simple assault. Thus, the subsequent prosecution for assault is barred. However, the remaining four counts of assault with intent to kill and threats to injure or kidnap are not barred. Each of those offenses contained a separate element, and the test for double jeopardy was not met. Thus, Dixon's (D) subsequent prosecution for cocaine possession, as well as Foster's (D) subsequent prosecution for simple assault violate the Double Jeopardy Clause and are barred. Affirmed [as to *Dixon*]. Affirmed in part; reversed in part [as to *Foster*].

CONCURRENCE AND DISSENT: (Rehnquist, C.J.) A defendant who is guilty of possession with intent to distribute cocaine or of assault has not necessarily satisfied any statutory element of criminal contempt. Nor can it be said that a defendant who is held in criminal contempt has necessarily satisfied any element of those substantive crimes. The offenses for which Dixon (D) and Foster (D) were prosecuted in this case cannot be analogized to greater and lesser included offenses; hence, they are separate and distinct for double jeopardy purposes.

Continued on next page.

CONCURRENCE AND DISSENT: (White, J.)
The Double Jeopardy Clause bars prosecution for an offense if the defendant already has been held in contempt for its commission. Thus, the subsequent prosecutions in both Dixon (D) and Foster (D) were impermissible as to all counts.

CONCURRENCE AND DISSENT: (Souter, J.)
Both the prosecution of Dixon (D) and the prosecution of Foster (D) on all counts against him should be barred by the Double Jeopardy Clause.

ANALYSIS

The same-elements test was first enunciated by the court in *Blockburger v. United States*, 284 U.S. 299 (1932), and is commonly referred to as the *Blockburger* test. In arriving at its ruling in the instant case, the majority overruled its recent decision in *Grady v. Corbin*, 495 U.S. 508 (1990), which held that in addition to passing the *Blockburger* test, a subsequent prosecution must satisfy a "same-conduct" test to avoid the double jeopardy bar. The *Grady* test provided that if, to establish an essential element of an offense charged in that prosecution, the government would prove conduct that constituted an offense for which the defendant had already been prosecuted, a second prosecution may not be had. In the majority's view, *Grady* was not only wrong in principle, but had already proved inconsistent in application.

Quicknotes

CONTEMPT An act of omission that interferes with a court's proper administration of justice.

DOUBLE JEOPARDY A prohibition against a second prosecution for the same offense after an acquittal or conviction for that offense in a prior proceeding or against multiple punishments for the same offense.

Ashe v. Swenson

Robbery convict (D) v. Court (P)

397 U.S. 436 (1970).

NATURE OF CASE: Petition for writ of habeas corpus after conviction of robbery.

FACT SUMMARY: Three or four men robbed six men and stole one of the victims' cars. Each alleged robber was charged with seven separate offenses. Ashe (D) was acquitted on the robbery charge as to one of the victims. At that trial, the state's proof that the robbery had occurred and that the alleged victim was one of the victims was unassailable. The evidence that Ashe (D) was one of the robbers was weak. At a second trial for the robbery of a second victim, Ashe (D) was convicted.

🏛 **RULE OF LAW**
The doctrine of collateral estoppel is embodied in the Fifth Amendment guarantee against double jeopardy, and, accordingly, an acquittal based on a factual issue that is also presented as an essential element of a second charge bars trial on that charge.

FACTS: Three or four men robbed six men who were playing poker and stole one of the victims' cars. (It was never clear whether there were three or four robbers.) Three men were arrested near the abandoned stolen car. Ashe (D) was arrested separately some distance away. Each of the four was charged with six robbery counts and the theft of the car. At Ashe's (D) trial for the robbery of Knight, the proof that the armed robbery had occurred and that Knight had been a victim was unassailable. The state's evidence that Ashe (D) had been one of the robbers was weak. The jury found Ashe (D) not guilty. Six weeks later, Ashe (D) was brought to trial for the robbery of Roberts. The witnesses were the same but their testimony on Ashe's (D) identification was much stronger. One of the victims whose identification testimony had been negative at the first trial was not called at the second. The jury found Ashe (D) guilty, and he was sentenced to 35 years.

ISSUE: Is collateral estoppel a part of the Fifth Amendment's guarantee against double jeopardy?

HOLDING AND DECISION: (Stewart, J.) Yes. Collateral estoppel is a part of the Fifth Amendment's guarantee against double jeopardy. Collateral estoppel means that when an issue of ultimate facts has once been determined by a valid and final judgment, that issue cannot be litigated again between the same parties in any future lawsuit. Although first developed in civil litigation, the doctrine has long been held applicable in criminal cases. Where a previous judgment of acquittal was based upon a general verdict, as is usually the case, the court must examine the records of the prior proceedings to determine

whether a rational jury could have grounded its verdict upon any issue other than the one which the defendant seeks to foreclose from consideration. Looking to the record here, there is no indication that the first jury could have rationally based its verdict on a finding that the robbery did not occur or that Knight had not been a victim. The only rationally conceivable issue in dispute before the jury was whether Ashe (D) had been one of the robbers. The jury, by its verdict, found that he had not. We hold that the doctrine of collateral estoppel is embodied in the Fifth Amendment guarantee against double jeopardy; a state could not constitutionally bring Ashe (D) before a second jury to decide whether he was one of the robbers after a first jury had already held that he was not. Reversed and remanded.

CONCURRENCE: (Brennan, J.) I agree with the majority's holding. However, even if collateral estoppel were not applicable here, the Double Jeopardy Clause bars the second trial, since the two prosecutions grew out of one criminal episode. The Double Jeopardy Clause requires the prosecution, except in most limited circumstances, to join at one trial all charges against a defendant that grow out of a single criminal act, occurrence, episode, or transaction. This "same transaction" test enforces the ancient prohibition against multiple prosecutions and also promotes the justice, economy and convenience that result from consolidation in one lawsuit of all issues arising out of a single transaction or occurrence.

DISSENT: (Burger, C.J.) Nothing in the language or any of the gloss previously placed on the Double Jeopardy Clause remotely justifies the majority's treatment of the collateral estoppel doctrine. The essence of the concurring opinion is that all that occurred in this case was one transaction or episode. "For me it demeans the dignity of the human personality and individuality to talk of a 'single transaction' in the context of six separate assaults on six individuals."

▶ **ANALYSIS**

Ashe deprives the prosecution of a major tactical advantage in trying separately, closely related offenses arising from a single transaction. The effect of the collateral estoppel doctrine is to prevent the prosecutor from "treating the first trial as no more than a dry run for a second prosecution" on a second charge. With this tactic eliminated, the prosecutor may find less advantage in separate

Continued on next page.

prosecutions in such situations. In *Harris v. Washington*, 404 U.S. 55 (1971), the Court held that the constitutional guarantee applies, irrespective of whether the jury considered all relevant evidence, and irrespective of the state's good faith in bringing successive prosecutions. There a bomb sent through the mails killed Burdick and the defendant's son. After his acquittal on a charge of murdering Burdick, the defendant was charged with murdering his son. It was contended that the issue of identity had not been fully litigated because the trial judge had wrongly excluded a threatening letter written by the defendant.

■══■

Quicknotes

COLLATERAL ESTOPPEL A doctrine whereby issues litigated and determined in a prior proceeding are binding upon all subsequent litigation between the parties regarding that issue.

DOUBLE JEOPARDY A prohibition against a second prosecution for the same offense after an acquittal or conviction for that offense in a prior proceeding or against multiple punishments for the same offense.

ULTIMATE FACT A fact upon which a judicial determination is made and which is inferred from the evidence presented at trial.

■══■

Schaffer v. United States

Prejudiced conspirator (D) v. Federal government (P)

362 U.S. 511 (1960).

NATURE OF CASE: Appeal from criminal conviction.

FACT SUMMARY: The defendants were charged with conspiracy and with individual substantive crimes. At the close of the prosecution's case, the defendants moved successfully for dismissal of the conspiracy charge. They now contend that continued joinder of the individual cases was unduly prejudiced.

> 🏛 **RULE OF LAW**
> Where the joinder of trials of multiple defendants is based on a charge of conspiracy, the failure of the conspiracy charge does not automatically mandate severance of the trials on the remaining substantive counts.

FACTS: The Schaffers (D), along with three others named Stracuzza, were charged with transporting stolen property across state lines. The Stracuzzas were also charged with separate interstate shipments involving two other individuals at separate times. All seven were also charged with conspiracy to commit the individual crimes charged and were tried in a joint trial. At the close of the prosecution's case, the seven moved for an acquittal on the conspiracy charge. The motion was granted on the basis that no connection, other than the common participation of the Stracuzzas, was shown between the Schaffers (D) and the other individual defendants. However, the motion for acquittal on the substantive crimes was denied along with a motion to sever the trials of the defendants.

ISSUE: Where the trial of multiple defendants is joined on the basis of a charge of conspiracy, must their trials thereafter be severed as to the substantive crimes charged if the conspiracy charge fails?

HOLDING AND DECISION: (Clark, J.) No. The trial was properly joined at the outset under Rule 8(b) of the Fed. R. Crim. P. and any severance thereafter was controlled by Rule 14 which provides for separate trials where it appears that a defendant is prejudiced by such joinder. The remaining substantive charges involved an almost identical outline with only the names of the particular defendants and the destination of the stolen goods being different in each count. The trial court was meticulously fair in pointing out to the jurors that evidence against one defendant could in no way be considered against another. This caveat was repeated in the charge to the jury. The trial judge did not abuse the discretion vested in him as to severance, since no prejudice can be shown by the trial record. While the trial judge must be particularly sensitive to the possibility of prejudice in cases such as these, we cannot hold as a hard and fast rule that the failure of a conspiracy charge that forms the basis for joinder must automatically result in severance of the trial on the remaining charges. Affirmed.

DISSENT: (Douglas, J.) While the initial charge of conspiracy was a proper foundation for joinder under Rule 8(b), the failure of proof of that charge removes the basis for joinder. This Court has previously held that joinder is not proper where the only connection between multiple defendants charged with similar offenses is the participation of one defendant in all the charged crimes. The possibility of prejudice by transferred inference of guilt is too strong to allow a joint trial. The showing of prejudice in such an instance is difficult, no matter how strong the possibility. The only sure way to protect against the subtle bond of guilt, and attendant prejudice, is to sever the trials. This circumstance is distinguishable from the case where both the conspiracy and substantive charges go to the jury and acquittal is rendered on the conspiracy charge but not on the substantive charge.

▶ ANALYSIS

Two critical views were expressed toward this decision. In one, the commentator found that an unscrupulous prosecutor might frame a totally groundless conspiracy charge to support joinder to save the time and expense of separate trials. Since bad faith on the part of the prosecutor is difficult to prove, actual misjoinder may be allowed to persist. Another commentator found that the dissent's view might very well be self-defeating. Since the trial judge may be very reluctant to dismiss and sever after failure of the conspiracy charge, he might very well refuse such dismissal and submit that charge to the jury, confident of an acquittal on that charge.

◼▬◼

Quicknotes

ACQUITTAL The discharge of an accused individual from suspicion of guilt for a particular crime and from further prosecution for that offense.

CONSPIRACY Concerted action by two or more persons to accomplish some unlawful purpose.

JOINDER The joining of claims or parties in one lawsuit.

◼▬◼

Gray v. Maryland

State (P) v. Accused murderer (D)

523 U.S. 185 (1998).

NATURE OF CASE: Appeal of a criminal conviction for murder.

FACT SUMMARY: When a jury convicted Gray (D) of murder following a trial at which a co-defendant's redacted confession had been introduced, Gray (D) appealed, claiming that his constitutional rights had been violated.

🏛 RULE OF LAW

Redacted confessions that replace the proper name with an obvious blank, the word "delete," a symbol, or similarly notify the jury that a name has been deleted, violate a defendant's Sixth Amendment rights if introduced into evidence insulated from cross examination.

FACTS: Gray (D) and a co-defendant were both indicted for murder. Gray's (D) motion for a separate trial was denied, and Gray (D) was convicted after the co-defendant's redacted confession incriminating Gray (D) was introduced at the joint trial with a limiting instruction. Gray (D) appealed the verdict, claiming that under *Bruton v. United States*, 391 U.S. 123 (1968), his Sixth Amendment rights had been violated.

ISSUE: Do redacted confessions that replace the proper name with an obvious blank, the word "delete," a symbol or similarly notify the jury that a name has been deleted violate a defendant's Sixth Amendment rights if introduced into evidence insulated from cross examination?

HOLDING AND DECISION: (Breyer, J.) Yes. Redacted confessions that replace the proper name with an obvious blank, the word "delete", a symbol or similarly notify the jury that a name has been deleted, violate a defendant's Sixth Amendment rights if introduced into evidence insulated from cross examination. Under *Bruton*, the introduction at trial of the powerfully incriminating extrajudicial statements of a co-defendant, who does not testify and cannot be cross-examined, violates a defendant's Sixth Amendment rights. The introduction of the redacted confession of Gray's (D) co-defendant with the blank prominent on its face "facially incriminated" Gray (D). There were no questions of policy to be considered here, since the connection of the defendant to the confession did not depend on the introduction of other evidence later in the trial. This case was not like *Richardson v. Marsh*, 481 U.S. 200 (1987), where the confession of the co-defendant had been redacted, eliminating all reference to his co-defendant and any indication that anyone else at all was implicated in the crime, and becoming incriminating only when linked

to other evidence. The powerfully incriminating effect of an out-of-court accusation creates a special, and vital, need for cross examination. Redactions that simply replace a name with a blank leave statements that, considered as a class, so closely resemble *Bruton*'s unredacted statements that, in our view, the law must require the same result. Reversed.

DISSENT: (Scalia, J.) The court's extension of *Bruton* to name-related confessions, "as a class," will seriously compromise society's compelling interest in finding, convicting, and punishing those who violate the law. The Court's analogizing of "deleted" to a physical description that clearly identifies the defendant does not survive scrutiny. By "facially incriminating," we have meant incriminating independent of other evidence introduced at trial. The issue is not whether the confession incriminated Gray (D), but whether the incrimination was so "powerful" that we must depart from the normal presumption that the jury follows its instructions. It was not, and the line for departing from the ordinary rule at the facial identification of the defendant makes more sense than drawing it anywhere else.

▶ ANALYSIS

Since the redacted confession in this case referred directly to the "existence" of the nonconfessing co-defendant, the court found more similarities with *Bruton* than with *Richardson*. In *Bruton*, the confession was held to be "incriminating on its face," while in *Richardson*, the confession became incriminating only by inference, and only when "linked" to other evidence. This "linkage" has proved problematic in other cases where the effect of a confession cannot be predicted until after the introduction of all the evidence.

■=■

Quicknotes

CROSS EXAMINATION The interrogation of a witness by an adverse party either to further inquire as to the subject matter of the direct examination or to call into question the witness's credibility.

LIMITING INSTRUCTION Directions given to a judge or jury prior to deliberation.

REDACTION Alteration of a confession to remove any reference by one joint defendant to any co-defendant.

SIXTH AMENDMENT Provides the right to a speedy trial by impartial jury, the right to be informed of the accusation, to confront witnesses and to have the assistance of counsel in all criminal prosecutions.

■=■

CHAPTER 20

Speedy Trial and Other Speed Disposition

Quick Reference Rules of Law

Barker v. Wingo

Murder convict (D) v. Court (P)

407 U.S. 514 (1972).

NATURE OF CASE: Petition for certiorari of a murder conviction.

FACT SUMMARY: Although Barker (D) made no objections during the first four years of a five-year delay between his arrest and conviction for murder, he subsequently claimed that his right to a speedy trial had been violated.

🏛 RULE OF LAW
The determination of whether a defendant has been deprived of his Sixth Amendment right to a speedy trial must be made on a case-by-case basis by balancing the following four factors: (1) length of delay, (2) reason for delay, (3) the defendant's assertion of his right, and (4) prejudice to the defendant.

FACTS: On July 20, 1958, an elderly couple was murdered. Shortly afterwards, Silas Manning and Willie Barker (D) were arrested as suspects. On September 15, they were indicted, counsel was appointed on September 17, and Barker's (D) trial was set for October 21. However, Barker (D) was not brought to trial for more than five years after his arrest due to numerous continuances by the prosecution. Initially, the continuances were for the purpose of first convicting Manning, against whom the Commonwealth had a stronger case, to assure his testimony at Barker's (D) trial (i.e., to eliminate problems of self-incrimination). However, Manning was not convicted until 1962. Afterwards, Barker's (D) trial was delayed another seven months due to the illness of the chief investigating officer in the case. During these continuances, Barker (D) was free for all but ten months in jail, and he made no objections during the first four years of delay. However, Barker (D) objected to the last few continuances, and, at his trial, he moved for dismissal on the basis that his Sixth Amendment right to a speedy trial had been violated. This motion was denied and Barker (D) was convicted of murder. Upon appeal to the Kentucky Court of Appeals, the conviction was affirmed. Barker (D) then petitioned for habeas corpus in the United States District Court. Upon denial of that petition, he appealed to the Court of Appeals for the Sixth Circuit. Upon affirmance of his conviction, Barker (D) brought a petition for certiorari.

ISSUE: Is a delay of five years between the arrest and trial of a defendant a violation per se of his Sixth Amendment right to a speedy trial?

HOLDING AND DECISION: (Powell, J.) No. The determination of whether a defendant has been deprived of his Sixth Amendment right to a speedy trial must

be made on a case-by-case basis by balancing the following four facts: (1) length of delay, (2) reason for delay, (3) the defendant's assertion of his right, and (4) prejudice to the defendant. Since the deprivation of the right to a speedy trial does not per se prejudice the ability of an accused to defend himself, it is impossible to state "with precision" when the right has been denied. Each factor, therefore, must be separately analyzed. First, it is true that a long delay before trial is more likely to be justified for a serious, complex crime (e.g., murder) than for a simple one. Here, however, the delay of over five years was extreme by any standard. Second, it is true that a delay in bringing an accused to trial may be justified by a showing of some strong reason for it. Here, however, there was a strong reason for delay (i.e., illness of the chief investigator) for only seven months of the five-year delay. Although some additional delay might also have been necessary to acquire Manning as a witness, over four years was clearly unreasonable. Third, it is true that failure to assert the right to a speedy trial will not constitute a waiver of that right, unless it is found to be an "intentional relinquishment or abandonment of a known right." Here, however, it is obvious that Barker (D) did not want a trial at all, hoping, rather, that the delays would ultimately result in dismissal of the charges against him. Fourth, it is true that the prejudice that results from a delay of a defendant's trial must be evaluated in the light of those interests that a speedy trial was designed to protect (i.e., prevention of "oppressive pretrial incarceration," minimization of anxiety and concern of the accused, and limitation on the possibility that the defense will be "impaired"). Here, however, prejudice was minimal. Although Barker (D) was prejudiced to some extent by spending some time in jail and by living for years under "a cloud of suspicion," none of his witnesses died or became unavailable. In conclusion, the facts that Barker (D) did not want a trial and was not prejudiced by the delay outweigh the unjustified length of delay. Judgment affirmed.

▶ ANALYSIS

This case illustrates the discretion available (through the balancing test) to the courts in determining when the right to a speedy trial has been violated, and the emphasis on the desire of an accused to have a speedy trial. Note, that an accused "waives" the right to a speedy trial if he flees the state after arraignment or request postponement of his trial. Note, also, that the right to a speedy trial attaches only after a person is accused (i.e., indicted or arrested), so

Continued on next page.

that it is not violated by a police delay in filing charges. However, if such a delay was purposeful, due process requires dismissal of the charges.

■=■

Quicknotes

BALANCING TEST A court's balancing of an individual's constitutional rights against the state's right to protect its citizens.

PRIVILEGE AGAINST SELF-INCRIMINATION A privilege guaranteed by the Fifth Amendment to the federal Constitution in a criminal proceeding for communications made by an accused and protecting an accused or witness from having to give testimony that may incriminate himself.

PROCEDURAL DUE PROCESS The constitutional mandate that if the state or federal government acts so as to deny a citizen of a life, liberty or property interest the individual is first entitled to notice and the right to be heard.

SIXTH AMENDMENT Provides the right to a speedy and public trial by impartial jury, the right to be informed of the accusation, the right to confront witnesses, and the right to have the assistance of counsel in all criminal prosecutions.

■=■

United States v. Lovasco

Federal government (P) v. Subsequent indictee (D)

431 U.S. 783 (1977).

NATURE OF CASE: Appeal from dismissal of a criminal indictment.

FACT SUMMARY: The district court dismissed the criminal indictment against Lovasco (D) due to the delay between the commission of the offense and the initiation of prosecution.

🏛 RULE OF LAW
To prosecute a criminal defendant following investigative delay does not deprive him of due process, even if his defense might have been somewhat prejudiced by the lapse of time.

FACTS: Although the offenses of possessing firearms stolen from the U.S. mail and dealing in firearms without a license allegedly occurred between July 25 and August 31, 1973, Lovasco (D) was not indicted for those crimes until March 6, 1975. The initial report noted that Lovasco (D) told Government (P) agents just one month after the alleged commission of the crimes that he had possessed and sold five of the stolen guns. By that time, there was also strong evidence linking him to the remaining three weapons. However, the agents were unable to confirm or refute his claim that he had found the guns in his car when he returned to it after visiting his son, a mail handler, at work. Little additional information was uncovered in the 17 months that followed before the initiation of prosecution. Thus, the district court granted Lovasco's (D) motion to dismiss the indictment on the ground that the unreasonable and unnecessary delay in initiating prosecution had prejudiced his defense and thus violated his due process rights. Evidence showed that the two witnesses whom Lovasco (D) claimed would have helped his defense died, one within nine months and the other more than a year after the initial investigative report on the crimes was completed.

ISSUE: Does it violate the Due Process Clause to prosecute a criminal defendant following investigative delay, even if his defense is somewhat prejudiced by the lapse of time?

HOLDING AND DECISION: (Marshall, J.) No. Even if his defense is somewhat prejudiced by the lapse of time between commission of the crimes and initiation of prosecution, prosecuting a defendant following investigative delay does not deprive him of due process. Proof of actual prejudice is a necessary prerequisite to, and makes, a due process claim concrete and ripe for adjudication, but it does not make the claim automatically valid. The determining question is whether compelling a particular defendant to stand trial after delay in a particular case violates those "fundamental conceptions of justice that lie at the base of our civil and political institutions." It does not in cases like this. Reversed.

▶ ANALYSIS

The court is careful not to say that prejudicial pre-accusation delay could never be a due process violation. This may prove most important in the future, since the Sixth Amendment right to a speedy trial has been found inapplicable to pre-indictment delays.

━━■

Quicknotes

PROCEDURAL DUE PROCESS The constitutional mandate that if the state or federal government acts so as to deny a citizen of a life, liberty or property interest the individual is first entitled to notice and the right to be heard.

RIPENESS A doctrine precluding a federal court from hearing or determining a matter, unless it constitutes an actual and present controversy warranting a determination by the court.

━━■

Pretrial Discovery and Related Rights

Quick Reference Rules of Law

Williams v. Florida

Robbery convict (D) v. State (P)

399 U.S. 78 (1970).

NATURE OF CASE: Appeal from conviction of robbery.

FACT SUMMARY: Florida law requires that a defendant submit to a limited form of pretrial discovery by the state whenever he intends to rely at trial on the defense of alibi.

RULE OF LAW
The constitutional privilege against self-incrimination is not violated by a requirement that defendant give notice of an alibi defense and disclose his alibi witnesses.

FACTS: Williams (D) was charged with robbery. Prior to his trial, Williams (D) sought a protective order to be excused from complying with a Florida law that requires a defendant, on written demand of the prosecution, to give notice in advance of trial if the defendant intends to claim an alibi, and to furnish the prosecution with information as to the place he claims to have been and with the names and addresses of the alibi witnesses he intends to use. Williams (D) wanted to declare his intent to use an alibi, but objected to further disclosure on the ground that the rule would compel him to be a witness against himself in violation of the Fifth and Fourteenth Amendments. The rule also obligated the State (P) to notify a defendant of any rebuttal witnesses to the alibi defense the State (P) will call. Failure to comply, by either side, results in the exclusion of the defendant's alibi evidence or the State's (P) rebuttal evidence. When Williams's (D) motion for the protective order was denied, he complied with the rule. On the morning of his trial, the State (P) interviewed a Mrs. Scotty, Williams's (D) chief alibi witness. At trial, Mrs. Scotty gave testimony that contradicted her pretrial statements. The State (P) also furnished a rebuttal witness. Williams (D) was convicted.

ISSUE: Is a notice-of-alibi rule violative of the Fifth and Fourteenth Amendments by compelling a defendant to be a witness against himself?

HOLDING AND DECISION: (White, J.) No. A notice-of-alibi rule is not violative of the Fifth and Fourteenth Amendments by compelling a defendant to be a witness against himself. The rule is fair to both the defendant and the state (P) in permitting liberal discovery. The State (P) has a legitimate interest in protecting itself against eleventh hour defenses: although based on an adversary system, a trial is not yet a poker game in which players may conceal their cards at will. No pretrial statements of Mrs. Scotty were introduced at trial; her pretrial testimony

was only urged to find rebuttal witnesses. A defendant is always in a dilemma whether to remain silent or present a defense that may prove disastrous. Nothing in the rule obligates the defendant to rely on an alibi or prevents him from abandoning it as a defense. The rule only requires that a defendant accelerate the timing of his disclosure of information that he would have revealed at trial anyway. A defendant is not entitled to await the end of the prosecution's case against him before announcing the nature of his defense any more than he can await the jury's verdict on the state's case before deciding to take the stand himself. Absent the rule, the prosecution would be entitled to a continuance at trial on the grounds of surprise; the rule thus serves to prevent a disrupted trial. Affirmed.

CONCURRENCE: (Burger, C.J.) The rule serves an added function of disposing of many cases before trial. If the prosecution interviews the defendant's alibi witnesses, and finds them to be reliable and unimpeachable, he might be strongly inclined to dismiss charges against the defendant. On the other hand a defendant, who knows that his alibi defense will be thoroughly investigated by the prosecution before trial, may well be induced to change his plea.

DISSENT: (Black, J.) Before trial the defense counsel can only guess at what the state's (P) case might be. The rule thus compels defendants with any thoughts at all of pleading alibi to be forced to disclose their intentions so as to preserve the possibility of later raising the defense—the decision goes to more than just "timing." Pretrial disclosure will adversely affect the defendant who then decides to forgo raising an alibi defense. His alibi witnesses will still help the prosecution to new leads or evidence. The rule is a clear violation of the Fifth Amendment because it requires a defendant to give information to the state that may destroy him. The entire burden of proving criminal activity rests on the state: no constitutional provision is designed to make conviction easier. The defendant need not do anything to defend or convict himself. While a criminal trial is in part a search for truth, it also is designed to protect "freedom" by ensuring that the state carries its burden. Efficiency is not a consideration. The majority's decision opens the way to compel complete pretrial discovery of a defendant's case, and any defenses he might raise.

ANALYSIS

At the time *Williams* was decided, fifteen states other than Florida had notice-of-alibi requirements of varying kinds.

Continued on next page.

One such rule, in *Wardins v. Oregon*, 412 U.S. 470 (1973), was struck down because it failed to provide reciprocal discovery rights to the defendant. The Court found this omission violative of the Due Process Clause of the Fourteenth Amendment. Because exclusion of the testimony of alibi witnesses is a drastic sanction for failure on the defendant's part to comply with the rule's disclosure requirements, other sanctions have been suggested. These include: (1) granting a continuance to the prosecution; (2) allowing the prosecution or court to comment on the defendant's failure to the jury; (3) placing the defense counsel in contempt when the failure was not in "good faith."

■=■

Quicknotes

ALIBI Provable documentation of an individual's activities at the time a criminal offense was committed, thereby relieving him of possible guilt.

DISCOVERY Pretrial procedure during which one party makes certain information available to the other.

FIFTH AMENDMENT Provides that no person shall be compelled to serve as a witness against himself, or be subject to trial for the same offense twice, or be deprived of life, liberty, or property without due process of law.

FOURTEENTH AMENDMENT Declares that no state shall make or enforce any law that shall abridge the privileges and immunities of citizens of the United States. No state shall deny to any person within its jurisdiction the equal protection of the laws.

PRIVILEGE AGAINST SELF-INCRIMINATION A privilege guaranteed by the Fifth Amendment to the federal Constitution in a criminal proceeding for communications made by an accused and protecting an accused or witness from having to give testimony that may incriminate himself.

■=■

Taylor v. Illinois

Attempted murder convict (D) v. State (P)

484 U.S. 400 (1988).

NATURE OF CASE: Appeal from conviction for attempted murder.

FACT SUMMARY: Taylor (D) contended he was deprived of his right to obtain favorable testimony by the trial court's refusal to allow a witness to testify whose identity had been withheld during pretrial discovery.

🏛 RULE OF LAW
A court may forbid a defense witness from testifying as a sanction for the defendant's failure to conduct pretrial discovery in good faith.

FACTS: Taylor (D) was charged with attempted murder. Well in advance of trial, the prosecution moved to compel a list of defense witnesses. Although Taylor's (D) attorney met with and spoke to Wormsley, he did not include this witness on the list. On the second day of trial, Taylor's (D) attorney sought to amend the list and add Wormsley, representing to the court that he (the defense attorney) had just been informed of Wormsley's existence. The court refused to allow Wormsley to testify and Taylor (D) was convicted. Taylor (D) appealed, contending he had been deprived of his right to present favorable evidence. The appellate court affirmed, and the United States Supreme Court granted a hearing.

ISSUE: May a court preclude defense witness testimony as a discovery sanction?

HOLDING AND DECISION: (Stevens, J.) Yes. A court may forbid a defense witness from testifying as a sanction for a lack of compliance with discovery. The Sixth Amendment grants defendants a right to subpoena witnesses. It does not otherwise grant a right to testimony. The Sixth Amendment cannot be used to circumvent the adversary system. The court in this case did not abuse its discretion in precluding the testimony. Judgment of the appellate court is affirmed.

DISSENT: (Brennan, J.) Precluding a criminal defense witness from testifying bears an arbitrary and disproportionate relation to the purposes of discovery, at least absent any evidence that the defendant was personally responsible for the discovery violations. Direct punitive measures, such as contempt, can be used to graduate the punishment to correspond to the severity of a discovery violation.

DISSENT: (Blackmun, J.) Specific remedies for suppression should be fashioned on a case-by-case basis.

▶ ANALYSIS

Criminal discovery is much different from civil discovery. Criminal discovery is greatly restricted and runs heavily in favor of the defense. In civil actions, discovery is very wide and arguably favors neither party. It is generally believed that the apparent willfulness of the behavior in this case was the deciding factor in the use of the rather harsh sanction.

■■■

Quicknotes

ATTEMPT An intent combined with an act falling short of the thing intended.

DISCOVERY Pretrial procedure during which one party makes certain information available to the other.

SIXTH AMENDMENT Provides the right to a speedy and public trial by impartial jury, the right to be informed of the accusation, the right to confront witnesses, and the right to have the assistance of counsel in all criminal prosecutions.

■■■

United States v. Bagley

Federal government (P) v. Criminal suspect (D)

473 U.S. 667 (1985).

NATURE OF CASE: Appeal from narcotics conviction.

FACT SUMMARY: Bagley (D) contended it was reversible error for the prosecution to fail to disclose a financial arrangement between the state and prosecution witnesses.

🏛 RULE OF LAW
Evidence is material and must be disclosed to the defense if there is a reasonable probability that, had the evidence been disclosed to the defense, the result of the proceeding would have been different.

FACTS: Bagley (D) was arrested for narcotics and fire-arm violations. His attorney filed a discovery motion seeking evidence of any deals made between the prosecution and witnesses for testimony. The prosecution failed to reveal a financial arrangement with two witnesses, and Bagley (D) appealed his conviction on the ground that he was denied the right to effectively cross-examine the witnesses due to this nondisclosure. The court of appeals reversed, and the United States Supreme Court granted certiorari.

ISSUE: Must evidence be disclosed if there is a reasonable likelihood that had it been disclosed, a different result would have resulted?

HOLDING AND DECISION: (Blackmun, J.) Yes. Evidence is material and must be disclosed to the defense if there is a reasonable probability that, had the evidence been disclosed to the defense, the result of the proceeding would have been different. The court of appeals held that the nondisclosure required automatic reversal. However, it made no determination regarding the materiality of the evidence so that application of the present rule could be performed. Reversed and remanded.

CONCURRENCE: (White, J.) The test of materiality does not depend upon the specificity of the defense request.

DISSENT: (Marshall, J.) A presumption of materiality should be adopted and a rule of automatic reversal applied.

DISSENT: (Stevens, J.) While the result here is correct, a new rule of materiality should not be fashioned.

▶ ANALYSIS

The Court in this case deemphasizes the manner in which the nondisclosure occurs in the analysis of reversible error. Previously, there were three situations analyzed separately which would provide difference levels of materiality. The first was where the prosecution knowingly introduced perjured testimony. The second was the failure to respond to a specific request, and the third was where no request was made.

Quicknotes

CROSS EXAMINATION The interrogation of a witness by an adverse party either to further inquire as to the subject matter of the direct examination or to call into question the witness's credibility.

PERJURY The making of false statements under oath.

Guilty Pleas

Quick Reference Rules of Law

Bordenkircher v. Hayes

Court (P) v. Forgery convict (D)

434 U.S. 357 (1978).

NATURE OF CASE: Appeal from a criminal conviction and penalty enhancement.

FACT SUMMARY: The prosecutor informed Hayes (D) that he would seek an indictment under the Kentucky Habitual Criminal Act if Hayes (D) did not plead guilty to the charge of uttering a forged instrument. Hayes (D) pled innocent, a jury convicted him, and his sentence was enhanced when the prosecutor initiated the Habitual Criminal indictment.

RULE OF LAW
A prosecutor can attempt to gain a defendant's assent to a plea bargain by informing the defendant that more severe charges will be brought if no bargain is struck.

FACTS: Hayes (D), who was charged with uttering a forged instrument (for $88.30), faced a sentence of two to ten years if convicted. The prosecutor offered a five-year sentence in return for a guilty plea and told Hayes (D) that refusal to take the "bargain" would result in his seeking an additional indictment under the Kentucky Habitual Criminal Act, which makes a life sentence mandatory if there are two prior felony convictions. When Hayes (D) declined the plea bargain, he was subjected to the additional indictment and sentenced to life imprisonment under the Habitual Criminal Act, after having been found guilty of the uttering charge. The two previous felonies in which Hayes (D) was involved had never resulted in his imprisonment; one was a rape charge reduced to a plea of detaining a female, and the other was a robbery conviction resulting in five years in a reformatory. Finding the prosecutor to have acted vindictively in securing the second indictment, the court of appeals reversed Hayes's (D) conviction for violation of due process of law.

ISSUE: Is it constitutionally permissible for a prosecutor to try to influence a defendant to accept a plea bargain by informing him that more severe charges will be brought if it is refused?

HOLDING AND DECISION: (Stewart, J.) Yes. As the constitutionality and utility of plea bargaining have been recognized, there is no bar to the prosecutor's use of the possibility of more severe charges being brought for purposes of persuading a defendant to accept a plea bargain. So long as the defendant is advised that the bringing of additional charges will accompany his refusal to bargain, the situation becomes similar to that where the prosecutor offers to drop a charge as part of the plea bargain. If plea bargaining is a recognized process, neither can be forbidden simply because the charging decision is influenced by what a prosecutor hopes to gain in plea bargaining negotiations. In accepting plea bargaining, it is implicit that there is acceptance of the notion that the prosecutor's interest is to persuade the defendant not to exercise his right to plead not guilty. So long as the prosecutor has probable cause to believe the accused committed the offense, and he properly exercises his discretion, decisions not being influenced by standards of race, religion, etc., there is no due process violation. Reversed.

DISSENT: (Blackmun, J.) Past cases indicate that prosecutorial vindictiveness resulting from a defendant's exercise of his rights is a constitutionally impermissible basis for discretionary actions. Here, it is admitted that such vindictiveness was the sole reason for the new indictment.

DISSENT: (Powell, J.) Discretion used to deter the exercise of constitutional rights is not constitutionally exercised. The prosecutor's initial failure to charge indicates his own appreciation of the unreasonableness of placing Hayes (D) in jeopardy of life imprisonment while many murderers and rapists face lighter sentences.

ANALYSIS

Brady v. United States, 397 U.S. 742 (1970), was the case in which the Court first recognized plea bargaining as a legitimate practice. While the majority here suggests that such an acceptance implies sanctioning of prosecutorial use of charging powers to influence a defendant to plead guilty, the *Brady* decision specifically states that it makes no reference to such use by the prosecutor or a similar use by the judge of his sentencing power.

■━━■

Quicknotes

PLEA BARGAIN An agreement between a criminal defendant and a prosecutor, which is submitted to the court for approval, generally involving the defendant's pleading guilty to a lesser charge or count in exchange for a more lenient sentence.

■━━■

Santobello v. New York

Convicted felon (D) v. State (P)

404 U.S. 257 (1971).

NATURE OF CASE: Review of sentence following plea of guilty to a felony.

FACT SUMMARY: After a prosecutor promised no recommendation regarding sentencing, as an inducement to a guilty plea, a different prosecutor did recommend a sentence.

> 🏛 **RULE OF LAW**
> When the prosecution makes a promise regarding sentencing recommendations as an inducement to a guilty plea, the prosecutor may not renege.

FACTS: Santobello (D) was charged with a felony. As an inducement to plead guilty, the prosecutor promised no recommendation regarding sentencing. Santobello (D) pled guilty. At the sentencing hearing, a different prosecutor recommended the maximum sentence, which the judge imposed. Santobello (D) moved to withdraw his plea. This was denied, and the court of appeals affirmed. The United States Supreme Court granted review.

ISSUE: When the prosecution makes a promise regarding sentencing recommendations as an inducement to a guilty plea, may the prosecution renege?

HOLDING AND DECISION: (Burger, C.J.) No. When the prosecution makes a promise regarding sentencing recommendations as an inducement to a guilty plea, the prosecution may not renege. To preserve the integrity of the plea bargaining process, due process requires the prosecution to live up to whatever promises it made to induce the guilty plea. Here, the prosecution reneged on a promise regarding sentencing. This was impermissible. [The Court then remanded to the trial court to determine whether Santobello (D) should be permitted to withdraw his guilty plea, or merely re-sentenced.)

CONCURRENCE: (Douglas, J.) The defendant's preference as to disposition in a case like this should be given considerable, if not controlling, weight.

CONCURRENCE AND DISSENT: (Marshall, J.) Where a defendant wishes to withdraw his plea of guilty after the prosecution reneges on a sentencing promise, he should be allowed to withdraw his plea as a matter of right.

▶ ANALYSIS

A plea bargain is, in essence, a contract. This being so, it is logical to analogize the law of contracts to cases of broken plea bargain. This is to a large extent the rule. Differences do exist between plea bargains and typical contracts. The most important of these is that plea bargains have a constitutional dimension not usually found in contract law.

◼◼◼

Quicknotes

FELONY A criminal offense of greater seriousness than a misdemeanor; felonies are generally defined pursuant to statute as any crime that is punishable by death or by a term of imprisonment exceeding one year.

PLEA BARGAIN An agreement between a criminal defendant and a prosecutor, which is submitted to the court for approval, generally involving the defendant's pleading guilty to a lesser charge or count in exchange for a more lenient sentence.

◼◼◼

Missouri v. Frye

State (P) v. Convicted individual claiming ineffective assistance of counsel (D)

566 U.S. _____ (2012), 132 S. Ct. 1399 (2012).

NATURE OF CASE: State's (P) appeal from state appellate court's decision to grant plaintiff postconviction relief.

FACT SUMMARY: Frye's (D) attorney failed to communicate to him a formal plea offer from the prosecution that included more favorable terms than the terms to which Frye (D) eventually pleaded guilty.

🏛 **RULE OF LAW**

Counsel for criminal defendants has the duty to communicate formal offers from the prosecution with terms and conditions that may be favorable to the defendants.

FACTS: In August 2007, Frye (D) was charged with driving with a revoked license. He had been convicted of the same offense on three other occasions. Under Missouri law, the fourth charge allowed the State (P) to charge him with a Class D felony. The felony charge carried a possible four-year prison term. In November, the prosecution sent a formal written plea offer to Frye's (D) counsel with two choices. First, the prosecutor offered a three-year sentence if Frye (D) plead guilty to the felony charge, without a recommendation for probation but a requirement that Frye (D) spend ten days "shock" time in jail. The second offer was to reduce the charge to a misdemeanor and have Frye (D) serve 90 days in jail. The misdemeanor charge had a possible one-year maximum sentence. The letter stated the offer would expire on December 28. Frye's (D) counsel never communicated the offer to him and the plea offers expired. A week before his preliminary hearing on the August 2007 charge, Frye (D) was again arrested for driving with a revoked license. At a subsequent hearing, Frye (D) eventually pleaded guilty to the felony charge and the trial court sentenced him to three years in prison. Following the conviction, Frye (D) filed for postconviction relief in state court on the grounds his attorney's failure to inform him of the plea offers constituted actionable ineffective assistance of counsel. The state trial court denied his petition, but the Missouri Court of Appeals reversed, finding that Frye (D) received ineffective assistance of counsel and that Frye (D) was prejudiced thereby. The United States Supreme Court granted the State of Missouri's (D) petition for review.

ISSUE: Does counsel for criminal defendants have the duty to communicate formal offers from the prosecution with terms and conditions that may be favorable to the defendants?

HOLDING AND DECISION: (Kennedy, J.) Yes. Counsel for criminal defendants has the duty to communi-

cate formal offers from the prosecution with terms and conditions that may be favorable to the defendants. When a defense counsel fails to communicate a plea offer to his or her client, that failure constitutes actionable ineffective assistance of counsel under the Constitution. This holding is supported by the reality that more than 94 percent of state criminal convictions are the result of guilty pleas. That is only one part of the analysis. The convicted defendant must also show the ineffective assistance of counsel caused him prejudice in the criminal proceedings. To show prejudice when an attorney fails to communicate a plea offer, the defendant must demonstrate a reasonable probability that he would have accepted the earlier plea offer had he been aware of it. Significantly, defendants must also show that the prosecution would not have canceled the plea deal or that the trial court would not have rejected the agreement. This is relevant because some states allow prosecutors the discretion to cancel a plea agreement up to the moment the agreement is accepted by the court. This further showing is also important because a defendant has no constitutional right to be offered a plea agreement and no right that the judge accepts the agreement. In the instant case, Frye (D) can show he would have accepted the offer to plead guilty to the lesser misdemeanor charge. However, Frye's (D) subsequent arrest for the same offense one week prior to his hearing complicates matters for him. It is not entirely clear that the prosecution would not have canceled the agreement based on that new arrest. Nor is it clear that the trial court would have agreed to the plea deal. Accordingly, it is appropriate to remand the case to the Missouri Court of Appeals for it to consider whether the prosecution and the trial court would have agreed to the plea offer of the lesser misdemeanor charge in light of Frye's (D) new arrest for the same offense. Remanded for consideration of state-law questions before an appeal decision.

DISSENT: (Scalia, J.) The majority improperly constitutionalizes the plea-bargaining process in criminal cases. While it is clear Frye (D) received ineffective assistance of counsel, it is not entirely clear he was prejudiced thereby. The majority's reasonability probability test is nothing more than crystal ball gazing masquerading as legal analysis. There are no cases that discuss the standard for a prosecutor's withdrawal from a plea agreement or a trial court's authority to accept or reject a plea deal. In most states, the trial court has broad discretion to accept or reject such agreements. The judicial branch should not

Continued on next page.

create precedents based upon what prosecutors and judges might have done in the past. State legislatures are better equipped to regulate the plea-bargain process, starting by imposing punishments upon a defense counsel's right to practice when they fail to communicate valid plea offers to their clients. However, in this case, Frye (D) was not prejudiced because he pleaded guilty to the felony charge after the usual colloquy with the trial court judge that assured his guilty plea was voluntary and truthful.

▶ ANALYSIS

The majority's decision was based on the prevalent use of plea bargains in criminal prosecutions, both at the state and federal level. In addition to the 94 percent of convictions in state cases resulting from plea bargains, 97 percent of convictions in federal court are similarly the result of plea negotiations. Note that the majority's holding is narrow: where a plea offer is made, the defense counsel must communicate it to their clients. The Court refrained from adjudicating on any strategic decisions defense counsel may make during those plea negotiations.

∎══∎

Quicknotes

INEFFECTIVE ASSISTANCE OF COUNSEL A claim brought by an accused in which it must be determined whether the attorney's rendering of representation was such that the ultimate disposition of the case may not be relied upon as fair.

PLEA BARGAIN An agreement between a prosecutor and a criminal defendant that is submitted to the court for approval, generally involves the defendant's pleading guilty to a lesser charge or count in exchange for a more lenient sentence.

∎══∎

Newman v. United States

Convicted accomplice (D) v. Federal government (P)

127 U.S. App. D.C. 263, 382 F.2d 479 (D.C. Cir. 1967).

NATURE OF CASE: Appeal from conviction of housebreaking and petty larceny.

FACT SUMMARY: The United States Attorney refused to consent to plead on reduced charges for Newman (D), although Newman's (D) accomplice had been allowed to plead to less serious charges.

🏛 RULE OF LAW
The United States Attorney, as attorney for the Executive, is not constitutionally obligated to treat every offense and every offender alike in discharging his prosecutorial duties. The judiciary will not review his discretionary judgments.

FACTS: Newman (D) and Anderson (D) were indicted for housebreaking and petty larceny. After negotiations with an assistant United States Attorney, Anderson (D) was allowed to plead guilty to a less serious charge of attempted housebreaking in return for having the housebreaking charge dropped. The United States Attorney, however, refused to consent to the same deal for Newman (D) who was then tried and convicted of housebreaking and petty larceny. Newman (D) claimed that because of the different treatment accorded him by the United States Attorney, he was denied "due process" and "equal protection" as guaranteed him by the Fourteenth Amendment, and "equal standing."

ISSUE: Is the decision of a United States Attorney to prosecute a defendant for a different offense than that charged against his accomplice reviewable by a federal court as an abuse of discretion?

HOLDING AND DECISION: (Burger, J.) No. The United States Attorney, as attorney for the Executive, is not constitutionally obligated to treat every offense and every offender alike in discharging his prosecutorial duties. The judiciary will not review his discretionary judgments. When federal offenses are involved, the Executive branch (the President and, through him, the Justice Department) is charged with instituting criminal proceedings, formulating criminal charges and dismissing charges once brought. In carrying out these duties, the President is given broad discretion. As attorney for the Executive, a United States Attorney is imbued with the same broad discretion. Although a United States Attorney is, in one sense, an officer of the court and is responsible for the manner of his conduct of a case (i.e., his demeanor, deportment, and ethical conduct), he is also an agent of the President, and accountable only to him for the execution of his duty within the framework of his professional employment.

When two persons have committed the same legal offense, the prosecutor is free to exercise his own discretion and common sense. Defendants' ages, criminal records, roles in perpetration of the crime, relationship to one another, and other factors might influence the prosecutor in deciding to prosecute each defendant differently. If a United States Attorney abuses his discretion, it is up to the President to deal with him. The conviction is affirmed.

▶ ANALYSIS

It has been suggested that the *Newman* Court would have had to reach a more difficult decision if Newman (D) could have shown that he and Anderson (D) came from almost identical backgrounds and played the same role in the commission of the alleged crime. A claim would thus arise under the Equal Protection Clause of the Fourteenth Amendment. Plea bargaining, in general, gives rise to a host of problems: (1) widely disparate sentences which engender bitterness, and not remorse, by those convicted; (2) serious offenders are "let off the hook" because their cases superficially resemble those who are not as disposed to criminality; (3) the opportunity for a prosecutor to over inflate his case in pretrial negotiations (the same may equally be said for defense attorneys).

■■■■

Quicknotes

EQUAL PROTECTION A constitutional guarantee that no person shall be denied the same protection of the laws enjoyed by other persons in similar life circumstances.

FOURTEENTH AMENDMENT Declares that no state shall make or enforce any law that shall abridge the privileges and immunities of citizens of the United States. No state shall deny to any person within its jurisdiction the equal protection of the laws.

PROCEDURAL DUE PROCESS The constitutional mandate that if the state or federal government acts so as to deny a citizen of a life, liberty or property interest the individual is first entitled to notice and the right to be heard.

■■■■

United States v. Ruiz

Federal government (P) v. Drug possessor (D)

536 U.S. 622 (2002).

NATURE OF CASE: Appeal by Government (P) from the vacating of a sentencing determination.

FACT SUMMARY: Angela Ruiz (D) argued that the Constitution prohibits a defendant from waiving the right to impeachment information before the defendant can enter into a plea agreement.

🏛 RULE OF LAW
The Fifth and Sixth Amendments do not require prosecutors, before entering into a plea bargain, to disclose impeachment information relating to any informants or other witnesses.

FACTS: After immigration agents found 30 kilograms of marijuana in Angela Ruiz's (D) luggage, federal prosecutors offered her a so-called "fast track" plea bargain in return for which the Government (P) agreed to recommend a more lenient sentence than otherwise would have been mandated. Such plea bargain agreement contained detailed terms, including that the defendant waive the right to receive impeachment information relating to any informants or other witnesses. Because Ruiz (D) would not agree to this waiver, the prosecutors withdrew their bargaining offer. Despite the absence of a plea agreement, Ruiz (D) pled guilty and requested that the sentencing judge grant her the same reduced sentence she would have received if she had accepted the "fast track" plea. The judge refused; however, the federal circuit court vacated the district judge's sentencing determination, taking the position that the Constitution prohibits defendants from waiving their right to impeachment information before they enter into a plea agreement. The Government (P) appealed.

ISSUE: Do the Fifth and Sixth Amendments require prosecutors, before entering into a plea bargain, to disclose impeachment information relating to any informants or other witnesses?

HOLDING AND DECISION: (Breyer, J.) No. The Fifth and Sixth Amendments do not require prosecutors, before entering into a plea bargain, to disclose impeachment information relating to any informants or other witnesses. Impeachment information is special in relation to the fairness of a trial, not in respect to whether a plea is voluntary ("knowing," "intelligent," and "sufficiently aware"). Of course, the more information the defendant has, the more aware he or she is of the likely consequences of a plea, waiver, or decision, and the wiser that decision will likely be. However, the Constitution does not require the prosecutor to share all useful information with the defendant. The law ordinarily considers a waiver knowing, intelligent, and sufficiently aware if the defendant fully understands the nature of the right and how it would likely apply in general in the circumstances—even though the defendant may not know the specific detailed consequences of invoking it. It is particularly difficult to characterize impeachment information as critical information of which the defendant must always be aware prior to pleading guilty given the random way in which such information may, or may not, help a particular defendant. The degree of help that impeachment information can provide will depend upon the defendant's own independent knowledge of the prosecution's potential case—a matter that the Constitution does not require prosecutors to disclose. Furthermore, since the proposed plea agreement provides that the government will provide any information establishing the factual innocence of the defendant, that fact along with other guilty-plea safeguards, diminishes the force of Ruiz's (D) concern that, in the absence of impeachment information, innocent individuals, accused of crimes, will plead guilty. Reversed.

▶ ANALYSIS

In *Ruiz*, the Supreme Court found no decisional authority to support the Ninth Circuit position of required disclosure of impeachment witnesses. To the contrary, noted the Supreme Court, it would be difficult to distinguish, in terms of importance, (1) a defendant's ignorance of grounds for impeachment of potential witnesses at a possible future trial from (2) the varying forms of ignorance that could be at issue in any particular case.

■—■

Quicknotes

FIFTH AMENDMENT Provides that no person shall be compelled to serve as a witness against himself, or be subject to trial for the same offense twice, or be deprived of life, liberty, or property without due process of law.

IMPEACHMENT The discrediting of a witness by offering evidence to show that the witness lacks credibility.

PLEA BARGAIN An agreement between a prosecutor and a criminal defendant that is submitted to the court for approval, generally involves the defendant's pleading guilty to a lesser charge or count in exchange for a more lenient sentence.

SIXTH AMENDMENT Provides the right to a speedy and public trial by impartial jury, the right to be informed of the accusation, the right to confront witnesses, and the right to have the assistance of counsel in all criminal prosecutions.

■—■

Trial by Jury

Quick Reference Rules of Law

Taylor v. Louisiana

Kidnapping convict (P) v. State (D)

419 U.S. 522 (1975).

NATURE OF CASE: Appeal from criminal conviction on the basis that the jury was unconstitutionally constituted.

FACT SUMMARY: A Louisiana statute provided that women would be exempt from jury duty unless they specifically requested to serve.

🏛 RULE OF LAW
The exclusion of a segment of society from jury duty is sufficient to establish a per se violation of a defendant's constitutional right to a trial by jury of his peers guaranteed under the Sixth Amendment.

FACTS: Louisiana enacted a statute that provided women should not be selected for jury duty unless they filed a specific request to serve. The practical effect of this provision was that women (constituting 53 percent of potential jurors) were virtually unrepresented on juries within Louisiana (D). Taylor (P) was convicted of aggravated kidnapping. Taylor (P) moved to quash the conviction on the basis that no women were available to sit on the jury that tried him. Taylor (P) claimed that this violated his rights to a trial by jury of his peers (i.e., a fair cross-segment of the community). This was violative of the Sixth Amendment that was made applicable to the states under the Fourteenth Amendment to the U.S. Constitution. The motion was denied by the trial court.

ISSUE: Where the exclusion of a class of potential jurors makes the jury pool unrepresentative of the community, does this violate a defendant's rights under the Sixth Amendment?

HOLDING AND DECISION: (White, J.) Yes. A defendant is entitled to be tried by a representative cross-section of his community. The failure to provide such a cross-section is violative of the Sixth Amendment's constitutional guarantee of a trial by jury. It does not matter that the defendant has not established discrimination, for it is immaterial. The fact that he is a man and only women are being excluded is also immaterial. A caucasian may complain that blacks are being excluded. The blanket exemption for women has the effect of practically excluding them from jury panels. The role of women in society (i.e., mothers) is insufficient grounds for the issuance of a blanket exemption. Liberal, specific exemptions are allowed where individual facts warrant. Since the jury was unrepresentative, the conviction must be overturned. Reversed and remanded.

DISSENT: (Rehnquist, J.) The conviction should not have been overturned without a showing of prejudice.

There is no sound policy ground for arbitrarily overturning this conviction.

▶ ANALYSIS

In *Hamling v. United States*, 418 U.S. 87 (1974), the Court held that exclusion of the young through a failure to update the master jury wheel for four years was not a per se violation of the defendant's Sixth Amendment guarantees. It would require a showing of prejudice to require a reversal of the conviction. The mere fact that persons who have become eligible for jury duty have been excluded is insufficient to establish purposeful discrimination. This last fact is what differentiates *Hamling* from *Taylor*.

Quicknotes

MOTION TO QUASH To vacate, annul, void.

RIGHT TO JURY TRIAL The right guaranteed by the Sixth Amendment to the federal Constitution that in all criminal prosecutions the accused has a right to a trial by an impartial jury of the state and district in which the crime was allegedly committed.

Batson v. Kentucky

Black defendant (D) v. State (P)

476 U.S. 79 (1986).

NATURE OF CASE: Appeal of rejection of challenge to practice of exercising peremptory challenges to keep certain races off juries.

FACT SUMMARY: The prosecutor exercised his peremptory challenges to keep blacks off the jury in the trial of Batson (D), a black man.

RULE OF LAW

A prosecutor cannot use peremptory challenges to keep members of the defendant's race off the jury on the assumption that they will not be impartial.

FACTS: During the jury selection process of the trial of Batson (D), the prosecutor used his peremptory challenges to disqualify all blacks from the jury. Batson (D), a black man, argued that this constituted a violation of equal protection. The trial court rejected his contentions, and the Kentucky Supreme Court agreed. Batson (D) appealed.

ISSUE: May a prosecutor use peremptory challenges to keep members of the defendant's race off the jury on the assumption that they will not be impartial?

HOLDING AND DECISION: (Powell, J.) No. A prosecutor may not use peremptory challenges to keep members of the defendant's race off the jury on the assumption that they will not be impartial. Such generalizations are precisely what the Equal Protection Clause was meant to remove and cannot be approved, even when a time-honored practice such as peremptory challenges is concerned. If a defendant can demonstrate a pattern of racially motivated peremptory challenges in the selection of his jury, the burden falls on the prosecutor to make a legitimate explanation. Here, the prosecutor made no explanation at all. Reversed.

CONCURRENCE: (Marshall, J.) Peremptory challenges offer such a great potential for abuse that they should be abolished in the criminal justice system entirely.

DISSENT: (Burger, C.J.) Peremptory challenges are inherently based on hunches and other intangibles and one exercising them should not have to explain his/her reasons. The rule announced here can interfere with the defendant's use of peremptories if it is ever applied to him, which is likely.

DISSENT: (Rehnquist, J.) Where a party of any race may exclude members of any other race through peremptories, equal protection is not violated.

▶ ANALYSIS

Justice Rehnquist makes an interesting argument. According to him, so long as no particular race is precluded from using peremptories to keep off the jury members of any other race, no discrimination exists. This argument obviously would be wrong in most contexts, but in as fluid an area as peremptory challenges, it makes some sense, although practically speaking, black defendants have suffered most from the practice.

Quicknotes

EQUAL PROTECTION A constitutional guarantee that no person shall be denied the same protection of the laws enjoyed by other persons in life circumstances.

PEREMPTORY CHALLENGE The exclusion by a party to a lawsuit of a prospective juror without the need to specify a particular reason.

First Amendment Rights vs. Fair Trial Rights

Quick Reference Rules of Law

Skilling v. United States

Convicted criminal (D) v. Federal government (P)

___ U.S. ___, 130 S. Ct. 2896 (2010).

NATURE OF CASE: Appeal from affirmance of conviction of conspiracy to commit "honest-services" wire fraud in violation of 18 U.S.C. §§ 371, 1343, and 1346.

FACT SUMMARY: Skilling (D), a former chief executive officer of the collapsed Enron Corporation who was convicted of conspiracy to commit "honest-services" wire fraud in violation of 18 U.S.C. §§ 371, 1343, and 1346 (among other crimes), contended that pretrial publicity and community prejudice prevented him from obtaining a fair trial and that the jury improperly convicted him of conspiracy to commit honest-services wire fraud.

RULE OF LAW

Pretrial publicity and community prejudice do not prevent a criminal defendant from obtaining a fair trial where the presumption of juror prejudice that these conditions create is rebutted by a showing that voir dire has been proper and thorough, so that an impartial jury has in fact been empaneled, and there is no showing that actual bias infected the jury that tried the defendant.

FACTS: Founded in 1985, Enron Corporation (Enron) grew from its headquarters in Houston, Texas, into the seventh highest revenue-grossing company in America. Skilling (D), a longtime Enron officer, was Enron's chief executive officer (CEO) for about half a year, when he resigned. Less than four months later, Enron crashed into bankruptcy, and its stock plummeted in value. After an investigation uncovered an elaborate conspiracy to prop up Enron's stock prices by overstating the company's financial well-being, the Government (P) prosecuted dozens of Enron employees who participated in the scheme. In time, the Government (P) worked its way up the chain of command, indicting Skilling (D) and two other top Enron executives. These three defendants, the indictment charged, engaged in a scheme to deceive investors about Enron's true financial performance by manipulating its publicly reported financial results and making false and misleading statements. Count 1 of the indictment charged Skilling (D) with, inter alia, conspiracy to commit "honest-services" wire fraud, 18 U.S.C. §§ 371, 1343, and 1346, by depriving Enron and its shareholders of the intangible right of his honest services. Skilling (D) was also charged with over 25 substantive counts of securities fraud, wire fraud, making false representations to Enron's auditors, and insider trading. Skilling (D) moved for a change of venue, contending that hostility toward him in Houston, coupled with extensive pretrial publicity, poisoned potential jurors. He

submitted hundreds of news reports detailing Enron's downfall, as well as affidavits from experts he engaged portraying community attitudes in Houston in comparison to other potential venues. The district court denied the motion, concluding that pretrial publicity did not warrant a presumption that Skilling (D) would be unable to obtain a fair trial in Houston. Despite incidents of intemperate commentary, the court observed, media coverage, on the whole, had been objective and unemotional, and the facts of the case were neither heinous nor sensational. Moreover, the court asserted, effective voir dire would detect juror bias. In the months before the trial, the court asked the parties for questions it might use to screen prospective jurors. Rejecting the Government's (P) sparer inquiries in favor of Skilling's (D) more probing and specific questions, the court converted Skilling's (D) submission, with slight modifications, into a 77-question, 14-page document. The questionnaire asked prospective jurors about their sources of news and exposure to Enron-related publicity, beliefs concerning Enron and what caused its collapse, opinions regarding the defendants and their possible guilt or innocence, and relationships to the company and to anyone affected by its demise. The court then mailed the questionnaire to 400 prospective jurors and received responses from nearly all of them. It granted hardship exemptions to about 90 individuals, and the parties, with the court's approval, further winnowed the pool by excusing another 119 for cause, hardship, or physical disability. The parties agreed to exclude, in particular, every prospective juror who said that a preexisting opinion about Enron or the defendants would prevent her from being impartial. Three weeks before the trial date, one of Skilling's (D) co-defendants, Causey, pleaded guilty. Skilling (D) renewed his change-of-venue motion, arguing that the juror questionnaires revealed pervasive bias and that news accounts of Causey's guilty plea further tainted the jury pool. The court again declined to move the trial, ruling that the questionnaires and voir dire provided safeguards adequate to ensure an impartial jury. The court also denied Skilling's (D) request for attorney-led voir dire on the ground that potential jurors were more forthcoming with judges than with lawyers. But the court promised to give counsel an opportunity to ask follow-up questions, agreed that venire members should be examined individually about pretrial publicity, and allotted the defendants jointly two extra peremptory challenges. When voir dire began, after it questioned the venire as a group, the court examined prospective jurors individually, asking each about her or his exposure to Enron-related news, the

Continued on next page.

content of any stories that stood out in her or his mind, and any questionnaire answers that raised a red flag signaling possible bias. The court then permitted each side to pose follow-up questions and ruled on the parties' challenges for cause. Ultimately, the court qualified 38 prospective jurors, a number sufficient, allowing for peremptory challenges, to empanel 12 jurors and 4 alternates. After a four-month trial, the jury found Skilling (D) guilty of 19 counts, including the honest-services-fraud conspiracy charge, and not guilty of nine insider-trading counts. On appeal, Skilling (D) contended that pretrial publicity and community prejudice prevented him from obtaining a fair trial. Second, he alleged that the jury improperly convicted him of conspiracy to commit honest-services wire fraud. The court of appeals determined that the volume and negative tone of media coverage generated by Enron's collapse created a presumption of juror prejudice. Stating, however, that the presumption was rebuttable, the court examined the voir dire, found it "proper and thorough," and held that the district court had empaneled an impartial jury. The United States Supreme Court granted certiorari.

ISSUE: Do pretrial publicity and community prejudice prevent a criminal defendant from obtaining a fair trial where the presumption of juror prejudice that these conditions create is rebutted by a showing that voir dire has been proper and thorough, so that an impartial jury has in fact been empaneled, and there is no showing that actual bias infected the jury that tried the defendant?

HOLDING AND DECISION: (Ginsburg, J.) No. Pretrial publicity and community prejudice do not prevent a criminal defendant from obtaining a fair trial where the presumption of juror prejudice that these conditions create is rebutted by a showing that voir dire has been proper and thorough, so that an impartial jury has in fact been empaneled, and there is no showing that actual bias infected the jury that tried the defendant. Although the Sixth Amendment and Art. III, § 2, cl. 3, provide for criminal trials in the state and district where the crime was committed, these place-of-trial prescriptions do not impede transfer of a proceeding to a different district if extraordinary local prejudice will prevent a fair trial. Thus, in the past, the Court has not hesitated to reverse convictions where the proceedings were so tainted by media prejudice that they were akin to the proceedings of a kangaroo court. However, the Court also has indicated that juror exposure to news accounts of the crime alone does not presumptively deprive a defendant of due process. In other words, prominence does not necessarily produce prejudice, and juror impartiality does not require ignorance. Thus, a presumption of prejudice attends only the extreme case. Important differences separate Skilling's (D) prosecution from those in which the Court has presumed juror prejudice. First, the Court has emphasized the size and characteristics of the community in which the crime occurred. In contrast to the small-town setting in past cases, Houston is the

country's fourth most populous city. Given the large, diverse pool of residents eligible for jury duty, any suggestion that 12 impartial individuals could not be empaneled in Houston is hard to sustain. Second, although news stories about Skilling (D) were not kind, they contained no blatantly prejudicial information. Third, unlike cases in which trial swiftly followed a widely reported crime, over four years elapsed between Enron's bankruptcy and Skilling's (D) trial. Although reporters covered Enron-related news throughout this period, the decibel level of media attention diminished somewhat in the years following Enron's collapse. Finally, and of prime significance, Skilling's (D) jury acquitted him of nine insider-trading counts. Similarly, earlier instituted Enron-related prosecutions yielded no overwhelming victory for the Government (P). Given all these circumstances, it would be odd for an appellate court to presume prejudice in a case in which jurors' actions run counter to that presumption, as here. The court of appeals presumed juror prejudice based primarily on the magnitude and negative tone of the media attention directed at Enron. However, "pretrial publicity—even pervasive, adverse publicity—does not inevitably lead to an unfair trial." Here, news stories about Enron did not present the kind of vivid, unforgettable information the Court has recognized as particularly likely to produce prejudice, and Houston's size and diversity diluted the media's impact. Nor did Enron's sheer number of victims trigger a presumption. Although the widespread community impact necessitated careful identification and inspection of prospective jurors' connections to Enron, the extensive screening questionnaire and follow-up voir dire yielded jurors whose links to Enron were either nonexistent or attenuated. Finally, while Causey's well publicized decision to plead guilty shortly before trial created a danger of juror prejudice, the district court took appropriate steps to mitigate that risk. For all these reasons, the district court did not violate the Constitution by refusing to order a change of venue. The next issue is whether actual prejudice contaminated Skilling's (D) jury. The short answer is that it did not. No hard-and-fast formula dictates the necessary depth or breadth of voir dire. Jury selection is "particularly within the province of the trial judge." When pretrial publicity is at issue, moreover, "primary reliance on the judgment of the trial court makes [especially] good sense" because the judge "sits in the locale where the publicity is said to have had its effect" and may base her evaluation on her "own perception of the depth and extent of news stories that might influence a juror." The in-the-moment voir dire affords the trial court a more intimate and immediate basis for assessing a venire member's fitness for jury service. Skilling (D) failed to show that his voir dire fell short of constitutional requirements. The jury-selection process was insufficient, Skilling (D) maintained, because voir dire lasted only five hours, most of the district court's questions

Continued on next page.

were conclusory and failed adequately to probe jurors' true feelings, and the court consistently took prospective jurors at their word once they claimed they could be fair, regardless of other indications of bias. A review of the record, however, yields a different appraisal. The district court initially screened venire members by eliciting their responses to a comprehensive questionnaire drafted in large part by Skilling (D). That survey helped to identify prospective jurors excusable for cause and served as a springboard for further questions; voir dire thus was the culmination of a lengthy process. Moreover, inspection of the questionnaires and voir dire of the seated jurors reveals that, notwithstanding the flaws Skilling (D) lists, the selection process secured jurors largely uninterested in publicity about Enron and untouched by the corporation's collapse. Whatever community prejudice existed in Houston generally, Skilling's (D) jurors were not under its sway. Skilling (D) also asserts the district court should not have accepted jurors' promises of fairness, but the district court did not have good reasons to discredit jurors' assurances of impartiality: News stories about Enron did not contain horrifying information; Houston is not, for example, a rural community; circulation figures for Houston media sources showed that not nearly everyone in Houston was reached by media reports about Enron; and Skilling's (D) seated jurors exhibited no display of unmitigated bias. In any event, the district court did not simply take venire members at their word. It questioned each juror individually to uncover concealed bias. This face-to-face opportunity to gauge demeanor and credibility, coupled with information from the questionnaires regarding jurors' backgrounds, opinions, and news sources, gave the court a sturdy foundation to assess fitness for jury service. On these facts, the voir dire did not fall short of constitutional requirements. Finally, Skilling's (D) allegation that several jurors were openly biased also fails. In reviewing such claims, the deference due to district courts is at its pinnacle. First, Skilling (D) unsuccessfully challenged only one of the seated jurors for cause. This is "strong evidence that he was convinced the [other] jurors were not biased and had not formed any opinions as to his guilt." Additionally, a review of the record reveals no manifest error regarding the empaneling of other jurors, each of whom indicated, inter alia, that he or she would be fair to Skilling (D) and would require the Government (P) to prove its case. Affirmed.

CONCURRENCE: (Alito, J.) Where there is extraordinary pretrial publicity, there is no presumption of juror prejudice. A properly conducted voir dire can ensure that the panel will be populated with impartial jurors. Trial judges can also take steps once a jury is seated to shield the jury from the media. There is no simply no way to measure the level of pretrial publicity that must be attained before a change in venue must occur.

CONCURRENCE AND DISSENT: (Sotomayor, J.) As a factual matter, the majority is incorrect about the level of hostility in Houston directed toward

Enron and Skilling (D), and about the adequacy of the district court's handling of voir dire. First, the majority understates the breadth and depth of community hostility toward Skilling (D) and Enron. For example, Enron's community ties were so extensive that the entire local U.S. Attorney's Office was forced to recuse itself from the Government's (P) investigation into the company's fall. With Enron's demise affecting the lives of so many Houstonians, local media coverage of the story saturated the community. While many of the thousands of media stories were straightforward news items, many others conveyed and amplified the community's outrage at the top executives perceived to be responsible for the company's bankruptcy. Articles deriding Enron's senior executives were juxtaposed with pieces expressing sympathy toward and solidarity with the company's many victims, and the media overwhelmingly indicated that Skilling's (D) indictment was overdue when it finally occurred. Given this acute state of animus, the district court's handling of voir dire fell short of constitutional requirements. The questionnaires returned to the court indicated that more than one-third of the prospective jurors indicated that they or persons they knew had lost money or jobs as a result of the Enron bankruptcy. Two-thirds of the jurors expressed views about Enron or the defendants that suggested a potential predisposition to convict. In many instances, they did not mince words, describing Skilling (D) as "smug," "arrogant," "brash," "conceited," "greedy," "deceitful," "totally unethical and criminal," "a crook," "the biggest liar on the face of the earth," and "guilty as sin." Ultimately, numerous individuals who had made harsh comments about Skilling (D) remained in the jury pool. From this, the court of appeals determined that prejudice was to be presumed, but that this presumption was rebuttable, thus turning the concept of presumptive prejudice into a burden-shifting framework: Once the defendant musters sufficient evidence of community hostility, the onus shifts to the Government (P) to prove the impartiality of the jury. However, the Court's precedents have never treated the notion of presumptive prejudice so formalistically. Instead, they convey the commonsense understanding that as the tide of public enmity rises, so too does the danger that the prejudices of the community will infiltrate the jury. The underlying question has, therefore, always been: Do we have confidence that the jury's verdict was "induced only by evidence and argument in open court, and not by any outside influence, whether of private talk or public print"? On one end of the spectrum, the Court has reversed, without considering the sufficiency of voir dire, a conviction where the Court found inherently prejudicial circumstances. In another case, the Court reversed the conviction where it found that voir dire did not suffice to counter the "wave of public passion" that had swept the community prior to the defendant's trial—despite the seated jurors' assurances of

Continued on next page.

impartiality. In that case, the Court emphasized that a juror's word on whether he or she can be impartial is not decisive, particularly when "the build-up of prejudice [in the community] is clear and convincing." Here, the majority was correct that the prospect of seating an unbiased jury in Houston was not so remote as to compel the conclusion that the district court acted unconstitutionally in denying Skilling's (D) motion to change venue—given the size and diversity of the Houston population; the media did not present smoking-gun evidence of Skilling's (D) guilt; and the courtroom proceedings themselves never turned into a "carnival." Still, the voir dire process itself fell short of constitutional requirements. First, the district court gave short shrift to the overwhelming evidence of hostility toward Skilling (D) and Enron. Second, that court, as well as the majority, downplayed the passions Enron's demise aroused in the public, characterizing the case as "neither heinous nor sensational" because no violence was involved. Economic crimes are certainly capable of rousing public passions, particularly when thousands of unsuspecting people are robbed of their livelihoods and retirement savings. Indeed, the record was replete with examples of visceral outrage toward Skilling (D) and other Enron executives, and some Houstonians compared Skilling (D) to, among other things, a rapist, an axe murderer, and an Al Qaeda terrorist. The situation was so hostile that Skilling (D) and the other executives had to hire private security, lest the public take matters into their own hands. Also, contrary to the majority's observation, the passage of time did little to soften community sentiment. If anything, the time that elapsed between the bankruptcy and the trial made the task of seating an unbiased jury more difficult, not less. Based on these circumstances, and perhaps because the district court did not perceive the intense animosity in the community, its short voir dire fell far short of identifying and removing biased jurors. First, it did not ask questions about the effect of Causey's guilty plea on the prospective jurors. Second, the questions the court did ask were addressed in a cursory fashion, primarily eliciting "yes" or "no" responses, instead of open-ended responses. Third, the district court failed to make a sufficiently critical assessment of prospective jurors' assurances of impartiality. Although the majority insists otherwise, the voir dire transcript shows that the district court essentially took jurors at their word when they promised to be fair. Indeed, the court declined to dismiss for cause any prospective juror who ultimately gave a clear assurance of impartiality, no matter how much equivocation preceded it. Worse still, the district court on a number of occasions accepted declarations of impartiality that were equivocal on their face, as where jurors "hoped" they could presume Skilling's (D) innocence, or did "not necessarily" think he was guilty. Finally, the mere fact that the jurors acquitted Skilling (D) of the insider trading charges does not necessarily indicate that they were impartial. Instead, it could just mean that there was a complete dearth of evidence to convict. For all these reasons, it is doubtful that Skilling's

(D) jury was indeed free from the deep-seated animosity that pervaded the community at large.

▶ ANALYSIS

The difficult issue in cases involving undisclosed self-dealing is the problem of proof. One reason for the court's limiting of the honest services doctrine is that federal criminal statutes have a better chance of surviving judicial scrutiny when they are limited in scope. Here, the Court sought to limit the statute's coverage to scenarios where there exists the possibility of concrete evidence to support the alleged crime, such as a bribe or a kickback.

■═■

Quicknotes

VENIREA list of jurors called to serve for a particular term.

VOIR DIRE Examination of potential jurors on a case.

■═■

The Criminal Trial

Quick Reference Rules of Law

Illinois v. Allen

State (P) v. Armed robbery convict (D)

397 U.S. 337 (1970).

NATURE OF CASE: Certiorari from reversal of a robbery conviction.

FACT SUMMARY: Allen (D) was convicted of armed robbery, after he was removed from the courtroom due to his disruptive behavior.

🏛 RULE OF LAW

The Sixth Amendment right of an accused to be present at his own trial and confront the witnesses against him can be lost if, after a warning by the judge, he continues to conduct himself in a manner so "disorderly, disruptive, and disrespectful of the court that his trial cannot be carried on with him in the courtroom."

FACTS: During his trial for armed robbery, Allen (D) argued with the judge continuously and in such an abusive, disruptive manner that it was impossible to carry on the trial. After repeated warnings from the judge that he would be removed, Allen (D) continued such behavior and was removed for most of his trial. Upon conviction and affirmation of the conviction by the Supreme Court of Illinois, Allen (D) brought a federal habeas corpus petition in the district court. The district court, finding no constitutional violation of Allen's (D) rights, declined to issue the writ, whereupon Allen (D) appealed to the court of appeals. The court of appeals reversed the conviction on the basis that an accused's Sixth Amendment right to "be confronted with the witnesses against him" can never be lost.

ISSUE: Where an accused is removed from his trial because of extremely disruptive behavior, after warnings by the judge that he would be removed if such behavior continued, has his right to be present at his trial been lost?

HOLDING AND DECISION: (Black, J.) Yes. The Sixth Amendment right of an accused to be present at his trial and confront the witnesses against him can be lost if, after a warning by the judge, he continues to conduct himself in a manner so "disorderly, disruptive and disrespectful of the court that his trial cannot be carried on with him in the courtroom." Of course, once the right is lost, it can be reclaimed when the accused is willing to conduct himself "consistently with the decorum and respect inherent in the concept of courts and judicial proceedings." It is essential to the proper administration of justice, that trial judges be given sufficient discretion to deal with disruptive behavior to preserve our system of justice, and there are at least three constitutionally permissible ways for a judge to handle such behavior: (1) bind and gag the accused in court, (2) cite him for contempt, or (3) take him out of

the courtroom until he agrees to conduct himself properly. Each of these possibilities has disadvantages and infringes to a different degree upon an accused's Sixth Amendment right to confront witnesses. Therefore, discretion must be allowed to the trial judge to determine the appropriate sanction under the circumstances. Here, the trial judge decided that it was best to remove the extremely disruptive Allen (D), and did so only after repeated warnings and after telling him that he could be present whenever he decided to act properly. This may not have been the only solution to the problem, but it was properly within the discretion of the trial judge. Under these circumstances, Allen (D) lost his right to be present throughout his trial. The judgment of the court of appeals is reversed.

▶ ANALYSIS

This case illustrates one situation in which an accused's absence from the courtroom does not violate his Sixth Amendment right to confront the witnesses against him. Generally, this right guarantees that an accused must be present in the courtroom during any time when "testimony" is offered against him (though not necessarily during arguments on questions of law), unless he "waives" that right. Waiver not only occurs when the accused is disruptive, but also, in most jurisdictions, when he voluntarily absents himself from the trial once it has started. Note, however, that if an accused is not present at the start of his trial, the court cannot proceed without him, even if his absence is deliberate. Note, finally, that the court here does not ignore the risk of prejudice to an accused, who is bound and gagged in front of a jury. Rather, the court states that this prejudice is one factor to be considered by the trial court when deciding whether such restraints should be applied or whether the disruptive accused should be removed from the court.

■■■

Quicknotes

CERTIORARI A discretionary writ issued by a superior court to an inferior court in order to review the lower court's decisions; the Supreme Court's writ ordering such review.

HABEAS CORPUS A proceeding in which a defendant brings a writ to compel a judicial determination of whether he is lawfully being held in custody.

SIXTH AMENDMENT Provides the right to a speedy and public trial by impartial jury, the right to be informed of

Continued on next page.

the accusation, the right to confront witnesses, and the right to have the assistance of counsel in all criminal prosecutions.

WAIVER The intentional or voluntary forfeiture of a recognized right.

■■■

Michigan v. Bryant

State (P) v. Individual (D)

562 U.S. 344 (2011).

NATURE OF CASE: Appeal from state court decision reversing conviction of an individual for murder.

FACT SUMMARY: After Bryant (D) shot victim Anthony Covington, Covington made statements before his death to the police implicating Bryant (D) as the shooter.

🏛 **RULE OF LAW**
Where the primary purpose of an interrogation of a witness is to allow police to respond to an ongoing emergency, statements made by a witness will not qualify as testimonial statements and the Confrontation Clause will not bar their admission at trial.

FACTS: Bryant (D) shot Covington. Police responding to a radio call found Covington and asked him what happened. Covington informed police that "Rick" Bryant (D) had shot him 25 minutes earlier through the back door of Bryant's house. The conversation between five police officers and Covington lasted five to ten minutes before an ambulance arrived and transported Covington to a hospital. He died several hours later. Police went to Bryant's (D) house and found blood and a bullet hole in the back door. At trial, the court allowed the police officers to testify as to Covington's statements regarding the identity of Bryant (D). A jury convicted Bryant (D) but the Michigan Supreme Court eventually reversed the conviction because the Confrontation Clause barred the use of Covington's statements, which that court held to be testimonial. The state (P) appealed to the United States Supreme Court.

ISSUE: Where the primary purpose of an interrogation of a witness is to allow police to respond to an ongoing emergency, do statements made by a witness qualify as testimonial statements and will the Confrontation Clause bar their admission at trial?

HOLDING AND DECISION: (Sotomayor, J.) No. Where the primary purpose of an interrogation of a witness is to allow police to respond to an ongoing emergency, statements made by a witness will not qualify as testimonial statements and the Confrontation Clause will not bar their admission at trial. To determine whether the primary purpose is to assist the police with an ongoing emergency courts should analyze the circumstances present, the statements of the parties, and their actions. It is an objective test. When an emergency situation is present, statements made to resolve the emergency are given indicia of reliability, thus shielding them from cross-examination usually required by the Confrontation Clause for out of

court statements. In addition to the circumstances, another factor is the informality of the questioning, including where the questioning took place. A review of both the questions and answers given during the alleged emergency situation is critical. Police officers have a duty to resolve emergency situations and serve as criminal investigators. A victim's statements often have a purpose of protecting themselves, particularly when an armed assailant remains at large. Another factor is the type of dispute. If the dispute is domestic, the level of emergency may be lower. That was not the case here. The police did not know if Covington's shooter was a threat only to Covington at the time. Nor did the police know the location or motive of Bryant (D) during the police officers' questioning of Covington. The questioning was also informal, and occurred in a public place. Accordingly, because the primary purpose of Covington's statements was to assist the police in resolving the emergency, the statements were not testimonial and the Confrontation Clause did not bar their admission at trial. The judgment of the Supreme Court of Michigan is vacated, and the case is remanded for further proceedings not inconsistent with this opinion.

CONCURRENCE: (Thomas, J.) Covington's statements were not testimonial because they occurred in an informal setting. The statements did not therefore "bear testimony" against Bryant (D). Analysis of the setting in which the statements were made is more appropriate, rather than the majority's primary purpose test.

DISSENT: (Scalia, J.) The majority's decision greatly distorts our prior Confrontation Clause jurisprudence. The focus of the inquiry should be on the intent of the declarant. Here, 25 minutes after the shooting, Covington found himself surrounded by five police officers. These five officers all asked Covington to describe what had happened, what the shooter looked like, and what events led to the shooting. The alleged "emergency situation" had ended 25 minutes earlier. It is unreasonable to think that Bryant (D) would attempt to fire upon Covington again. Covington, aware that the threat had ended, had the sole of purpose of identifying his shooter to the police. Even if the perspective of the officers is taken into account, none of the officers testified that they were in danger of any imminent threat. At a minimum, the questions from the officers became investigative, thus rendering Covington's statements testimonial in nature. The majority's decision greatly expands the definition of emergency situations in violation of the Confrontation Clause. Pursuant to this decision,

Continued on next page.

prosecutors and police may be able to argue that statements given in the hours after an incident but before a suspect is arrested are not testimonial because an ongoing emergency still exists. Finally, the Court's reversion to a reliability standard has been previously rejected by this Court. Reliability of a statement does not mean it is testimonial or nontestimonial. Per the Sixth Amendment, the proper analysis is whether the statements are testimonial, not reliable. If they are testimonial, the Confrontation Clause bars the admission of such statements because the defendant has not been given the right to cross-examine.

▶ *ANALYSIS*

The significance of this case is that it deals solely with the Confrontation Clause analysis. The Court remanded the case to the Michigan courts for a determination of whether the statements could be admitted through another hearsay exception, such as a dying declaration or an excited utterance. The *Crawford v. Washington,* 541 U.S. 36 (2004), decision rejected the notion that out of court statements were admissible over Confrontation Clause objections if they were shown to be reliable. Justice Scalia's dissent argued that the majority's decision was a return to the improper reliability standard.

■━━■

Quicknotes

CONFRONTATION CLAUSE A provision in the Sixth Amendment to the United States Constitution that an accused in a criminal action has the right to confront the witnesses against him, including the right to attend the trial and to cross-examine witnesses called on behalf of the prosecution.

EXCITED UTTERANCE An exception to the hearsay rule for statements made or caused by the happening of a startling occurrence and that is related to that occurrence.

■━━■

Griffin v. California

First-degree murder convict (D) v. State (P)

380 U.S. 609 (1965).

NATURE OF CASE: Certiorari from a murder conviction.

FACT SUMMARY: Griffin (D), during his trial for first-degree murder, did not testify on the issue of his guilt, and both the prosecutor and judge subsequently commented on this failure to the jury before it convicted him.

🏛 RULE OF LAW

The Fifth Amendment Self-Incrimination Clause implicitly forbids comment by the prosecution on an accused's failure to testify, or instructions by the court that such failure is evidence of guilt.

FACTS: Griffin (D) refused to testify at his trial for first-degree murder, invoking the Fifth Amendment privilege against self-incrimination. Before the jury deliberated on the issue of guilt, the prosecutor commented on this failure to testify and suggested that guilt should be inferred therefrom. During instructions to the jury, the court stated that if Griffin (D) failed to explain facts within his knowledge which tended to indicate his guilt, then the jury could take that failure as "tending to indicate the truth of such evidence," but that such failure alone does not by itself "warrant an inference of guilt." Upon conviction, and affirmance of that conviction by the California Supreme Court, Griffin (D) brought a petition for certiorari to the United States Supreme Court.

ISSUE: Do comments by a judge or prosecutor on an accused's failure to testify violate his Fifth Amendment privilege against self-incrimination?

HOLDING AND DECISION: (Douglas, J.) Yes. The Fifth Amendment Self-Incrimination Clause forbids comment by the prosecution on an accused's failure to testify, or instructions by the court that such failure is evidence of guilt. Such comment by the prosecution or court is a "remnant of the inquisitorial system of criminal justice which the Fifth Amendment protects against." Such comment penalizes the exercise of a constitutional privilege to refrain from self-incrimination and, as such, cannot be allowed. It may be true that there is a natural inference of guilt from a failure to testify as to facts within the knowledge of an accused, but the jury must make this inference on its own without comment from the court. Here, therefore, Griffin's (D) conviction must be reversed.

DISSENT: (Stewart, J.) In examining if an accused's privilege against self-incrimination has been violated "compulsion" is the focus of inquiry (i.e., such privilege has only been violated if the accused was "compelled to be a witness against himself"). The Court, however, fails to identify any such compulsion in the comments of the court and prosecutor. First, such comments do not compel an accused's testimony by creating awareness in the jury of his failure to testify, since that failure is obvious by itself. Second, no compulsion may be assumed on the ground that the inferences drawn by the jury that has heard such comments will be detrimental to an accused, especially where the court has carefully controlled its comments. The trial court here carefully instructed the jury that Griffin's (D) failure to testify "does not by itself warrant an inference of guilt." It is doubtful that a jury without such instructions would have observed such a limitation. The comment in this case was a means of articulating and rationally discussing a fact that is necessarily impressed on the jury's consciousness (i.e., the failure to testify). The state has an important interest in such discussion, which should not arbitrarily be cut off.

▶ ANALYSIS

This case illustrates the rule applicable to "direct comment" on an accused's failure to "testify." Note, however, that it does not prevent a prosecutor from commenting on an accused's "failure to offer evidence" on critical aspects of the case. It has been held that a court's comment that an accused's "failure to explain" possession of recently stolen property should be considered in determining whether he knew the goods were stolen, does not violate *Griffin* (*Barnes v. United States*, 412 U.S. 837 (1973)). Of course, what is considered permissible depends upon the wording of the prosecutor's comments. If he emphasizes an accused's failure to present other evidence instead of the fact that he "personally" offered no explanation, there is probably no violation of *Griffin*. Note, further, that *Griffin* does not prevent a prosecutor from commenting to a jury upon an accused's "refusal to submit to reasonable tests or examinations," the results of which would have been admissible on the issue of guilt or innocence. Note, finally, that *Griffin* does prevent counsel for one of several codefendants from commenting on the failure of other co-defendants to testify.

■=■

Quicknotes

PRIVILEGE AGAINST SELF-INCRIMINATION A privilege guaranteed by the Fifth Amendment to the federal Constitution in a criminal proceeding for communications made by an accused and protecting an accused or witness from having to give testimony that may incriminate himself.

■=■

Darden v. Wainwright

Murder convict (D) v. Court (P)

477 U.S. 168 (1986).

NATURE OF CASE: Appeal of denial of habeas corpus.

FACT SUMMARY: At the guilt phase of a murder trial, the prosecution made improper closing statements concerning the crime.

🏛 RULE OF LAW
Improper closing statements by counsel will void a conviction only if they make the trial so unfair as to violate due process.

FACTS: Darden (D) was charged with a particularly vicious series of crimes, including murder. At his trial, counsel for the prosecution made various improper closing arguments, which appealed to passion rather than to facts, although evidence was not misstated, and no comments were made about the exercise of rights. Darden (D) was sentenced to death. This was affirmed on appeal, and the court of appeals denied habeas corpus. Darden (D) appealed.

ISSUE: Will improper closing statements by counsel void a conviction only if they make the trial so unfair as to violate due process?

HOLDING AND DECISION: (Powell, J.) Yes. Improper closing statements by counsel will void a conviction only if they make the trial so unfair as to violate due process. It is not enough to void a conviction that remarks by counsel are improper or incorrect. The relevant question is whether the remarks made the trial so unfair as to violate due process. Here, the remarks, while appealing to the passion of the jurors, did not misstate the evidence, and did not comment on the exercise of constitutional rights. The trial still was fundamentally fair. Affirmed.

DISSENT: (Blackmun, J.) The prosecution in this case offered personal opinions as to guilt, injected broader issues into the trial, and used arguments designed to inflame the passions of the jury. The result of all this was an unfair trial.

▌ ANALYSIS

The dissent did not appear to question the standard of review used by the court. Due process would appear to be the standard the dissent proposed. However, the dissent disagreed with the court's conclusion that the trial was not fundamentally unfair.

Quicknotes

PROCEDURAL DUE PROCESS The constitutional mandate that if the state or federal government acts so as to deny a citizen of a life, liberty or property interest the individual is first entitled to notice and the right to be heard.

CHAPTER 26

Reprosecution and Double Jeopardy

Quick Reference Rules of Law

Illinois v. Somerville

State (D) v. Re-trial defendant (P)

410 U.S. 458 (1973).

NATURE OF CASE: Appeal of a judgment granting a petition for habeas corpus.

FACT SUMMARY: The judge declared a mistrial of Somerville's (P) first trial and Somerville (P) claimed that the second trial amounted to double jeopardy.

🏛 RULE OF LAW
If a trial judge grants a mistrial, over the objections of the defendant, because there is a manifest necessity to grant a mistrial or in order to meet the ends of public justice, a second trial for the same offense does not amount to double jeopardy.

FACTS: Somerville (P) was indicted by an Illinois grand jury for the crime of theft. Before any evidence was presented at his trial, the prosecuting attorney asked the court to declare a mistrial because Somerville's (P) indictment was found to be fatally defective. The defect could not be cured by an amendment and Somerville (P) could not waive the error as it was considered jurisdictional. The court felt that further proceedings under this indictment would be useless, and therefore declared a mistrial. Two days later, the grand jury handed down a second indictment. Somerville (P) claimed that the second trial constituted double jeopardy. The court rejected this contention and convicted Somerville (P), and the state appellate court upheld the verdict. Somerville (P) then sought a writ of habeas corpus in the federal district court, but the writ was denied and the Seventh Circuit Court of Appeals affirmed that decision. Somerville's (P) petition for certiorari was granted and the case was remanded for reconsideration in light of two recent court decisions. On remand, the Seventh Circuit held that Somerville's (P) petition for habeas corpus should have been granted because jeopardy had attached when the jury was impaneled and sworn in. A declaration of a mistrial by the court over Somerville's (P) objections precluded a retrial. Somerville (P) claims that once a jury has been selected and sworn in that jeopardy attaches, and that he has a right to have his case completed by the first court.

ISSUE: If a trial judge grants a mistrial, over the objections of the defendant, is a second trial for the same offense prohibited under the doctrine of double jeopardy because the mistrial was granted in order to meet the ends of public justice?

HOLDING AND DECISION: (Rehnquist, J.) No. If the court finds that there is manifest necessity for calling a mistrial or the ends of public justice would otherwise be defeated if a mistrial were not declared, the court may declare a mistrial over the objections of the defendant. The court must consider all the circumstances in making its decision. In this case, it would have been useless to complete the first trial under the defective indictment because, on appeal, the decision would have been reversed and the case would have had to be retried. By declaring a mistrial, all parties were saved considerable time and expense. The court also appointed out that the public has an interest in seeing all trials end in either a conviction or an acquittal. The court held that even though a defendant has a valued right to have his trial completed by a particular tribunal, that right must, in some instances, be subordinated to the public's interest in fair trials ending in just judgments. Since the declaration of a mistrial implemented a reasonable state policy, Somerville's (P) interest in proceeding to verdict was outweighed by the competing and equally legitimate demand for public justice. The decision of the court of appeals was therefore reversed.

DISSENT: (White, J.) The right of the defendant not to be put in double jeopardy outweighs the public's interest in fair trials and there was no manifest necessity to grant the mistrial. Somerville (P) had the right to be tried by the jury chosen in the first trial.

▶ ANALYSIS

This case illustrates one of the situations in which a second trial is permissible, even though jeopardy would normally have been held to have attached at the first trial. Jeopardy attaches when the jury has been sworn in a jury trial, or when the first witness has been sworn in a trial without a jury. Usually, once jeopardy has attached, a second trial would constitute double jeopardy. Note, however, that there are several other situations in which a second trial is permissible after jeopardy has attached: (1) after a successful appeal by the defendant, (2) where a jury is unable to reach a verdict due to some "evident necessity" (e.g., death of judge or juror), (3) where there is a "hung jury," or (4) where "misconduct of a witness or a defendant" personally causes a mistrial.

■━■

Quicknotes

DOUBLE JEOPARDY A prohibition against a second prosecution for the same offense after an acquittal or conviction for that offense in a prior proceeding or against multiple punishments for the same offense.

Continued on next page.

HABEAS CORPUS A proceeding in which a defendant brings a writ to compel a judicial determination of whether he is lawfully being held in custody.

JEOPARDY The subjection to potential conviction and punishment in a trial for a criminal act.

MISTRIAL An erroneous or invalid trial.

Renico v. Lett

State (P) v. Individual (D)

559 U.S. 766 (2010).

NATURE OF CASE: Appeal from Sixth Circuit Court of Appeals decision in favor of the plaintiff.

FACT SUMMARY: After a nine-hour trial spread out over a week, jurors deliberated for a period of four hours. After sending a note to the trial judge referring to their inability to agree, the foreperson informed the judge that the jury would not reach a unanimous verdict. The judge then declared a mistrial.

> ### 🏛 RULE OF LAW
> A trial judge may declare a mistrial when, considering all of the circumstances, there is a high degree of necessity for doing so.

FACTS: After a nine-hour trial spread out over a week, jurors deliberated for a period of four hours. After four hours of deliberations, the jurors sent a note asking, "What if we can't agree? Mistrial? Retrial?" The jurors also sent a separate note stating that they had a concern their raised voices were disturbing other court proceedings. The judge then brought the jury out and asked the foreperson if the jury would be able to reach a verdict. The foreperson replied, "No, Judge." Without any objections from defense counsel or the prosecution, the judge declared a mistrial. A second jury later convicted Lett (D) of second-degree murder. Lett (D) eventually filed this petition for habeas corpus relief, which the Sixth Circuit Court of Appeals granted. The State (P) appealed to the United States Supreme Court.

ISSUE: May a trial judge declare a mistrial when, considering all of the circumstances, there is a high degree of necessity for doing so?

HOLDING AND DECISION: (Roberts, C.J.) Yes. A trial judge may declare a mistrial when, considering all of the circumstances, there is a high degree of necessity for doing so. The trial court judge has broad discretion to issue a mistrial. The judge is in the best position to assess whether a jury will be able to reach a verdict. Without such discretion, trial court judges would employ coercive measures that may force the jury into reaching a verdict it otherwise may not have reached. The trial judge's exercise of that discretion must be sound. The trial judge need not make any findings to support his or her decision, nor must the judge force the jury to deliberate for some time period before declaring a mistrial. Here, the jurors' notes were evidence of a significant disagreement among the jury. Moreover, the foreperson clearly answered that the jury would be unable to reach a verdict. While the judge could have used her discretion to have the jury deliberate

for additional time or consulted with trial counsel before proceeding, she was under no obligation to do so. The writ of habeas corpus should be denied. Reversed.

DISSENT: (Stevens, J.) The trial judge cut off deliberations before it was evident that further deliberations would be useless. The judge did not poll the jurors, instruct the jury to conduct further deliberations, query counsel on their thoughts for proceeding forward, or make any findings on the record regarding the declaration of a mistrial. A judge has a duty to exercise sound discretion, which did not occur here.

▶ ANALYSIS

When the standard of review is abuse of discretion, it is often difficult on appeal to overturn a decision made by a trial court judge. Appellate courts typically grant trial court judges broad discretion to make decisions based upon the conduct of the trial as it occurs in front of them. Even the majority noted the trial court judge should have instructed the jury to continue deliberations, but the judge was not required to do so.

■■■

Quicknotes

ABUSE OF DISCRETION A determination by an appellate court that a lower court's decision was based on an error of law.

HABEAS CORPUS A proceeding in which a defendant brings a writ to compel a judicial determination of whether he is lawfully being held in custody.

■■■

Oregon v. Kennedy

State (P) v. Re-tried theft convict (D)

456 U.S. 667 (1982).

NATURE OF CASE: Appeal from dismissal of prosecution for theft.

FACT SUMMARY: After being granted a mistrial, Kennedy (D) contended the Double Jeopardy Clause barred re-prosecution.

🏛 RULE OF LAW
Following a defendant's successful motion for a mistrial, the Double Jeopardy Clause will bar retrial only when the prosecution's objectionable conduct was done with the intent to provoke a mistrial motion.

FACTS: Kennedy (D) was charged with theft. During redirect of a State's (P) witness, the prosecutor made certain improper comments that resulted in a mistrial. It did not appear that the prosecutor intentionally provoked the motion. Kennedy (D) was retried and convicted. Kennedy (D) appealed, contending the Double Jeopardy Clause barred retrial. The Oregon Supreme Court agreed, and reversed the conviction. Oregon (P) appealed.

ISSUE: Following a defendant's successful motion for a mistrial, will the Double Jeopardy Clause bar retrial only when the prosecution's objectionable conduct was done with the intent to provoke a mistrial motion?

HOLDING AND DECISION: (Rehnquist, J.) Yes. Following a defendant's successful motion for a mistrial the Double Jeopardy Clause will bar retrial only when the prosecution's objectionable conduct was done with the intent to provoke a mistrial motion. The protection against double jeopardy is largely waived when the defendant himself moves for a mistrial. However, prosecutorial conduct may compel a defendant to move for a mistrial. There will always be an element of prejudicial prosecutorial conduct toward a defendant, so this alone does not justify barring retrial. A standard of intent by the prosecutor to provoke a mistrial motion is one easily applied. Any other standard would be very difficult to quantify. Only when the prosecutor intentionally provokes a motion should the prosecutor's conduct be such that a retrial should be barred. Reversed.

CONCURRENCE: (Powell, J.) A court should rely on objective evidence of intent.

CONCURRENCE: (Stevens, J.) Prosecutorial harassment or overreaching should also bar retrial.

▶ ANALYSIS

It is basic constitutional law that the United States Supreme Court is the final word on federal law. Several states have adopted rules broader than that enunciated here, based on state law. Oregon (P) did so later in this action. Kennedy (D) lost the battle but won the war.

■=■

Quicknotes

DOUBLE JEOPARDY A prohibition against a second prosecution for the same offense after an acquittal or conviction for that offense in a prior proceeding or against multiple punishments for the same offense.

MISTRIAL An erroneous or invalid trial.

■=■

United States v. Scott

Federal government (P) v. Narcotics indictee (D)

437 U.S. 82 (1978).

NATURE OF CASE: Appeal from dismissals of two counts of a criminal indictment.

FACT SUMMARY: Two of the three counts in the indictment against Scott (D) were dismissed on the ground that his defense had been prejudiced by preindictment delay, and the Government (P) sought to appeal.

🏛 RULE OF LAW

There is no violation of the Double Jeopardy Clause if the government appeals when the defendant has successfully sought to have his trial terminated without any submission to either judge or jury as to his guilt or innocence, whether it be by dismissal of the count or otherwise.

FACTS: Scott (D) successfully moved to have two of the three counts in his indictment for distributing narcotics dismissed on the ground that his defense had been prejudiced by preindictment delay. The offense allegedly occurred in September 1974, and the indictment was issued on March 5, 1975. A guilty verdict as to the third count was returned, but the Government (P) sought to appeal the dismissal of the first two counts. Concluding that any further prosecution on those counts was barred by the Double Jeopardy Clause, the appeal was dismissed and the Government (P) then sought review of that decision only as to the first count.

ISSUE: Can the government appeal when a defendant is successful in having the trial terminated without submission to judge or jury for determination of guilt or innocence?

HOLDING AND DECISION: (Rehnquist, J.) Yes. If a defendant manages to have his trial terminated without his guilt or innocence being submitted to judge or jury, as when he successfully moved for dismissal of a charge, the government may appeal without violating the Double Jeopardy Clause. The Double Jeopardy Clause looks askance at the government repeatedly seeking to try a person, but it does not come into play when the government is quite willing to continue a trial to conclusion but the defendant elects to seek termination of the trial on grounds unrelated to guilt or innocence. Unlike an insanity or entrapment defense, dismissal of a charge for preindictment delay represents a legal judgment that a defendant, although criminally culpable, may not be punished because of a supposed constitutional violation. It is a termination of a trial on grounds unrelated to guilt or innocence, and the Double Jeopardy Clause is not offended when such a

dismissal is appealed by the government. In such a case, it is the government which has lost its right to "one complete opportunity to convict those who have violated its laws"; the defendant has voluntarily given up, as opposed to being deprived of, his valued right to go to the first jury. Judgment reversed.

DISSENT: (Brennan, J.) The majority's attempt to draw a distinction between "true acquittals," supposedly subject to the Double Jeopardy bar of government appeals, and other final judgments, supposedly subject to the bar, favoring the accused, is unsupported in logic or policy. The definition adopted for "acquittal" is overly restrictive, as is evidenced by the attempted distinction between a dismissal based on preaccusation delay and one based on a defense of insanity or entrapment. The Double Jeopardy Clause mandates the government has just one complete opportunity to convict an accused and that retrial be barred when the first proceeding terminates in a final judgment favorable to the defendant, which is what occurred in this case. The reasons underlying preclusion of retrial after an acquittal are equally applicable to a final judgment entered on a ground "unrelated to factual innocence," so their disparate treatment is untenable. Furthermore, in this case, one of the "factual elements of the offense charged" was delay. If, indeed, acquittal is resolution of some or all of these elements, there was an acquittal and retrial is barred. In fact, there are few instances where defenses can be deemed unrelated to factual innocence.

▶ ANALYSIS

Prior to this case, the court had determined that an appeal by the government is barred by double jeopardy considerations when there is a pre-verdict judgment of acquittal based on the court's determination of the sufficiency of the evidence. Since the same result could be obtained by dismissing the indictment for failure to charge an offense, which would be more like a mistrial and could make appeal possible in certain circumstances, the court would be left with two options on how to treat a particular case. One option would bar government appeal and the other would not. Regarding this situation, Wright, Miller, and Cooper, 15 *Federal Practice and Procedure* § 3919 (1978) (pocket part) states: "If this conclusion is correct, it means that the trial court has discretion to control the double jeopardy consequences of its ruling. It also means that the government must be astute to argue for a disposition that leaves it free to appeal or start over. Although it is

Continued on next page.

troubling that trial judges should be left free of appellate review, procedural punctilio at least has the advantage of helping the defendant to know whether further proceedings may be possible. Even this virtue may be reduced, however, until the 'manifest necessity' standard that limits retrials after a mistrial or dismissal without the defendant's consent is elaborated in the context of defective indictments."

■═■

Quicknotes

ACQUITTAL The discharge of an accused individual from suspicion of guilt for a particular crime and from further prosecution for that offense.

MISTRIAL An erroneous or invalid trial.

■═■

Lockhart v. Nelson

State (P) v. Burglary convict (D)

488 U.S. 33 (1988).

NATURE OF CASE: Review of habeas corpus invalidating a conviction under a recidivist statute.

FACT SUMMARY: Nelson (D) was convicted under a recidivist statute, and when the conviction was shown to have been invalid, the State (P) attempted to retry him.

🏛 RULE OF LAW
When a conviction is based on evidence erroneously admitted and is reversed on appeal, the Double Jeopardy Clause does not prohibit retrial.

FACTS: Nelson (D) was convicted of burglary. Under a state recidivist statute, which required four prior felony convictions to be applicable, an enhanced sentencing hearing was held. Evidence of four prior convictions was introduced, although Nelson (D) contended one had been pardoned. Nelson was convicted under the recidivist law. In a habeas proceeding, Nelson (D) introduced proof of the pardon. The district court granted habeas. The State (P) announced an intention to retry, substituting another felony for the pardoned one. The district court held this to be barred by the Double Jeopardy Clause. The Eighth Circuit affirmed, and the United States Supreme Court granted review.

ISSUE: When a conviction is based on evidence erroneously admitted and is reversed on appeal, does the Double Jeopardy Clause prohibit retrial?

HOLDING AND DECISION: (Rehnquist, C.J.) No. When a conviction is based on evidence erroneously admitted and is reversed on appeal, the Double Jeopardy Clause does not prohibit retrial. It has long been settled that the clause does not bar retrial if a conviction is reversed on appeal. An exception to this rule has been created, that where a reversal is based on insufficiency of evidence, no retrial should occur, as such a reversal is tantamount to an acquittal. However, a reversal based on the erroneous admission of evidence is not the same situation. It may be that other evidence was not introduced for tactical reasons, because of the evidence that was erroneously admitted. The prosecution is entitled to present its best case. This differs from the above exception, because there the prosecution presumably has introduced its best case and still failed to obtain a conviction. Here, the prosecution wishes to introduce evidence of another, valid conviction, and it should be permitted to do so. Reversed.

DISSENT: (Marshall, J.) The decision here seems to rest on the notion that prosecutors held back evidence, which is a questionable supposition at best.

▶ ANALYSIS

The rule that a defendant may be retried following a reversal is relatively new. Up until the latter part of the nineteenth century, there could be one trial, one judgment, and one appeal. If exonerating evidence was later found, there was no judicial remedy. Appeals for executive clemency were much more important then than now. There have been calls among a minority of authorities for a return to such a system.

Quicknotes

DOUBLE JEOPARDY A prohibition against a second prosecution for the same offense after an acquittal or conviction for that offense in a prior proceeding or against multiple punishments for the same offense.

HABEAS CORPUS COLLATERAL REVIEW An independent review of whether a prisoner is being lawfully imprisoned.

RECIDIVIST A habitual criminal.

Heath v. Alabama

Murder convict (D) v. State (P)

474 U.S. 82 (1985).

NATURE OF CASE: Review of murder conviction.

FACT SUMMARY: After being convicted of murder in Georgia, Heath (D) was convicted of murder in Alabama (P) for the same homicide.

🏛 RULE OF LAW
Successive prosecutions by two states for the same conduct are not barred by the Double Jeopardy Clause.

FACTS: Heath (D) was charged in Georgia with murder, arising out of his allegedly hiring certain individuals to kill his wife, who was in fact killed. Part of the crime occurred in Alabama. Heath (D) was convicted by a Georgia jury and sentenced to life imprisonment. He was then charged with murder in Alabama. He was convicted and sentenced to death. His double jeopardy claims were rejected at the trial level and on appeal as well. The United States Supreme Court accepted review.

ISSUE: Are successive prosecutions by two states for the same conduct barred by the Double Jeopardy Clause?

HOLDING AND DECISION: (O'Connor, J.) No. Successive prosecutions by two states for the same conduct are not barred by the Double Jeopardy Clause. A crime is an offense against the sovereignty of a government. When an individual breaks the laws of two states, he has committed two distinct offenses. Each sovereign is entitled to have its law adjudicated in its own courts, so it is no answer to the above principle that the trial in Georgia regarded the same sort of offense involved in Alabama. Essentially, when two laws derive from two different ultimate sources, two separate offenses occur when the laws of each ultimate source are broken. Here, two separate sovereigns, Alabama and Georgia, are involved, and consequently two different offenses occurred. Affirmed.

▶ ANALYSIS

The analysis of the Court here does not apply in all cases where the laws of multiple jurisdictions are broken. For instance, if a single act violates similar laws in a county and a state, the violator may not be tried twice. Counties are not sovereigns, but rather subdivisions of a sovereign state.

■■■

Quicknotes

DOUBLE JEOPARDY A prohibition against a second prosecution for the same offense after an acquittal or conviction for that offense in a prior proceeding or against multiple punishments for the same offense.

FULL FAITH AND CREDIT Doctrine judgment by a court of one state shall be given the same effect in another.

■■■

Quick Reference Rules of Law

Williams v. New York

Defendant (D) v. State (P)

337 U.S. 241 (1949).

NATURE OF CASE: Appeal from a death sentence.

FACT SUMMARY: The judge imposed a death sentence for a murder conviction after a jury had recommended life imprisonment.

RULE OF LAW
A sentencing judge can exercise a wide discretion in the sources and types of evidence used to assist him in determining the kind and extent of punishment to be imposed within limits fixed by law.

FACTS: Williams (D) was found guilty of murder in the first degree. The jury recommended life imprisonment. The trial judge, after considering information from the presentence investigation, imposed the death sentence. Williams (D) appealed, alleging that the judge's consideration of information obtained outside the courtroom, from persons whom Williams (D) had not been permitted to confront or cross-examine, violated his due process rights under the Fourteenth Amendment.

ISSUE: May a sentencing judge exercise a wide discretion in the sources and types of evidence used to assist him in determining the kind and extent of punishment to be imposed within limits fixed by law?

HOLDING AND DECISION: (Black, J.) Yes. A sentencing judge can exercise a wide discretion in the sources and types of evidence used to assist him in determining the kind and extent of punishment to be imposed within limits fixed by law. In addition to the historical basis for different evidentiary rules governing trial and sentencing procedures, there are sound practical reasons for the distinction. Modern concepts individualizing punishment have made it necessary that a sentencing judge not be denied an opportunity to obtain pertinent information by a requirement of rigid adherence to restrictive rules of evidence properly applicable to the trial. Affirmed.

DISSENT: (Murphy, J.) In our criminal courts the jury sits as the representative of the community; its voice is that of the society against which the crime was committed. A judge, even though vested with the statutory authority to do so, should hesitate indeed to increase the severity of such a community expression.

▶ ANALYSIS

The court relied on information that Williams (D) had committed thirty other burglaries in the same areas, some to which he had confessed. His probation report revealed certain sexual activities that the judge considered to be morbid. The judge found Williams (D) to be a menace to society, based on this information. Rule 32 of the Fed. R. Crim. P. permits federal judges to consider reports made by probation officers in imposing sentences, reflecting the historical position.

■=■

Quicknotes

DISCRETION The authority conferred upon a public official to act reasonably in accordance with his own judgment under certain circumstances.

FIRST-DEGREE MURDER The willful killing of another person with deliberation and premeditation; first-degree murder also encompasses those situations in which a person is killed within the perpetration of, or attempt to perpetrate, specified felonies.

FOURTEENTH AMENDMENT DUE PROCESS CLAUSE Provides that protections mandated by the Constitution and observed by the federal government are equally applicable, and therefore must be observed by the States.

■=■

Apprendi v. New Jersey

Convicted accused (D) v. State (P)

530 U.S. 466 (2000).

NATURE OF CASE: Appeal from sentence.

FACT SUMMARY: Apprendi (D) contended that any fact that increases the penalty for a crime beyond the statutory maximum must be submitted to a jury and proved beyond a reasonable doubt.

RULE OF LAW

The Due Process Clause of the Fourteenth Amendment requires that any fact that increases the penalty for a crime beyond the statutory maximum must be submitted to a jury and proved beyond a reasonable doubt.

FACTS: Apprendi (D) pleaded guilty to a shooting, and at sentencing the government produced evidence that the shooting was racially motivated. The sentencing judge found evidence of racial bias by a preponderance of the evidence and imposed an enhanced sentence on the basis of the hate crime law. That sentence was well above what Apprendi (D) could have received for the crime to which he pled guilty. The sentence was upheld by the New Jersey appellate court, which concluded that the state had the authority to define racial motivation as a "sentencing factor" rather than as "an element of the crime." Apprendi (D) appealed.

ISSUE: Does the Due Process Clause of the Fourteenth Amendment require that any fact that increases the penalty for a crime beyond the statutory maximum must be submitted to a jury and proved beyond a reasonable doubt?

HOLDING AND DECISION: (Stevens, J.) Yes. The Due Process Clause of the Fourteenth Amendment requires that any fact that increases the penalty for a crime beyond the statutory maximum must be submitted to a jury and proved beyond a reasonable doubt. The New Jersey procedure here challenged is an unacceptable departure from the jury tradition that is an indispensable part of our criminal justice system. At stake in this case are constitutional protections of surpassing importance: the proscription of any deprivation of liberty without due process of law and the guarantee, inter alia, of public trial by an impartial jury. Taken together, these rights indisputably entitle a criminal defendant to a jury determination that he or she is guilty of every element of the crime with which charged, beyond a reasonable doubt. In this regard, this Court does not recognize any distinction between an "element" of a felony offense and a "sentencing factor." This court has previously made clear that due process and associated jury protections extend, to some degree, to determinations that go not to a defendant's guilt or inno-cence, but simply to the length of his or her sentence. Reversed.

DISSENT: (O'Connor, J.) This Court has long recognized that not every fact that bears on a defendant's punishment need be charged in an indictment, submitted to a jury, and proved by the government beyond a reasonable doubt. Rather, the legislature's definition of the elements of the offense is usually dispositive. (Breyer, J.) There are, to put it simply, far too many potentially relevant sentencing factors to permit submission of all (or even many) of them to a jury. Even the Federal Sentencing Guidelines themselves note that a sentencing system tailored to fit every conceivable wrinkle of each case can become unworkable and seriously compromise the certainty of punishment and its deterrent effect. To ask a jury to consider all, or many, such matters would do the same.

ANALYSIS

As the Supreme Court makes clear in *Apprendi*, the historic link between verdict and judgment and the consistent limitations of judges' discretion to operate within the limits of the legal penalties highlight the novelty of a legislative scheme, such as that of New Jersey, that removes the jury from the determination of a fact that, if found, exposes the criminal defendant to a penalty exceeding the maximum he or she would receive if punished according to the facts reflected in the jury verdict alone. It is for this articulated reason that the Supreme Court emphasizes that the "reasonable doubt" requirement has such a vital role in American criminal procedure for cogent reasons. Hence, the Court requires, among other things, procedural protections in order to provide concrete substance for the presumption of innocence and to reduce the risk of imposing such deprivations erroneously.

Quicknotes

DUE PROCESS CLAUSE Clauses, found in the Fifth and Fourteenth Amendments to the United States Constitution, providing that no person shall be deprived of "life, liberty, or property, without due process of law."

REASONABLE DOUBT Enough doubt on the part of jurors to acquit a defendant based on the absence of evidence.

Quick Reference Rules of Law

North Carolina v. Pearce

State (P) v. Assault convict (D)

395 U.S. 711 (1969).

NATURE OF CASE: Petitions for writs of habeas corpus.

FACT SUMMARY: Pearce (D) obtained a reversal of his conviction. Upon retrial, he was sentenced to eight years in prison which, when added to the time he had already served, amounted to a longer total sentence than that originally imposed. Rice (D) also obtained a reversal of his conviction. Upon retrial, he was sentenced to a harsher sentence than his original sentence, and no credit was given for the time he had already served.

🏛 RULE OF LAW

(1) The Double Jeopardy Clause does not prohibit, upon a defendant's reconviction, the imposition of a harsher sentence than that imposed after the first conviction, but whenever a judge does impose a more severe sentence upon a defendant's reconviction, his reasons for doing so must be shown.

(2) The Double Jeopardy Clause requires that in computing a new sentence on retrial, credit be given for that part of the original sentence already served.

FACTS: Pearce (D) was sentenced to 12 to 15 years in prison for assault with intent to rape. He obtained a reversal of his conviction. Upon retrial, he was convicted and sentenced to eight years, which, when added to the time he had already served, amounted to a longer sentence than that originally imposed. Rice (D) was sentenced to ten years in prison after pleading guilty to burglary. He obtained a reversal of his conviction. Upon his retrial, he was convicted on three of the original four counts and sentenced to a term totaling 25 years. No credit was given for the time he had already served. Pearce (D) was granted habeas corpus on the ground that the longer sentence was unconstitutional. Rice (D) was also granted habeas corpus as it was found that the state was punishing him for his having exercised his post-conviction right of review.

ISSUE:
(1) Does the Fifth Amendment prohibit the imposition of a more severe punishment after conviction for the same offense upon retrial?

(2) Does the Fifth Amendment require that, in computing a new sentence on retrial, credit must be given for that part of the original sentence already served?

HOLDING AND DECISION: (Stewart, J.)
(1) No. The Fifth Amendment does not prohibit the imposition of a more severe punishment after conviction

for the same offense upon retrial. The guarantee against double jeopardy does not include restrictions upon the length of a sentence imposed upon reconviction. This rule rests upon the premise that the original conviction has, at the defendant's behest, been wholly nullified. However, it would be a flagrant violation of the Fourteenth Amendment for a state court to impose a heavier sentence upon every reconvicted defendant to the explicit purpose of punishing the defendant for his having gotten his original conviction set aside. The very threat inherent in the existence of such a policy would "chill the exercise of basic rights" by those still in prison. A court cannot put a price on an appeal, and a defendant's exercise of a right of appeal must be free and unfettered. In order to insure the absence of a motivation to punish, whenever a judge imposes a more severe sentence upon a defendant after a new trial, he must affirmatively show his reasons for doing so. These reasons must be based upon objective information concerning identifiable conduct on the part of the defendant after the original proceeding.

(2) Yes. The Fifth Amendment requires that, in computing a new sentence on retrial, credit must be given for that part of the original sentence already served. The Double Jeopardy Clause protects against multiple punishments as well as multiple prosecutions. This basic constitutional guarantee is violated when punishment already exacted is not fully credited in imposing sentence upon a new conviction for the same offense. In both of these cases before us, no reason was offered to justify the imposition of the harsher sentence. The judgment below must be affirmed.

▶ ANALYSIS

In *Green v. United States*, 355 U.S. 184 (1957), mentioned in one of the concurring opinions, the defendant had originally been charged with first-degree murder, but was convicted of second-degree murder. His appeal resulted in the reversal of his conviction, and he was retried on the original charge. The second jury convicted him of first-degree murder. The Supreme Court held that double jeopardy barred conviction on that charge, since Green had already been in peril of being convicted and punished for first-degree murder at his first trial. In *Tucker v. Peyton*, 357 F.2d 115 (1966), it was held that where a prisoner serving consecutive sentences succeeded in having one of the sentences invalidated after it had been fully or partially

Continued on next page.

served, the state must give credit on the sentence remaining for the time served. In *Miller v. Cox*, 443 F.2d 1019 (4th Cir. 1971), it was held that a defendant who had served 21 years on a void conviction was not entitled to credit against subsequently committed felonies.

■═■

Quicknotes

DOUBLE JEOPARDY A prohibition against a second prosecution for the same offense after an acquittal or conviction for that offense in a prior proceeding or against multiple punishments for the same offense.

FIRST DEGREE MURDER The willful killing of another person with deliberation and premeditation; first-degree murder also encompasses those situations in which a person is killed within the perpetration of, or attempt to perpetrate, specified felonies.

HABEAS CORPUS A proceeding in which a defendant brings a writ to compel a judicial determination of whether he is lawfully being held in custody.

PROCEDURAL DUE PROCESS The constitutional mandate that if the state or federal government acts so as to deny a citizen of a life, liberty or property interest the individual is first entitled to notice and the right to be heard.

SECOND-DEGREE MURDER The unlawful killing of another person, without premeditation, and characterized by either intent to kill or a reckless disregard for human life.

■═■

Chapman v. California

Defendant who fails to testify (D) v. State (P)

386 U.S. 18 (1967).

NATURE OF CASE: Appeal from conviction of robbery, kidnapping and murder.

FACT SUMMARY: Chapman (D) and others contended that because the prosecutor committed a constitutional error by commenting on his failure to testify in his own behalf, as a matter of law such error was reversible.

🏛 RULE OF LAW
A federal constitutional error may be found to be harmless where such is shown beyond a reasonable doubt.

FACTS: Chapman (D) and others were arrested for kidnapping, robbery, and murder. None of the defendants testified at trial. The prosecution commented heavily on Chapman's (D) failure to testify, and they were convicted. While the case was on appeal, the United States Supreme Court held that it was a deprivation of a defendant's constitutional rights for the prosecution to comment on his failure to testify. Chapman (D) contended that because the error was constitutional, as a matter of law it was reversible error. The California Supreme Court held the error to be harmless. The United States Supreme Court granted review.

ISSUE: May constitutional error be held harmless where such is shown beyond a reasonable doubt?

HOLDING AND DECISION: (Black, J.) Yes. It must be shown beyond a reasonable doubt that constitutional error was harmless or such will be considered reversible. Not all federal constitutional errors are reversible. However, the highest level of proof must be presented to hold such an error harmless. It is not harmless error to effectively deprive a defendant of his right against self-incrimination. By commenting on Chapman's (D) failure to testify, the prosecution suggests that such failure is an admission of guilt. Thus this is reversible error. Reversed.

▶ ANALYSIS

Some commentators suggest this opinion implies that constitutional errors are, by their nature, more important errors than others. The abuse of constitutional as opposed to statutory or state common law standards is considered fundamentally more erosive of the justice system.

■■■

Quicknotes

HARMLESS ERROR An error committed during trial that is not sufficient in nature or effect to warrant reversal, modification, or retrial.

■■■

Neder v. United States

Criminal (D) v. Federal government (P)

527 U.S. 1 (1999).

NATURE OF CASE: Appeal from a guilty verdict and appellate court's holding that district court committed harmless error.

FACT SUMMARY: A jury found Neder (D) guilty on various charges and a judge sentenced him (D) to 147 months in prison. The defendant appealed and the court of appeals held that the district court's failure to instruct the jury on materiality was harmless error.

> **RULE OF LAW**
> When a trial judge omits an element of an offense in a jury instruction, the proper review on appeal is the harmless error analysis.

FACTS: Neder (D) was tried and convicted of fraud and tax offenses, and sentenced to 147 months of imprisonment, five years of supervised release, and $25 million in restitution. On appeal, the court of appeals affirmed the conviction and held that the district court erred when it failed to submit the materiality element of the tax offense to the jury. The error, however, was harmless because materiality was not in dispute, therefore, the error did not contribute to the jury's verdict. Neder (D) appealed.

ISSUE: Is the harmless error analysis appropriate in reviewing a trial court's failure to instruct a jury on each and every element of an offense?

HOLDING AND DECISION: (Rehnquist, C.J.) Yes. The harmless error analysis is appropriate in reviewing a trial court's failure to instruct a jury on each and every element of an offense. Federal Rule of Criminal Procedure 52(a) states that any error, defect, irregularity, or variance that does not affect substantial rights will be disregarded. Although this rule applies to all alleged errors, there is a class of fundamental constitutional errors that goes beyond the harmless error examination. The error at issue here is a jury instruction that fails to include an element of an offense and is not an error that necessarily renders a criminal trial fundamentally unfair. The harmless error analysis is properly applied to an error as is involved in this case. The harmless error inquiry is whether it is clear beyond a reasonable doubt that a rational jury would have found the defendant guilty without the error. When an element of the offense is omitted from a jury instruction but supported by overwhelming and uncontroverted evidence, the above analysis balances society's interest in punishing the guilty and the method by which such decisions of guilt are made. Affirmed.

CONCURRENCE AND DISSENT: (Scalia, J.) A failure to include each element of the crime charged in an instruction can never be harmless error. The right to be tried by a jury necessarily means the right to have a jury determine whether one has been proved guilty of a charged offense, and that means a jury must determine all elements that were proved or not. The Court does not specify exactly how many elements of an offense can be omitted before the error is not viewed as harmless. Failure to prove one element should be treated the same as a failure to prove all elements of an offense and prevent a conviction.

▶ **ANALYSIS**

Justice Stevens's concurrence noted that the Court took a narrow perspective in identifying those errors that required automatic reversal. For example, racial discrimination in the selection of grand juries is not to be tolerated, even if the defendant's guilt is later established in a fair trial with overwhelming evidence. Our Constitution and criminal justice system respects other values besides the reliability of a determination of guilt.

Quicknotes

HARMLESS ERROR An error taking place during trial that does not require the reviewing court to overturn or modify the trial court's judgment in that it did not affect the appellant's substantial rights or the disposition of the action.

MATERIALITY Importance; the degree of relevance or necessity to the particular matter.

Post-Conviction Review: Federal Habeas Corpus

Quick Reference Rules of Law

Stone v. Powell

Accused (D) v. State (P)

428 U.S. 465 (1976).

NATURE OF CASE: Writ for federal habeas corpus.

FACT SUMMARY: A prisoner sought habeas corpus relief on the grounds that he was convicted based on evidence obtained in an illegal search or seizure.

🏛 RULE OF LAW
Where the state has provided an opportunity for full and fair litigation of a Fourth Amendment claim, the Constitution does not require that a state prisoner be granted federal habeas corpus relief on the ground that evidence obtained in an unconstitutional search or seizure was introduced at his trial.

FACTS: Stone (D) alleged that his conviction was based on evidence illegally obtained, and requested habeas corpus review. After state habeas corpus proceedings, Stone (D) filed a writ for federal habeas corpus, alleging violation of Fourth Amendment rights guaranteed through the Fourteenth Amendment.

ISSUE: Where the state has provided an opportunity for full and fair litigation of a Fourth Amendment claim, does the Constitution require that a state prisoner be granted federal habeas corpus relief on the ground that evidence obtained in an unconstitutional search or seizure was introduced at his trial?

HOLDING AND DECISION: (Powell, J.) No. Where the state has provided an opportunity for full and fair litigation of a Fourth Amendment claim, the Constitution does not require that a state prisoner be granted federal habeas corpus relief on the ground that evidence obtained in an unconstitutional search or seizure was introduced at his trial. The primary justification for the exclusionary rule is the deterrence of police conduct that violates Fourth Amendment rights; the Fourth Amendment itself is not a personal constitutional right. Fourth Amendment concerns support the implementation of the exclusionary rule at trial and its enforcement on direct appeal of state court convictions. The additional contribution, if any, of the consideration of search and seizure claims of state prisoners on collateral review is small in relation to the costs. Writ denied.

DISSENT: (Brennan, J.) The Court today is ignoring the settled principle that for purposes of adjudicating constitutional claims, Congress, which has the power to do so under Article III of the Constitution, has effectively cast the district courts sitting in habeas in the role of surrogate Supreme Courts. The procedural safeguards mandated by the Congress are not admonitions to be tolerated only to the extent they serve functional purposes. Every guarantee enshrined in our Constitution is endowed with an independent vitality and value, and the Court is not free to curtail those Constitutional guarantees even to punish the most obviously guilty.

▶ ANALYSIS

The Court has not extended the holding from this case to bar habeas corpus review of other claims based on violations of the Constitution. The Antiterrorism and Effective Death Penalty Act enacted in 1996 limited successive habeas corpus petitions. This Act did not, however, repeal the authority of the Court to entertain original habeas corpus petitions.

■—■

Quicknotes

FOURTH AMENDMENT Provides that persons be secure as to their person and private belongings against unreasonable searches and seizures.

HABEAS CORPUS A proceeding in which a defendant brings a writ to compel a judicial determination of whether he is lawfully being held in custody.

SEARCH An inspection conducted in order to obtain evidence to be utilized for the prosecution of a crime.

SEIZURE The removal of property from one's possession due to unlawful activity or in satisfaction of a judgment entered by the court.

■—■

Wainwright v. Sykes

Court (P) v. Murder convict (D)

433 U.S. 72 (1977).

NATURE OF CASE: Habeas corpus challenge to a murder conviction.

FACT SUMMARY: Sykes (D) sought a review of his murder conviction via a habeas corpus proceeding, but he had failed to comply with state procedural rules in not raising the underlying claim at trial.

🏛 **RULE OF LAW**
One who did not comply with state procedural rules by not raising his federal claim at trial cannot obtain federal habeas corpus review of his state criminal conviction unless he shows "cause" for noncompliance and shows "prejudice" as a result of the claimed error in the original proceeding.

FACTS: Sykes (D) violated a state procedural rule by not raising, at trial, his claim that the incriminating statements admitted against him were involuntary because he did not understand the *Miranda* warnings [*Miranda v. Arizona*, 384 U.S. 436 (1966)] that he had been given. When he was convicted in state court for murder, Sykes (D) then presented a federal habeas corpus challenge to that conviction based on the aforementioned contention. Opposing such action, Wainwright (P) argued that the rule in *Francis v. Henderson*, 425 U.S. 536 (1976), should be extended to cover this case. That rule was that federal habeas corpus review was barred absent a showing of "cause" and "prejudice" where the challenge was to the makeup of a grand jury. Sykes (D) argued that *Fay v. Noia*, 372 U.S. 391 (1963), had laid down an all-inclusive rule rendering state timely-objection rules ineffective to bar review of underlying federal claims in federal habeas corpus proceedings absent a showing of "knowing waiver" or a "deliberate bypass" of the right to so object.

ISSUE: In order to obtain federal habeas corpus review of his state criminal conviction, must one who did not comply with state procedural rules in raising his federal claim at trial show "cause" for noncompliance and show "prejudice" resulting from the claimed error in the original proceeding?

HOLDING AND DECISION: (Rehnquist, J.) Yes. If one who suffered a state criminal conviction did not comply with state procedural law by bringing up his federal claim at trial, he cannot obtain federal habeas corpus review of the conviction unless he shows "cause" for noncompliance and shows "prejudice" as a result of the claimed error in the original proceeding. A state's contemporaneous objection rule is designed to ensure that constitutional claims are heard when they are fresh, not years later in a federal habeas corpus proceeding. Furthermore, to apply the "knowing waiver" or "deliberate bypass" standard, the more lenient of those suggested, would encourage "sandbagging" by lawyers who would take their chances on a not guilty verdict at trial with the intent to raise their constitutional claims in a federal habeas corpus court if their initial gamble does not pay off. The "cause" and "prejudice" rule herein adopted attempts to make the state trial on the merits the "main event" rather than a "tryout on the road." In this case, the required showing of cause was not made. Reversed and remanded with instructions to dismiss the petition for a writ of habeas corpus.

CONCURRENCE: (Stevens, J.) In applying the "deliberate bypass" standard, courts have found the client impliedly consents where, as here, his attorney decides as a tactical ploy not to raise a constitutional objection at trial. Furthermore, there is no evidence that the trial lacked fundamental fairness. So, there is no reason to allow collateral attack in this case regardless of which rule is chosen.

DISSENT: (Brennan, J.) The Court is not justified in imposing a stricter standard than the deliberate bypass test. It is the harshest test possible which still distinguishes between intentional and inadvertent noncompliance by counsel with procedural rules. Most procedural defaults are born of the inadvertence, negligence, inexperience, or incompetence of trial counsel; and it is unfair to make the criminal defendant accountable for the naked errors of his attorney. The mistakes of a trial attorney should be visited on the head of a federal habeas corpus applicant only when this Court is convinced that the lawyer actually exercised his expertise and judgment in his client's service, and with his client's knowing and intelligent participation, where possible.

▌ *ANALYSIS*

One possible result of this case may be that defendants are pushed into making more claims based on ineffectiveness of counsel to fulfill the requirement that they show "cause." That is, a particular procedural default will simply be cited as an example of general incompetence of counsel. The effect would be merely to transform the old claims alleging deprivation of constitutional rights to new claims alleging ineffectiveness of counsel, with all the attendant problems that will engender.

▄▬▬

Continued on next page.

Quicknotes

HABEAS CORPUS A proceeding in which a defendant brings a writ to compel a judicial determination of whether he is lawfully being held in custody.

KNOWING AND INTELLIGENT WAIVER The intentional or voluntary forfeiture of a recognized right.

■▬■

Teague v. Lane

Black felony convict (D) v. Court (P)

489 U.S. 288 (1989).

NATURE OF CASE: Review of denial of habeas corpus.

FACT SUMMARY: Teague (D) argued in a habeas proceeding that a post-conviction judicial decision had rendered his conviction invalid.

🏛 RULE OF LAW
Except in special circumstances, case law will not be retroactively applied in collateral review.

FACTS: Teague (D) was charged with various felonies. An all-white jury convicted Teague (D), a black man, of attempted murder, robbery, and battery. The prosecution had used all its peremptory challenges to exclude blacks from the jury. Teague (D) appealed, contending that this denied him due process. On appeal the conviction was upheld. Teague (D) subsequently petitioned for habeas corpus, contending that he had been entitled to a jury consisting of a cross-section of the community. The district court denied his petition on the merits, as did the court of appeals. The United States Supreme Court granted review.

ISSUE: Will case law be retroactively applied in collateral review?

HOLDING AND DECISION: (O'Connor, J.) No. Except in special circumstances, case law will not be retroactively applied in collateral review. Habeas corpus provides an avenue for upsetting judgments that otherwise would be final. It is not intended to be a substitute for direct review. Both the state and criminal defendants have an interest in leaving concluded litigation in a state of repose. If new rules of constitutional law were to be applied retroactively, any litigation might be reopened if the new rule were to be applicable. Further, the purpose of habeas is that its presence creates an incentive for trial and appellate judges to conduct their proceedings in a manner consistent with established constitutional principles. To apply new principles retroactively would actually subvert this purpose. Therefore, the Court concludes that, unless the post-conviction rule announced is so fundamental to the concept of ordered liberty that it would be unconscionable not to retroactively apply it, retroactive application will not be given. A necessary corollary to this rule is that no new rule of constitutional criminal procedure should be announced in a habeas proceeding. Here, to rule as Teague (D) urges would amount to that. Therefore, without ruling on the merits of the claim, the denial of habeas must be affirmed.

CONCURRENCE: (Stevens, J.) The test adopted by the court is essentially proper. However, as to the Court's discussion of the "fundamental fairness" exception, the Court gives an excessively result-oriented analysis.

DISSENT: (Brennan, J.) The 1867 Habeas Corpus statute was, from its inception, given an extremely broad jurisdictional reach. Nothing done by Congress since has indicated a wish to narrow its reach. Further, the ruling by the Court will foreclose decision upon important constitutional issues.

▌ ANALYSIS

The opinion in fact announces two rules, the first being that stated above and the second being that new constitutional issues cannot be announced in a habeas proceeding. The latter rule is potentially much more significant than the first. It is important to note, however, that only four justices joined the section announcing that rule, which limits its precedential value.

■■■

Quicknotes

HABEAS CORPUS A proceeding in which a defendant brings a writ to compel a judicial determination of whether he is lawfully being held in custody.

■■■

Harrington v. Richter

State (P) v. Individual (D)

562 U.S. 86 (2011).

NATURE OF CASE: Appeal from habeas decision in favor of the plaintiff.

FACT SUMMARY: A jury convicted Richter (D) of murder, attempted murder and armed robbery. Richter (D) then brought a petition for habeas corpus relief directly to the California Supreme Court. That court denied his petition without full explanation.

🏛 **RULE OF LAW**
Under 28 U.S.C. Section 2254 as amended by the Antiterrorism and Effective Death Penalty Act (AEDPA) of 1996, federal habeas relief may not be granted unless it is shown that an earlier state court's decision was contrary to clearly established federal law or involved an unreasonable application of such federal law.

FACTS: In 1994, police in California arrived at the home of Joshua Johnson, a known drug dealer. Johnson had been shot. Another man, Klein, had also been shot and lay on a couch in the living room. Klein later died from his injuries. Johnson informed the police that two men came into his house and one of them named Christian Branscombe shot Johnson near the door of Johnson's bedroom. Johnson also informed the police that Richter (D) allegedly shot Klein in the living room. The police later searched Richter's (D) residence and found items stolen from Johnson's home as well as similar ammunition used in the murder of Klein. At trial, Richter's (D) attorney argued Branscombe fired at Johnson in self-defense and that Klein was shot in the crossfire by Johnson near the bedroom door. Klein was then allegedly moved to the couch. At trial, the prosecution put on expert witnesses to prove that the blood near the door was that of Johnson, and not Klein. This evidence supported Johnson's story and damaged the credibility of Richter's (D) version of events. Fifteen years after his conviction and imposition of a life sentence, Richter (D) filed a petition for habeas corpus relief at the California Supreme Court on the grounds of ineffective assistance of counsel. The basis of Richter's (D) claim was that his attorney did not call any expert witnesses of his own to rebut the expert testimony of the prosecution. The California Supreme Court denied his application with a one-line rejection of his claims. Richter (D) then filed a new habeas petition in federal district court which denied his claim. On appeal, however, the Ninth Circuit Court of Appeals reversed, holding that the California Supreme Court unreasonably applied the federal standard for ineffective assistance of counsel claims. The State (P) appealed to the United States Supreme Court.

ISSUE: Under 28 U.S.C. Section 2254 as amended by the Antiterrorism and Effective Death Penalty Act (AEDPA) of 1996, may federal habeas relief be granted only if it is shown that an earlier state court's decision was contrary to clearly established federal law or involved an unreasonable application of such federal law?

HOLDING AND DECISION: (Kennedy, J.) Yes. Under 28 U.S.C. Section 2254 as amended by the Antiterrorism and Effective Death Penalty Act (AEDPA) of 1996, federal habeas relief may not be granted unless it is shown that an earlier state court's decision was contrary to clearly established federal law or involved an unreasonable application of such federal law. First, 28 U.S.C. 2254 applies because Richter (D) is in state custody. Moving to the substantive issue, Richter's (D) burden is to show that the state court's application of the standard this court laid out in *Strickland v. Washington*, 466 U.S. 668 (1984), for ineffective assistance of counsel claims was unreasonable. The issue here is not a relitigation of whether Richter's (D) counsel actually performed at a level below the standard set in *Strickland*. This Court is not adjudicating an ineffective assistance of counsel claim under direct review. Rather, under AEDPA, the state court's review of the habeas petition is granted deference. A state court's denial of habeas relief will preclude relief in the federal courts if fair-minded jurists could disagree about the correctness of the state court's determination. A federal habeas court must consider what arguments the state court could have used to support its decision. Here, a state court could have made the determination that defense counsel reasonably decided to forego the use of his own experts and rely upon cross examination only of the prosecution experts. Richter's (D) counsel clearly had reason to question his client's account. Use of their own expert may possibly have proved that Richter's (D) version of events was wrong. It was thus a reasonable strategic decision to instead rely upon cross-examination in the hopes of creating reasonable doubt in the minds of the jury. Because the state court's review of the *Strickland* standard was reasonable, federal courts must defer to the state courts and deny Richter's (D) habeas petition as well. Reversed and remanded.

▎ **ANALYSIS**

Habeas petitioners relying upon ineffective assistance of counsel claims face a very difficult burden. AEDPA added another layer by requiring that federal courts may not

Continued on next page.

grant habeas relief unless the state court decision was essentially unreasonable. As this decision noted, unreasonable is different from incorrect.

━━━

Quicknotes

RIGHT TO COUNSEL Right conferred by the Sixth Amendment that the accused shall be provided effective legal assistance in a criminal proceeding.

━━━

Glossary

Common Latin Words and Phrases Encountered in the Law

A FORTIORI: Because one fact exists or has been proven, therefore a second fact that is related to the first fact must also exist.

A PRIORI: From the cause to the effect. A term of logic used to denote that when one generally accepted truth is shown to be a cause, another particular effect must necessarily follow.

AB INITIO: From the beginning; a condition which has existed throughout, as in a marriage which was void ab initio.

ACTUS REUS: The wrongful act; in criminal law, such action sufficient to trigger criminal liability.

AD VALOREM: According to value; an ad valorem tax is imposed upon an item located within the taxing jurisdiction calculated by the value of such item.

AMICUS CURIAE: Friend of the court. Its most common usage takes the form of an amicus curiae brief, filed by a person who is not a party to an action but is nonetheless allowed to offer an argument supporting his legal interests.

ARGUENDO: In arguing. A statement, possibly hypothetical, made for the purpose of argument, is one made arguendo.

BILL QUIA TIMET: A bill to quiet title (establish ownership) to real property.

BONA FIDE: True, honest, or genuine. May refer to a person's legal position based on good faith or lacking notice of fraud (such as a bona fide purchaser for value) or to the authenticity of a particular document (such as a bona fide last will and testament).

CAUSA MORTIS: With approaching death in mind. A gift causa mortis is a gift given by a party who feels certain that death is imminent.

CAVEAT EMPTOR: Let the buyer beware. This maxim is reflected in the rule of law that a buyer purchases at his own risk because it is his responsibility to examine, judge, test, and otherwise inspect what he is buying.

CERTIORARI: A writ of review. Petitions for review of a case by the United States Supreme Court are most often done by means of a writ of certiorari.

CONTRA: On the other hand. Opposite. Contrary to.

CORAM NOBIS: Before us; writs of error directed to the court that originally rendered the judgment.

CORAM VOBIS: Before you; writs of error directed by an appellate court to a lower court to correct a factual error.

CORPUS DELICTI: The body of the crime; the requisite elements of a crime amounting to objective proof that a crime has been committed.

CUM TESTAMENTO ANNEXO, ADMINISTRATOR (ADMINISTRATOR C.T.A.): With will annexed; an administrator c.t.a. settles an estate pursuant to a will in which he is not appointed.

DE BONIS NON, ADMINISTRATOR (ADMINISTRATOR D.B.N.): Of goods not administered; an administrator d.b.n. settles a partially settled estate.

DE FACTO: In fact; in reality; actually. Existing in fact but not officially approved or engendered.

DE JURE: By right; lawful. Describes a condition that is legitimate "as a matter of law," in contrast to the term "de facto," which connotes something existing in fact but not legally sanctioned or authorized. For example, de facto segregation refers to segregation brought about by housing patterns, etc., whereas de jure segregation refers to segregation created by law.

DE MINIMIS: Of minimal importance; insignificant; a trifle; not worth bothering about.

DE NOVO: Anew; a second time; afresh. A trial de novo is a new trial held at the appellate level as if the case originated there and the trial at a lower level had not taken place.

DICTA: Generally used as an abbreviated form of obiter dicta, a term describing those portions of a judicial opinion incidental or not necessary to resolution of the specific question before the court. Such nonessential statements and remarks are not considered to be binding precedent.

DUCES TECUM: Refers to a particular type of writ or subpoena requesting a party or organization to produce certain documents in their possession.

EN BANC: Full bench. Where a court sits with all justices present rather than the usual quorum.

EX PARTE: For one side or one party only. An ex parte proceeding is one undertaken for the benefit of only one party, without notice to, or an appearance by, an adverse party.

EX POST FACTO: After the fact. An ex post facto law is a law that retroactively changes the consequences of a prior act.

EX REL.: Abbreviated form of the term "ex relatione," meaning upon relation or information. When the state brings an action in which it has no interest against an individual at the instigation of one who has a private interest in the matter.

FORUM NON CONVENIENS: Inconvenient forum. Although a court may have jurisdiction over the case, the action should be tried in a more conveniently located court, one to which parties and witnesses may more easily travel, for example.

GUARDIAN AD LITEM: A guardian of an infant as to litigation, appointed to represent the infant and pursue his/her rights.

HABEAS CORPUS: You have the body. The modern writ of habeas corpus is a writ directing that a person (body) being detained (such as a prisoner) be brought before the court so that the legality of his detention can be judicially ascertained.

IN CAMERA: In private, in chambers. When a hearing is held before a judge in his chambers or when all spectators are excluded from the courtroom.

IN FORMA PAUPERIS: In the manner of a pauper. A party who proceeds in forma pauperis because of his poverty is one who is allowed to bring suit without liability for costs.

INFRA: Below, under. A word referring the reader to a later part of a book. (The opposite of supra.)

IN LOCO PARENTIS: In the place of a parent.

IN PARI DELICTO: Equally wrong; a court of equity will not grant requested relief to an applicant who is in pari delicto, or as much at fault in the transactions giving rise to the controversy as is the opponent of the applicant.

IN PARI MATERIA: On like subject matter or upon the same matter. Statutes relating to the same person or things are said to be in pari materia. It is a general rule of statutory construction that such statutes should be construed together, i.e., looked at as if they together constituted one law.

IN PERSONAM: Against the person. Jurisdiction over the person of an individual.

IN RE: In the matter of. Used to designate a proceeding involving an estate or other property.

IN REM: A term that signifies an action against the res, or thing. An action in rem is basically one that is taken directly against property, as distinguished from an action in personam, i.e., against the person.

INTER ALIA: Among other things. Used to show that the whole of a statement, pleading, list, statute, etc., has not been set forth in its entirety.

INTER PARTES: Between the parties. May refer to contracts, conveyances or other transactions having legal significance.

INTER VIVOS: Between the living. An inter vivos gift is a gift made by a living grantor, as distinguished from bequests contained in a will, which pass upon the death of the testator.

IPSO FACTO: By the mere fact itself.

JUS: Law or the entire body of law.

LEX LOCI: The law of the place; the notion that the rights of parties to a legal proceeding are governed by the law of the place where those rights arose.

MALUM IN SE: Evil or wrong in and of itself; inherently wrong. This term describes an act that is wrong by its very nature, as opposed to one which would not be wrong but for the fact that there is a specific legal prohibition against it (malum prohibitum).

MALUM PROHIBITUM: Wrong because prohibited, but not inherently evil. Used to describe something that is wrong because it is expressly forbidden by law but that is not in and of itself evil, e.g., speeding.

MANDAMUS: We command. A writ directing an official to take a certain action.

MENS REA: A guilty mind; a criminal intent. A term used to signify the mental state that accompanies a crime or other prohibited act. Some crimes require only a general mens rea (general intent to do the prohibited act), but others, like assault with intent to murder, require the existence of a specific mens rea.

MODUS OPERANDI: Method of operating; generally refers to the manner or style of a criminal in committing crimes, admissible in appropriate cases as evidence of the identity of a defendant.

NEXUS: A connection to.

NISI PRIUS: A court of first impression. A nisi prius court is one where issues of fact are tried before a judge or jury.

N.O.V. (NON OBSTANTE VEREDICTO): Notwithstanding the verdict. A judgment n.o.v. is a judgment given in favor of one party despite the fact that a verdict was returned in favor of the other party, the justification being that the verdict either had no reasonable support in fact or was contrary to law.

NUNC PRO TUNC: Now for then. This phrase refers to actions that may be taken and will then have full retroactive effect.

PENDENTE LITE: Pending the suit; pending litigation under way.

PER CAPITA: By head; beneficiaries of an estate, if they take in equal shares, take per capita.

PER CURIAM: By the court; signifies an opinion ostensibly written "by the whole court" and with no identified author.

PER SE: By itself, in itself; inherently.

PER STIRPES: By representation. Used primarily in the law of wills to describe the method of distribution where a person, generally because of death, is unable to take that which is left to him by the will of another, and therefore his heirs divide such property between them rather than take under the will individually.

PRIMA FACIE: On its face, at first sight. A prima facie case is one that is sufficient on its face, meaning that the evidence supporting it is adequate to establish the case until contradicted or overcome by other evidence.

PRO TANTO: For so much; as far as it goes. Often used in eminent domain cases when a property owner receives partial payment for his land without prejudice to his right to bring suit for the full amount he claims his land to be worth.

QUANTUM MERUIT: As much as he deserves. Refers to recovery based on the doctrine of unjust enrichment in those cases in which a party has rendered valuable services or furnished materials that were accepted and enjoyed by another under circumstances that would reasonably notify the recipient that the rendering party expected to be paid. In essence, the law implies a contract to pay the reasonable value of the services or materials furnished.

QUASI: Almost like; as if; nearly. This term is essentially used to signify that one subject or thing is almost analogous to another but that material differences between them do exist. For example, a quasi-criminal proceeding is one that is not strictly criminal but shares enough of the same characteristics to require some of the same safeguards (e.g., procedural due process must be followed in a parole hearing).

QUID PRO QUO: Something for something. In contract law, the consideration, something of value, passed between the parties to render the contract binding.

RES GESTAE: Things done; in evidence law, this principle justifies the admission of a statement that would otherwise be hearsay when it is made so closely to the event in question as to be said to be a part of it, or with such spontaneity as not to have the possibility of falsehood.

RES IPSA LOQUITUR: The thing speaks for itself. This doctrine gives rise to a rebuttable presumption of negligence when the instrumentality causing the injury was within the exclusive control of the defendant, and the injury was one that does not normally occur unless a person has been negligent.

RES JUDICATA: A matter adjudged. Doctrine which provides that once a court of competent jurisdiction has rendered a final judgment or decree on the merits, that judgment or decree is conclusive upon the parties to the case and prevents them from engaging in any other litigation on the points and issues determined therein.

RESPONDEAT SUPERIOR: Let the master reply. This doctrine holds the master liable for the wrongful acts of his servant (or the principal for his agent) in those cases in which the servant (or agent) was acting within the scope of his authority at the time of the injury.

STARE DECISIS: To stand by or adhere to that which has been decided. The common law doctrine of stare decisis attempts to give security and certainty to the law by following the policy that once a principle of law as applicable to a certain set of facts has been set forth in a decision, it forms a precedent which will subsequently be followed, even though a different decision might be made were it the first time the question had arisen. Of course, stare decisis is not an inviolable principle and is departed from in instances where there is good cause (e.g., considerations of public policy led the Supreme Court to disregard prior decisions sanctioning segregation).

SUPRA: Above. A word referring a reader to an earlier part of a book.

ULTRA VIRES: Beyond the power. This phrase is most commonly used to refer to actions taken by a corporation that are beyond the power or legal authority of the corporation.

Addendum of French Derivatives

IN PAIS: Not pursuant to legal proceedings.

CHATTEL: Tangible personal property.

CY PRES: Doctrine permitting courts to apply trust funds to purposes not expressed in the trust but necessary to carry out the settlor's intent.

PER AUTRE VIE: For another's life; during another's life. In property law, an estate may be granted that will terminate upon the death of someone other than the grantee.

PROFIT A PRENDRE: A license to remove minerals or other produce from land.

VOIR DIRE: Process of questioning jurors as to their predispositions about the case or parties to a proceeding in order to identify those jurors displaying bias or prejudice.